OCR HISTORY A

Liberals and Conservatives 1846–95

David Paterson | Series editors: Martin Collier | Rosemary Rees

www.heinemann.co.uk

✓ Free online support
✓ Useful weblinks
✓ 24 hour online ordering

01865 888080

Official Publisher Partnership

Heinemann is an imprint of Pearson Education Limited, a company incorporated in England and Wales, having its registered office at Edinburgh Gate, Harlow, Essex, CM20 2JE. Registered company number: 872828

www.heinemann.co.uk

Heinemann is a registered trademark of Pearson Education Ltd

Text © David Paterson 2008

12 11 10 09 08
10 9 8 7 6 5 4 3 2 1

British Library Cataloguing in Publication Data is available from the British Library on request.

ISBN 978-0-435-31262-6

Typeset by Tek-Art
Original illustrations © Pearson Education 2008
Illustrated by Tek-Art
Cover design by Pearson Education
Cover illustration © Mary Evans Picture Library
Edited by Kirsty Taylor
Index compiled by Ian D. Crane
Printed in the UK by Henry Ling Ltd

Acknowledgements

The author and publisher would like to thank the following individuals and organisations for permission to reproduce photographs:

Alamy/Mary Evans Picture Library (Wellington picture): p. 3; Alamy/Classic Images (Peel picture): p. 3; Corbis/Michael Nicholson: p. 7; Alamy/Mary Evans Picture Library: p. 17; Alamy/Alan King Engraving: p. 19; Topfoto/Fortean Picture Library/Janet & Colin Bond: p. 21; Corbis/Bettmann: p. 23; Mary Evans Picture Library: p. 28; Alamy/Visual Arts Library (London): p. 48; The Bridgeman Art Library/Manchester City Art Galleriees, UK: p. 59; Punch: p. 69; Alamy/Mary Evans Picture Library: p. 72; Alamy/Mary Evans Picture Library: p. 76; Getty/Hulton Archive: p. 91; Cartoon Stock/Sir John Tenniel: p. 101; Alamy/ INTERFOTO Pressebildagentur: p. 105; Alamy/The Print Collector: p. 121; Alamy/ Mary Evans Picture Library: p. 166; Alamy/Lebrecht Music & Arts Photo Library: p. 184; Alamy/Mary Evans Picture Library: p. 203.

Written sources

p. 147; The Eastern Question in the 1870s. From: Lord Salisbury: A Political Biography, David Steele, © 2001 Routledge. Reproduced by permission of Taylor & Francis Books UK.

Every effort has been made to contact copyright holders of material reproduced in this book. Any omissions will be rectified in subsequent printings if notice is given to the publishers.

Websites

There are links to relevant websites in this book. In order to ensure that the links are up to date, that the links work, and that the sites are not inadvertently linked to sites that could be considered offensive, we have made the links available on the Heinemann website at www.heinemann.co.uk/hotlinks. When you access the site, the express code is 2626P.

CONTENTS

HOW TO USE THIS BOOK

This book is primarily designed to meet the requirements of OCR AS History Unit F961 Option B: Liberals and Conservatives 1846–95. The origin, meaning and significance of the Conservative and Liberal parties in nineteenth-century British political history are examined and particular attention is paid to the development of the ideas and careers of William Gladstone and Benjamin Disraeli. The aim is to provide an explanatory narrative of the major political developments of the later nineteenth century. Six of the chapters focus on the six key issues highlighted by the examination board but there are separate, relevant chapters on parliamentary reform, foreign policy and Ireland. It is hoped that the book deals with a historical theme in a historical way so that it can also be read with profit by those who are not studying for this particular examination.

Key Issue 1: How were the Whigs transformed into the Liberals (1846–68)?
This is the focus of Chapter 2.

Key Issue 2: What was Gladstonian Liberalism and how successful was Gladstone's first ministry (1868–74)?
This is the focus of Chapters 5 and 6.

Key Issue 3: Why did Disraeli become the Conservatives' leader?
This is covered in Chapters 3, 4 and 7.

Key Issue 4: What was Disraelian Conservatism?
This is the focus of Chapter 7.

Key Issue 5: How successful was Disraeli's second ministry?
This is covered in Chapters 8 and 9.

Key Issue 6: How successful were Gladstone's later ministries (1880–5, 1892–5)?
This is covered in Chapters 9, 10 and 11.

Features

There are many features in the margins of the book which are directly linked to the text and will help stimulate the students' imagination and enhance their overall understanding of the period.

Key Issues – these highlight areas which are particularly relevant to a Key Issue (see above)

Key Terms – these pick out and define key words

Key People – these give a brief biography of important people

Key Events – these give a brief overview of important events

Key Places – these give brief explanation of why certain areas are important for this topic

Key Concepts – these outline important concepts of the time

Key Themes – these pick out important themes of the period

Exam Café

There are Period Study style activities at the end of each chapter to help candidates develop essay writing skills as well as knowledge of the period.

The text in the book is supplemented by an exciting **Exam Café** feature. The Exam Café is split into three areas: Relax, Refresh, Result!

- **Relax** is a place for students to share revision tips.
- **Refresh** your memory is an area for revising content.
- **Result** provides examiner's tips and sample answers with comments.

Planning and Delivery Resource

The Liberals and Conservatives chapter of this resource contains guidance and advice for ways to approach and teach this topic for the OCR specification. There are student worksheets which help to build up essay writing skills for the examination requirements. The resource also contains lots of additional material and an Exam Café with more tips, sample answers and detailed examiner commentary.

INTRODUCTION

The year 1846 was a significant one in British history. Tragically, it saw a major famine in British-controlled Ireland: linked with this crisis were heated parliamentary debates in the House of Commons. Would the starving Irish benefit from removing customs duties on imported corn? What effect would such a removal have on the aristocratic landed interest? Subsequent events led to the downfall of the Conservative government of Sir Robert Peel and a time of relative party political confusion. Yet it eventually became apparent that the political scene was to be dominated by Conservatives and Liberals and competition between them would be a major political theme for at least the next 50 years. The year 1846 also witnessed the emergence of the increasingly Liberal William Gladstone as a loyal defender of Peel, and the sudden rise to fame of Conservative Benjamin Disraeli, who took a leading part in attacking Peel: the two became prominent parliamentary and political figures.

Since the extension of the right to vote in 1832, political debates in the Houses of Parliament had taken on a new importance and there were to be further reforms to the way the House of Commons was elected in both 1867 and 1884. It was a time when the class below the landed aristocracy but above the working class, the middle class, became increasingly important and active in political terms.

By 1895, however, there were signs of this era coming to an end. A Labour Party to represent working people was about to emerge and the right of the House of Lords to vote against measures passed by the House of Commons was being questioned, especially after its rejection of Irish Home Rule in 1893. **Queen Victoria**, who had given a unity – and her name – to the last two-thirds of the nineteenth century, was now an ageing figure.

However, in the intervening period, the Conservative and Liberal parties dominated the politics of much of the Victorian era. In the late 1870s the writer W.S. Gilbert penned the words to a song in an operetta called *Iolanthe*, set to music by the most famous mid-Victorian British composer, Arthur Sullivan. It ran:

I often think it comical,
How nature always does contrive,
That every boy and every girl
That's born into this world alive,
Is either a little Liberal
Or else a little Conservative.

Contemporaries were very well aware of the importance and domination of Liberals and Conservatives.

This book will attempt to answer the following questions:

- What did Conservatism and Liberalism stand for in the nineteenth century?
- How did these names come to be used for the two main political parties?
- Who were the leading politicians most identified with their ideas?
- What were the overall philosophies of these parties if they had them?
- What did they believe and achieve in foreign policy?
- How did they view the dramatic economic expansion and urban development of the nineteenth century?
- Where did they stand on such issues such as the extension of the vote?
- What views did they have on the amount that governments should interfere in the social questions of the day, such as public health, working conditions and the problems of poverty?
- How successful were they in their attempts to hold power and govern the country at this time? Why did their contrasting fortunes ebb and flow?
- What kinds of people in the country were attracted to support these groupings?

KEY TERMS

Conservative
The word conservative can be used with a small 'c' to describe a particular attitude to a problem, question or situation. This attitude:

- is cautious, careful and apprehensive of too much change all at once;
- has regard for past traditions and ideas;
- believes that rapid upheaval may produce instability and uncertainty;
- feels that, at national level, this kind of alteration could result in the loss of valuable ideas or institutions.

Liberal
Likewise, the word liberal with a small 'l' suggests:

- an open-minded and flexible approach to a problem;
- plenty of scope for free interpretation of the question in hand;
- that tradition, though respected, should not be adhered to over-rigidly;
- that change may be seen as desirable to prevent frustration and anger from building up.

Whig and Tory Like many names that stick they were not intended at first to be complimentary: a Tory was an Irish robber and a Whig his Scottish equivalent.

CHAPTER 1

What were Conservatism and Liberalism?

INTRODUCTION

The words **Conservative** and **Liberal** are used in a number of ways today. When they are used with capital letters in their political sense, their precise definition may change a little and vary according to time and circumstance. Nevertheless, in this political context, their meaning is likely to bear some resemblance to the more general explanation outlined in the margin.

Today in the early twenty-first century we are familiar with the words Conservative and Liberal with a large 'C' and a large 'L' to describe two of our major political parties. The Conservatives remain one of the major players in the political game: the Liberals, however (who have changed their name to Liberal Democrats), have long been displaced as the second of two major parties by the Labour Party. This was a twentieth-century development. In the second half of the nineteenth century the Conservative and Liberal parties were the two dominant parties in the British parliamentary system. Yet at the start of the century, in 1800, the words were only being used with a small 'c' and a small 'l' and the two main parties were known as the Tories and the Whigs.

WHAT WERE WHIG AND TORY?

The terms **Whig and Tory** had been in use ever since the second half of the seventeenth century and stood largely unchallenged until the 1830s in describing the two major political groupings of the day. Parties and groupings emerged gradually after 1660 when it was clear that the role of the king after the **restoration of the monarchy** was not going to be all-dominant and there were different views on how he ought to be advised and how far his powers should be restricted.

Parties began as informal groupings rather than being founded as an organisation in a formal manner with rules and regulations and a balance sheet. These parties were very different from today:

- Only a small number of Members of Parliament would have identified with being Whig or Tory.
- Many MPs would regard themselves as independent country gentlemen who were above party and would vote as they chose.
- Those who did think about it frequently regarded themselves as Whig or Tory rather than members of the Whig or Tory parties. There was no mass membership of the parties in the country as a whole and little formal organisation.
- The proportion of adult males who were entitled to vote for MPs was quite small under **the old electoral system before 1832**. Moreover, many candidates who stood for Parliament were elected unopposed because of the property or land they owned and/or influence they possessed in a particular area. They did not have to win voters over to the policies they supported by the politics of persuasion.

When a dispute emerged as to whether Parliament should be reformed in 1831–2, the differences between Whig and Tory were clearly demonstrated. Tories opposed what they saw as an unwarranted, sudden and drastic interference with the stable and well-established **British constitution** and Whigs supported what they felt was a moderate, prudent and necessary change to include the respectable middle class among those privileged to vote for their choice of elected Member of Parliament. In passing the **Great Reform Bill of 1832** the Whigs seemed to have won an important struggle and taken advantage of the growing demand for reform, especially from the industrial middle classes.

THE CHANGE TO 'CONSERVATIVE'

In the 1830s the use of the terms 'Conservative' and 'Liberal' began to challenge the terms 'Whig' and 'Tory'.

Restoration of the monarchy In 1660 the English monarchy was restored to the throne in the shape of Charles II. His father Charles I had been executed in 1649 and the monarchy abolished. Charles II never had absolute power and three years after his death in 1685 his Roman Catholic brother, reigning as James II, was deposed. The Bill of Rights of 1689 laid down further restrictions on the new monarch's freedom of action.

Electoral system before 1832 The all-male electorate was only about 6 per cent of the adult male population. In the small number of seats where there was a contest the system was both violent and corrupt. Bribery was common and landowning influence apparent. Despite a major shift in population to the new northern industrial areas, no redistribution of parliamentary seats had taken place, so these areas were usually much under-represented.

The British constitution Constitutions outline the rules by which a country is governed. They were rare at the start of the nineteenth century and the British constitution was distinctive for being partially unwritten and allowing (very unevenly) some degree of representation for ordinary people in an elected Parliament.

The **Great Reform Bill of 1832** successfully proposed an extension of the vote in English boroughs to a group of men known as £10 householders. In effect this gave the franchise (right to vote) to the middle classes in the towns – shopkeepers, merchants, traders and small businessmen who had generally been excluded from voting before. It also abolished some of the very smallest borough seats and partially redistributed these to the new industrial towns in the north.

This challenge came at slightly different times, in different ways and with different results. The historian of the Conservative Party, Robert Blake, records that the first use of the word Conservative to describe the Tory party was in an article in January 1830. This was at the start of the Reform Bill crisis and related to the idea of 'conserving', or preserving, the old electoral system. However, the term came into common use soon afterwards in the mid-1830s when the dust was beginning to settle on the Reform Bill crisis.

In 1834 the **Duke of Wellington**, who had been Tory Prime Minister up to 1830, was replaced as leader by **Sir Robert Peel.** Peel, in seeking re-election to Parliament, wrote an address (known as the Tamworth Manifesto) to his **constituents** in the Staffordshire **borough** of Tamworth in which he outlined his proposals. Peel made it clear that he accepted the 1832 Reform Act as an established fact and something that could not be reversed. He also established the idea that the Tories would accept change where it could be proven to be beneficial to the country. However, although he did not use the word, he indicated that

The old Tory and the new Conservative; Wellington and Peel.

What were Conservatism and Liberalism? 3

conservation of what was worthwhile from the old system would have a high priority. He promised that the Tories (or Conservatives) would undertake 'a *careful* review of all institutions civil and ecclesiastical ... in a *friendly* temper for the maintenance of *established* rights' (author's italics).

The word 'Tory' never disappeared and still appears today as meaning essentially the same as Conservative, but it is clear that by 1846 the Conservative Party was the most common term and it was already in frequent use when Peel succeeded in regaining real power for the Party in 1841, defeating the Whigs at a general election in that year. Peel had managed to modify the image of the Tories so that, while they could still be seen as a party primarily representing the landowning interest, they could also claim to govern for the interests of the country as a whole.

BELIEFS OF THE CONSERVATIVES

Parties at this time stood for broad principles rather than specific policies. At the start of Peel's Conservative ministry of the early 1840s it appeared clear what these were.

1. Conservatives greatly revered the position of the monarchy in the British political system: the monarch was entitled to exert real power and should do so when appropriate. There could be no dispute about the ultimate authority in the country: Queen Victoria was entitled to select her own ministers and the government was Her Majesty's Government.
2. Conservatives had a high regard for the British constitution and the workings of the traditional political system. Many Conservatives regretted the passing of the 1832 Great Reform Bill but they were prepared to accept its changes. They believed further adjustments were unlikely to be necessary. The place of the House of Lords was seen as equally significant as that of the House of Commons and democracy was associated with the USA and mob rule, which were both seen as powerful disincentives to adopt it or anything remotely resembling it.
3. The landowning aristocracy were the given rulers of the country. Their background, education and wealth

KEY PEOPLE

Duke of Wellington 1759–1852 He defeated Bonaparte at Waterloo in 1815 but his subsequent political career as a Tory politician was less successful. Prime Minister 1828–30, his refusal of even the smallest degree of reform when faced with evidence of the corrupt nature of the electoral system secured his downfall. 1835–52 a senior yet background figure in the Conservative Party. He was a member of Peel's cabinet 1841–6 without holding office.

Sir Robert Peel 1788–1850 From a wealthy Lancashire manufacturing family. His father was in Parliament before 1832. After brilliant academic success at Oxford, Peel was Irish Secretary 1813–20 and a reforming Home Secretary in the 1820s, but opposed parliamentary reform. Prime Minister 1834–5 and 1841–6. In the political wilderness for the last few years of his life.

KEY TERMS

Constituents All the people who live in the constituency (area) represented by an MP.

Borough A town or village granted a Royal Charter giving it the privilege of electing its own two MPs.

entitled them to this status. The stability of the country depended upon a landowning class that had a sufficient stake in the system to act in its best interests. The main desires of landowners would always take precedence over the manufacturing or commercial interest. The landed aristocracy and the House of Lords both depended on the hereditary system whereby titles and land were inherited in their entirety by the eldest sons.

4. The **established Church of England** was to be strongly maintained as a central plank in the social system. The monarch was the earthly head of the Church and was derived from the basis of society's organisation and principles and the Church's Christian beliefs. The senior bishops were members of the House of Lords. Since appointment of bishops tended to be political and the Tories had been in office for most of the period 1784–1830, the majority of the bishops were of that political persuasion for at least the first part of the nineteenth century and often beyond. Not for nothing was the Church of England described as 'the Conservative Party at prayer'.

All in all there was an admiration for the British constitution, a British Protestant monarch as head of a national Church and an English-based landowning aristocracy with numerous estates in Wales, Scotland and Ireland, all very much seen as part of one United Kingdom.

Some of these beliefs were not quite as rigid as they might sound. With a young Queen on the throne since 1837, it was expected that her ministers (the Ministers of the Crown) would now take more initiative. After the extension of the vote in 1832 the greater authority of the House of Commons was coming to be accepted. In contrast to the French aristocracy before the Revolution, the British landed classes were not totally opposed to some political role for the wealthy merchant middle class: indeed Peel himself was one of them. **Free trade** measures favouring the commercial middle classes had been passed by the Tories in the mid-1820s.

Whilst the privileges of the Church of England were to be stoutly maintained, there was to be religious toleration for

What were Conservatism and Liberalism?   5

other churches, although suspicion of Roman Catholics as foreign agents still lurked among the darker corridors of some of the great aristocratic houses. Nonetheless it had been a Tory government under Wellington and Peel that had passed **Catholic Emancipation** in 1829, albeit under threat of revolt in Ireland.

THE BEGINNING OF THE LIBERALS

The displacement of Whigs by Liberals took a slightly different course and longer to establish its full effect. However, later in the century it was clear that the change had become complete and permanent. The label 'Whig', unlike the word 'Tory', was eventually to disappear completely from use but the word remained to describe particular political characteristics.

'Liberal' was a word used in the aftermath of the French Revolution of 1789; it was used to describe a political attitude in general rather than one party in particular. The term 'Whig' was always a fairly exclusive one that could be applied to a particular set of aristocratic families who, in the early nineteenth century, took a more 'liberal' view of the workings of the British political system than did the Tories. Whigs such as Earl Grey, for instance, while not condoning the violence of the French Revolution, admired its removal of **absolute monarchy** and regretted that it had not been able to maintain the **constitutional monarchy** of its early days. When Grey was invited to form a ministry to govern the country in 1830 he was seen as the Whig most able to put through a reform of Parliament. He achieved this (though not without difficulty) and one of his principal arguments was that a liberal rather than rigid approach to the British political system was the one most likely to preserve its essentials. Liberals were not revolutionaries.

Although the use of the word remained vague and a little inconsistent 'Liberals' (sometimes with a capital 'L') were increasingly to be found on the Whig rather than Tory or Conservative side in the 1830s and the word was sometimes used interchangeably with **Radical**. By the time of the Corn Law crisis in 1846 'liberal' was increasingly used to

Constitutional monarch? Queen Victoria.

describe those who supported the move to free trade and their economic philosophy of **laissez-faire.**

Beliefs of the Liberals

Whig-Liberal beliefs were not always as clear-cut as Conservative ones. However, there were some discernible trends.

1. A greater acceptance of reform and amendment of the political system than the Conservatives, as seen in 1832. Earl Grey, the Prime Minister of the time, argued that the Reform Act was 'the most aristocratic measure ever put before parliament'. Whilst this was clearly a remark designed to win over waverers to the cause of parliamentary reform it reflected his belief that change was necessary in order to preserve the essentials of the political system.

2. A greater suspicion of the monarch's use of power and a high regard for the 'liberties' of the ordinary Englishman. The restrictions on the powers of the monarch dating from the Bill of Rights of 1689 (see page 2) were seen as central to the political system. The British system was seen by Whigs such as Lord John Russell as superior both to the despotisms (dictatorships) of continental Europe and the democratic 'excesses' of the United States. The system upheld the right of Parliament to be consulted on all major issues of policy including taxation. The **rule of law** was upheld in normal circumstances, as was the right of free speech and of a free press.

3. A more open attitude to allowing the middle classes into the heart of the political framework. The £10 householder (see page 3) to whom the Whigs gave the vote in 1832 was essentially the middle-class merchant and manufacturer as well as the small trader/shopkeeper who, henceforth, were all seen as natural political allies of the Liberals. This resulted in economic polices that were more inclined to free trade by removing **tariff barriers** and a general suspicion of unnecessary expense in government.

4. Less emphasis on the privileges of the Church of England and more attention to religious liberty. The Liberals showed greater sympathy towards **Nonconformist denominations** and sometimes the Roman Catholics: they were beginning to believe in what today is called equality of opportunity for all, regardless of which christian denomination a person belonged to. This was coupled with a concern to use the propertied wealth of the Church for the wider good, in areas such as education. The greater acceptance of the commercial industrial and urban changes which Britain was going through led to a concern with such issues.

KEY TERMS

Rule of law The idea that everyone, whatever their status or position in society, must keep to the laws of the land.

KEY TERMS

Tariff barriers Limit put on the free movement of goods by a government-imposed duty on their importation. This could be either to increase government revenue or to restrict imports of goods that might compete with British-made ones.

Nonconformist denominations
Denomination: a particular religious grouping. Nonconformist: those Protestants who did not wish to conform to the beliefs and organisation of the Church of England. Among the most numerous and influential of these groups were Methodists, Presbyterians, Congregationalists, Baptists, Unitarians and Quakers.

5. Less emphasis on the role of government. Pre-1832 Tories were seen as having prosecuted an expensive war with France before 1815 and Liberals remained keen on low taxation and cheap government throughout the nineteenth century. In this respect they were more reminiscent of the late-twentieth-century Conservative Party than modern Liberal Democrats.

Prime Ministers and their parties 1830–95

Name	Party	Dates
Grey	Whig	1830–4
Peel	Conservative	1834–5
Melbourne	Whig	1835–41
Peel	Conservative	1841–6
Russell	Whig	1846–52
Derby	Conservative	1852 (Feb. to Dec.)
Aberdeen	Whig-Peelite Coalition	1852–5
Palmerston	Whig	1855–8
Derby	Conservative	1858–9
Palmerston	Liberal	1859–65
Russell	Liberal	1865–6
Derby	Conservative	1866–8
Disraeli	Conservative	1868
Gladstone	Liberal	1868–74
Disraeli	Conservative	1874–80
Gladstone	Liberal	1880–5
Salisbury	Conservative	1885–6
Gladstone	Liberal	1886
Salisbury	Conservative	1886–92
Gladstone	Liberal	1892–4
Rosebery	Liberal	1894–5

Organisation of the parties The 1832 Reform Act was to encourage Whig-Liberals and Tory-Conservatives to employ Party Agents to try to maximise support. F.R. Bonham (Tory) and Joseph Parkes (Whig) became significant political figures. London clubs, the Carlton (Tory) and the Reform (Whig) were used as places for meetings and discussions and attempts were made in Parliament to get party supporters out for controversial votes. However, party organisation remained much less significant than after the Second Reform Act of 1867 (See Chapter 4).

By 1846 **the organisation of the parties** was developing and the words 'Conservative' and 'Liberal' were being increasingly used in political circles: the events of 1846–66 were to produce changes that brought them to the forefront of political talk.

QUESTIONS TO CONSIDER

1. How were the names 'Tory' and 'Whig' replaced by the terms 'Conservative' and 'Liberal'?
2. What were the essential differences between the beliefs of the Conservatives and Liberals in the first half of the nineteenth century?

KEY PEOPLE

Lord John Russell 1792–1878 Third Son of the Duke of Bedford, an MP at the age of 21 and a leading Whig politician. He played the principal role in drawing up the terms of the Great Reform Bill in 1830–2; Home Secretary 1835; Prime Minister 1846–52 and 1865–6; Foreign Secretary 1852–3 and 1859–66; and Colonial Secretary in 1855. Nicknamed 'Finality Jack' after insisting, at length, that the 1832 Reform Act was a final settlement of the reform question. In fact, Russell was fairly consistently interested in moderate reform from 1850 to his retirement from active politics in 1868.

Henry John Temple: Viscount Palmerston 1784–1865 His peerage was of Irish origin and did not entitle him to sit in the House of Lords. Originally a Tory and Secretary at War 1809–1830. He then became a Whig. He was Foreign Secretary 1830–4, 1835–41, 1846–51 and Home Secretary 1852–3. He resigned over government conduct with regard to the Russo-Turkish dispute leading to the Crimean War. Prime Minister 1855–8, 1859–65. Died in office having just been re-elected.

CHAPTER 2

How were Whigs transformed into Liberals over the period 1846–68?

INTRODUCTION

A Whig ministry was formed in 1846 when **Lord John Russell** became Prime Minister after the downfall in the Commons of Sir Robert Peel's Conservative government. A year later, in 1847, a General Election was held which confirmed Russell in power, though with the party allegiance of many MPs uncertain his majority was difficult to calculate.

However, when Lord John (later, Earl) Russell replaced **Lord Palmerston** nearly twenty years later in 1865, circumstances had altered. Russell was clearly regarded as leading a Liberal Government even though it may have contained some Whigs. A modern two party system was in the process of developing and the change from Whig to Liberal appeared to symbolise it. How had this come about? Was it actually as clear-cut and complete a change as this seems to suggest? The real position is a little more complex and it was slightly later, in 1868, that the Liberal Party truly emerged under **William Gladstone,** never a Whig but most definitely now a Liberal.

This chapter will chart the move from Whig to Liberal. After a brief look at the formal change which occurred in 1859 it will delve more deeply to examine:

- the political situation in 1846;
- the composition of the Whig Party and its relationship with the Radicals and the Liberals on major issues;
- the extent to which the Whigs followed Liberal and Radical policies between 1846 and 1859;
- why the Radicals failed to form a party separate from Whigs and Liberals;
- the moves towards the development of a strong Liberal Party between 1859 and 1866.

LIBERAL REPLACES WHIG?

The word 'Liberal' took longer than 'Conservative' to establish itself as the name of one of the two main political parties. The formal change to Liberal did not come until 1859.

- Russell's ministry from 1846–52 was usually regarded at the time as Whig, though individual members would have called themselves Liberal.
- Following a brief Conservative ministry under Lord Derby, the non-Conservative grouping that was formed by **Lord Aberdeen** in December 1852 was called a Whig-**Peelite** coalition. This lasted until January 1855.
- The government of Lord Palmerston between 1855 and 1858 was still seen as Whig, but when he re-formed his government in 1859, after another brief Conservative intermission of 16 months, it was regarded as Liberal.

Thus, the formal start of the Liberal Party occurred at the meeting on 6th June 1859 in Willis's Rooms in London when non-Conservative MPs of varying types formally pledged themselves to unite to defeat Lord Derby's Conservative government and oppose his policy towards **the question of Italian Unification**. However, though significant, we should not assign excessive importance to this meeting in the history of the Liberal Party. This is because:

- many Liberal ideas had already been forming well before this;
- Lord Palmerston's views after 1859 were not really different from the ones he had held in his earlier Ministry;
- it was left to Gladstone nearly ten years later in 1868 to become leader of a more coherent Liberal Party.

THE SITUATION IN 1846

The issue of the repeal of the Corn Laws complicated the position of the main political parties in 1846. Up to this

Earl of Derby 1799–1869 Family had extensive landed estates in Lancashire. Originally a Whig, he resigned from office in 1834, disapproving of the government's more liberal religious policy towards Ireland, and joined the Conservatives. Opposed Corn Law repeal and resigned in 1845. Leader of Conservatives 1846–68. Prime Minister 1852, 1858–9, 1866–8. Regarded politics as an aristocratic duty rather than a career. Keener on horse racing, billiards and translating the Greek classics.

point the Whigs and Tories who had fought over the merits of the Reform Bills in 1830–2 had still been the principal groupings. The party position in the House of Commons at the end of 1846 was as follows:

- **Conservatives** – Tory **protectionists** who had opposed repeal and did not favour free trade. They were led by the **Earl of Derby,** the most prominent of the Conservatives who split with Peel over repeal. They were the largest single group in the Commons but were outnumbered by others who all accepted free trade.
- Peelites – A group of Conservatives who stayed loyal to their leader. Their number was distinguished rather than large. They included future Prime Ministers Aberdeen and Gladstone as well as a number of other ex-ministers of Peel's Government. Peel steadfastly refused to ally with either Russell's Whigs or his old Conservative colleagues until his death in 1850.
- Whigs – Led by Lord John Russell: now the party of government. The Whigs had increasingly come to accept the necessity of repeal of the Corn Laws, even though their previous leader, Lord Melbourne, had called it 'the wildest and maddest scheme' as late as 1839.
- Radicals – Whigs also had the broad support of independent MPs over Free trade. These regarded themselves as Radicals but had not formed themselves into a coherent party and their numbers had fallen since the more reforming and exciting atmosphere of the mid 1830s.

After the election of 1847 the numbers were about:

- 325 Whig/Liberal/Radical supporters
- 230 Protectionist Conservatives
- 100 Peelites.

These numbers did not vary enormously over the next twenty years though the Peelite vote was gradually absorbed by both Conservatives and Liberals.

HOW FAR WERE THE WHIGS ARISTOCRATIC RATHER THAN MIDDLE CLASS?

In terms of their social background the Whigs were just as aristocratic as the Tories; that is, their core membership was wealthy, landed, titled aristocracy. Lord John Russell's **cabinet** in 1846 consisted of two marquises, four earls, one viscount, two barons, three knights and just two untitled **commoners**. Many leading Whig aristocratic families like the Grosvenors, the Russells, the Spencers and the Cavendishes had intermarried and were a closely knit group, though not numerous. To match the Tory/Conservative support in Parliament they had to rely on outside assistance from more independent and radical members as well as on **Irish support**.

Backing from more radically-minded MPs was certainly forthcoming. By 1846, their tradition of supporting religious liberty had gained Whigs the support of a wide sector of the industrial middle classes: this included Nonconformists who favoured religious liberty and were also attracted to the Whigs' free trade commitment. Only by appealing to this increasingly important sector of society could the Whigs hope to gain the support they needed to keep out the Tory-Conservative Protectionists.

What attracted the more liberal-thinking middle-classes to the Whigs?

The new political participation by the liberal middle classes in the political process was a major feature of mid-century politics. The middle classes would see the Whigs, for all their aristocratic attitudes, as the natural party with which to ally. After all, why were the middle classes playing a more substantial role in the political affairs of the nation in the first place?

• They owed their opportunity for greater participation partly to the changes introduced by the Whigs in the 1830s. In the 1832 Reform Act the £10 householder in the boroughs (see page 3) was enfranchised (given the vote).
• The middle classes were playing a central role in the growing area of local government. Although they may

KEY TERMS

Cabinet The most important ministers in a government who meet regularly together and agree on important policy decisions.

Commoners Ordinary citizens who did not possess a peerage (title). Entitled to sit in the House of Commons rather than the House of Lords.

KEY CONCEPTS

Irish Support Members of the House of Commons elected in Ireland (about 100), who sat in the English Parliament. Many of these were nationalists and wished to see major reforms in the way the country was run. They generally linked up with English Radicals and advanced Liberals showing that, before 1870, some Irish MPs were generally quite well integrated into the British political system. In the period 1846–68 Irish nationalism was weakened severely by the Famine of 1846.

Municipal Corporations Act of 1835 Corporations were town Councils. The Act set up better organised local government for many urban areas (though not London) and all men who paid rates were normally entitled to a vote. This fact was often used to argue for a ratepayer franchise for the Westminster Parliament.

Poor Law Board of Guardians Locally elected administrators of the workhouses set up by the 1834 Poor Law Act.

not have been actively seeking membership of the House of Commons in any significant numbers, they were increasingly being elected to local Corporations thanks to the Whig **Municipal Corporations Act of 1835**. Alternatively, they might seek election to the **Poor Law Board of Guardians** set up by the Poor Law Amendment Act of 1834. The middle classes dominated these organisations and the aristocracy played little part in such urban developments.

- The middle class factory owner may have been less keen on the Factory Act of 1833: by restricting the hours of work for women and children in factories this would also restrict his freedom of operation, but this was hardly a reason for supporting the Conservatives who had extended the legislation in 1844. The 1833 Act was supported by many Tories.

- The Whigs had not only passed political reform, they also seemed more likely to maintain and develop free trade and extend religious liberty. The Conservatives had opposed all three.

- The economic benefits of free trade were seen as central to middle class prosperity. While Peel had repealed the Corn Laws he had broken with the Conservatives in doing so. The Whig/Peelite coalition of 1852 effectively identified the clear supporters of free trade.

WHAT WAS THE POSITION OF THE RADICALS?

One of the major changes in the process of moving from Whig to Liberal was that in 1846, middle-class Radicals in parliament tended, like the Irish, to operate separately from the established parties. By the late 1860s, however, they were attaching themselves more formally to the emerging 'Liberal' Party. After 1832, middle-class Radicals had been elected in a number of seats, though they did not form a tightly knit group. Their number fell in the 1837 election and still further in 1841. After the repeal of the Corn Laws (partly attributable to the radical agitation of the Anti-Corn Law League) their numbers revived but barely reached more than 50 MPs even at their peak. With the election of 1847, however, they optimistically anticipated further radical reform.

They were to be disappointed. The repeal of the Corn Laws had been seen as a measure passed by the wish of Peel's Government and by the supporters of repeal in Parliament, rather than through the pressure of the Anti-Corn Law League. Russell did not feel obliged to let the middle classes into his government in large numbers. One member of the Anti-Corn Law League agitation, Milner Gibson (see page 53), was given a minor government office but the administration remained essentially a Whig one.

What did the middle-class Radicals want?

- Further political changes to the representative system of the country were required. The 1832 Reform Act had been a sound start but had not gone far enough.
- Religious liberty needed extending so that there was not merely **toleration** for Nonconformists but absolute equality.
- There was a need for more tariff reductions in order to develop free trade policies further.
- Administrative reform leading to greater equality of opportunity was desired. The aristocratic stranglehold on government had to be broken.

But in these areas the more radical middle-class Liberals felt unable to commit themselves fully to a Whig government led by a man such as Russell.

- While Radicals wanted parliamentary reform to go further than it had with extensions of the franchise (to at least **household suffrage**), **re-distribution of seats** and a **secret ballot**, Russell's proposals for reform were seen as inadequate and half-hearted.
- There were still major Nonconformist grievances such as the compulsory payment of Church rates (see page 95) that the Russell government seemed unlikely to introduce.
- The Whig's rather uninspiring Chancellor, Sir Charles Wood, did take action on free trade but was not seen to go far enough in reducing tariffs. This belief was central to middle-class Radicals, especially those of the **Manchester School**.

Manchester School
Originally a group who came from Manchester and industrial Lancashire who believed in a school of thought which championed free trade and as little government interference with the workings of the British economy as possible. Cobden and Bright were leading representatives (see page 24).

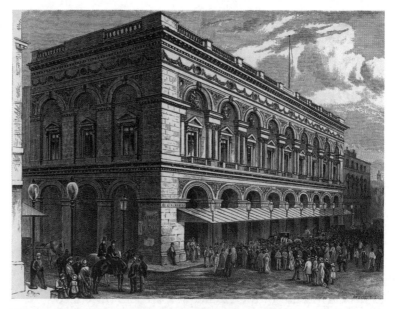

The only public building dedicated to a proposition? Free Trade Hall, Manchester, 1847.

- Whig governments such as Russell's seemed to them far too dominated by the aristocracy and unwilling to let in new middle class talent to a sufficient degree. It was left to Gladstone's governments after 1868 to fulfil many of the earlier Radical demands (see Chapter 5).

HOW FAR DID THE WHIGS SHOW SIGNS OF FOLLOWING LIBERAL POLICIES BETWEEN 1846 AND 1859?

The Whigs and free trade

Russell's ministry from 1846–52 was not a strong one. It lacked a clear majority and temporarily collapsed in 1851: but it *did* maintain free trade principles. It passed:

- The Sugar Act in 1848 which removed the trading privileges of British sugar planters in the West Indies.
- The repeal of the Navigation Laws in 1849. This meant that overseas traders could use any ships they wished to transport their goods abroad: they were not confined to the British Merchant Navy.

The **Great Exhibition of 1851** also advertised the importance of British manufacture and international trading to the world and significantly was only opposed by a few very traditional Conservative MPs such as **Colonel Sibthorp**. Although it was, ironically, the monarchy in the guise of **Prince Albert** that pushed for the Exhibition, it helped the middle classes feel they were playing a part in progress and change.

The Whigs, with the significant aid of the Peelites, extended their reputation as the party supporting free trade in the early fifties. The brief Conservative administration of Lord Derby in 1852 had been uncertain whether to drop their policy of protection. When Lord Aberdeen formed a ministry at the end of 1852 he appointed Gladstone as his Chancellor of the Exchequer: an acknowledged financial expert now thoroughly committed to extending the principles of free trade and with the technical mastery to accomplish his aims. Gladstone produced **budgets** that lowered tariff duties on a number of goods in order to encourage trade expansion. The Budget of 1853 removed duties on 123 articles and reduced them on 133 more.

Such was the growing prosperity of the country that Gladstone felt he could do this without increasing the basic rate of **income tax** despite the loss of government revenue the tariff reduction would bring. Gladstone argued that trade would be encouraged so much by the change that this would cancel out the need for any increases in income tax. Indeed, Gladstone forecast that, if present trends continued, the income tax itself could be abolished by 1860. This certainly pleased the commercial middle classes for two reasons:

- Income tax was not popular and the prospect of its eventual abolition was encouraging news.
- Not only this, the fact that Gladstone was *planning ahead* as Chancellor and actually bringing government financial policy in line with current economic trends sent a message to those same middle classes that government was now acting in their interests and not merely concerned with the well-being of the landed interest. The repeal of the Corn Laws had not been a one-off concession.

KEY EVENTS

Great exhibition of 1851
A special event held for several months in Hyde Park for which the original Crystal Palace was designed by Joseph Paxton. The idea was to display examples of the great variety of industrial products that were the fruits of modern technology.

KEY PEOPLE

Colonel Charles Sibthorp 1783–1855 MP for Lincoln (a family tradition) first elected 1826. Well known for opposing almost all new ideas suggested in Parliament. It was said that he opposed the introduction of free libraries as he didn't much like reading.

Prince Albert 1820–61
Second son of the Duke of Saxe-Coburg Gotha, a small German state. Cousin of Queen Victoria who met him when he first visited England in 1836. They married in 1840. He became popular despite initial anti-German prejudice. A major support for the Queen, he guided her to a style of constitutional monarchy. Made Prince Consort in 1857. Serious minded and hard working, he died of typhoid fever. Victoria was lost without him.

KEY TERMS

Budgets Annual financial statement by the Chancellor of the Exchequer. In the mid-nineteenth century the normal aim of these Budgets was to ensure that government expenditure was matched by government income from taxation and trade.

A building to impress the nations: the Crystal Palace, opened 1851.

Income Tax Tax paid by individuals to government in proportion to the size of their own income. First used in wartime 1797–1816 it was re-introduced as a temporary measure in 1842. In the 1850s it had still not been established as a permanent tax.

Chartists Chartism was a working class movement most prominent between 1838 and 1848. It requested universal male suffrage and related demands such as the secret ballot in the form of three petitions in 1839, 1842, and 1848. Its near collapse in 1848 weakened the working class movement for political reform until the 1860s. However, its absence also meant that governments could now propose parliamentary reform without being accused of caving in to Chartist demands.

Gladstone had begun the process (by no means inevitable at this stage) of becoming a friend of liberal-thinking people. In the 1860s he was to complete the task. However, in other important areas the Whigs (or Peelites in Gladstone's case) had not gone far enough to gain regular Radical support.

The Whigs and political reform

On the question of further parliamentary reform there were some signs of movement after 1848 when the final major **Chartist** demonstration had ended in a heavy rain on Kennington Common. Russell had previously argued that no more reform of parliament would be necessary after the changes of 1832 but reform was increasingly seen as a possibility. However, the various ideas put forward soon after this never got very far:

- In 1851 he made a very modest proposal for reform of Parliament whereby the £10 household franchise would be reduced to £6. This never got to the vote.
- A similar proposal in 1852 bit the dust with the fall of the ministry.
- Another one disappeared without trace in 1854 with the outbreak of the Crimean War.

For the more radical Liberals these proposals were inadequate. They looked to see:

- a substantial increase in the franchise to at least household suffrage;
- a redistribution of seats that would help break the aristocratic domination composition of Parliament;
- a secret ballot to enable voters to cast their votes freely.

The Whigs and religious reform

On the question of religious liberty, the Whigs were seen as less dogmatic upholders of the privileges of the Church of England than the Tories but had not gained the support of the religious dissenters (Nonconformists). In particular the more radical Nonconformists wished to see:

- abolition of compulsory Church Rates;
- **voluntaryism** in education so that the Church of England schools did not have the advantage of state funding;
- the opportunity to attend Oxford and Cambridge Universities on equal terms with Anglicans. Fellowships (teaching posts) at these institutions for example were barred to them;
- they questioned the establishment of the Anglican Church in Ireland where the majority of people were Roman Catholic and wished to see the wealth of the Church endowments go elsewhere. Increasingly many were coming to the view that there should be no establishment in England either.

These were significant issues: religious issues were much discussed in mid-nineteenth century Britain and were central to the lives of many people.

The Religious Census of 1851 indicated that about half of total Church attendance was not to the established Church of England but to Nonconformist denominations supported by the industrial middle class. However the Whig governments of Russell, and later Palmerston, did not wish to move towards this degree of radical reform. The year of the Religious Census also saw Russell pass an Ecclesiastical Titles Bill, which was an illiberal measure. It prevented the English Roman Catholic Bishops from taking up titles with the same name as their Church of England counterparts. Here, Russell may well have appealed to some of the protestant Nonconformist middle classes in a negative way, since their liberal attitude to differences

KEY CONCEPTS

Voluntaryism The idea that funding of education should be by voluntary means rather than state assistance. Government funding of education was increasing and the fear of Nonconformists was that the lion's share of this state assistance would go to Church of England schools.

The growth of nonconformity: Pendre Congregational Chapel, South Wales, built in 1820.

in belief did not always extend at this time to Roman Catholics. But he did not impress more consistent Liberal thinkers such as John Bright who thought the measure 'absurd'.

The Whigs and administrative reform

The desire of Liberals to enter the heart of the aristocratic establishment was as strong as ever. Although the middle classes had received the vote in 1832, the composition of Parliament did not reflect their proportion of the electorate. The kind of reforms desired, included a widening of opportunity for the middle classes:

- Civil Service appointments should no longer be reserved solely for those of upper-class backgrounds. Promotion on merit by competitive examination should be introduced.
- Top positions in the army should again be on merit and **Commissions** should not only be available to those who purchased them.
- A more open government prepared to reveal details of Departmental business, especially that of the Foreign Office.

Again, there was little sign of concession from the Whigs in this area. The Northcote-Trevelyan Report of 1854 did recommend competitive entry into the Civil Service but major change had to wait for Gladstone's government after 1868 (see Chapter 6). The **Crimean War** (1854–6) highlighted administrative inefficiencies starkly: uncertain generalship in the army and a lack of communication with government back home. For a time radical demands for reform surfaced strongly with the founding of the Administrative Reform Association in 1855 by figures such as Bright but the momentum did not last. Palmerston's government (strictly speaking the last Whig one) between 1855 and 1858 did not take up the challenge of major administrative reform. Again, it was only when Gladstone became Prime Minister in 1868 that reformist action was taken with regard to the purchase of army commissions (see Chapter 6).

Foreign policy and the importance of Palmerston's popularity

Palmerston, however, was a surprisingly popular figure with the Radicals despite a reputation (not always completely deserved, see Chapter 3) for being near Conservative in his domestic views and a well-known opponent of further parliamentary reform. He managed to maintain the voting support of many of the Radicals with a popular foreign policy. The English middle classes were decidedly patriotic and Palmerston's vigorous foreign policy was already well known to them, as he had previously been Foreign Secretary in Russell's ministry from 1846–51 (see page 11). In showing some sympathy with **1848 revolutionaries** and less concern for their governments on occasions, he gained a Liberal image. Whether this reputation was deserved is extremely questionable but a Liberal interpretation was generally made of Palmerston's actions. Arguably it was not so much his liberalism as his general championing of English interests abroad that endeared him to the middle classes.

The result was that, at the age of 70, **Palmerston was reluctantly invited by Queen Victoria** to be Prime Minister in 1855. The Whig-Peelite coalition of Lord Aberdeen had fallen with the Government's defeat in Parliament, largely because of its weaknesses in running the Crimean War. When the Conservative, Derby, was unwilling to become prime

KEY EVENTS

Crimean War 1854–6
Started from a dispute between Russia and Turkey in which Britain intervened on the Turkish side. Britain had strong trading links with Turkey. The war was largely confined to the Crimean peninsula where British forces suffered heavy causalities and there was much criticism at home about how the conflict was conducted. It ultimately brought down Aberdeen's Whig-Peelite coalition early in 1855.

KEY EVENTS

1848 revolutions In the year 1848 revolutionary disturbances swept through the entire continent of Europe west of Russia. Many were protesting about their dictatorial and illiberal governments. The absence of this kind of protest in Britain was seen by those in power as confirmation of the soundness and stability of the British political system.

KEY THEMES

Palmerston and Queen Victoria The Queen was reluctant to invite Palmerston to become Prime Minister because she disliked him intensely. Her playful name for him was Lord Pumicestone (see also page 51).

minister, the fact that a number of other leading figures had been at least temporarily discredited by their involvement in Aberdeen's government allowed Palmerston to emerge.

The Radicals were disappointed. They did not even have the consolation of Gladstone as Chancellor, since after at first accepting office he decided he could not serve in the new Ministry, objecting to Palmerston's approach to government in general and to his foreign policy in particular.

But there is no doubting the popularity of Palmerston's policy with the middle class electorate (see pages 47–55). Even when he was defeated on a foreign policy issue in Parliament in 1857, he immediately called a General Election. His supporters, Whigs and Liberals, were returned with a comfortable majority, but such was the uncertainty of party allegiance at this time that Palmerston was defeated in parliament the following year. Lord Derby then formed the third of his brief administrations only to fall after another triumph for Palmerston's supporters at the polls in 1859.

The attitude to Palmerston's foreign policy among Radicals was mixed, as were their views on the Crimean War. This division was not confined to foreign policy and helps explain the lack of a properly organised Radical Party.

The dominant mid-nineteenth-century parliamentarian: Lord Palmerston addresses the House of Commons, 1863.

WHY WERE RADICALS UNABLE TO FORM THEIR OWN PARTY?

Radicals were too diverse a group and too divided to form their own party with any chance of lasting unity and effectiveness. They were interested in a number of different questions and different Radical members emphasised different issues as being of prime importance. On some of these matters, like foreign policy, Radicals took opposing sides and would never have reached sufficient agreement to work together as a group. Only on free trade did there seem to be clear agreement. Their coherent differences can be grouped as follows.

1. **The range and degree of parliamentary reform.**
   Moderate Liberals favoured a lowering of the £10 household suffrage level to around £6 or £7. This would have included the very top end of the skilled working class. **More advanced Liberals,** now almost indistinguishable from Radicals, saw no objection to household suffrage with certain residence qualifications and up-to-date payment of Poor Rates. The most extreme Radicals favoured manhood suffrage. The Radicals John Stuart Mill and Henry Fawcett (see table) argued powerfully for female suffrage, though on this point they were in a minority. Some felt a secret ballot was essential to overcome aristocratic influence, while others regarded the secrecy involved as 'un-English'. Some, such as Mill, actually changed their views on the secret ballot question in the 1850s and decided the disadvantages of secrecy outweighed its advantages.

2. **Foreign policy**
   Some Radicals such as John Arthur Roebuck were strong supporters of Palmerston's foreign policy and fully believed Britain to be championing the interests of small nations abroad against mighty despotisms like Russia. Others, like Richard Cobden and John Bright, were near **pacifists** who had strong moral and religious objections to fighting that risked heavy casualties and felt the spread of international free trade would make the world so interdependent economically that war would be suicidal. Bright, a great orator, delivered a powerful **anti-war speech** in the House of Commons in February 1855. Despite his eloquent plea, however, the peace-

KEY TERMS

Advanced Liberals Liberals whose views bordered on Radical. They were generally more open to the idea of parliamentary reform, especially after 1850, and suspicious at what they saw as the excessive caution of many Whigs.

Pacifists Those opposed to war in all circumstances: Bright was a member of the Society of Friends (Quakers) whose views are usually pacifist. Bright, however, (unlike Cobden) strongly supported the northern states in the American Civil War 1861–5.

Anti-war speech John Bright delivered this speech in the House of Commons 23rd February 1855 'The angel of death has been abroad throughout the land: you can almost hear the beating of his wings…he takes his victims from the castle of the noble, the mansion of the wealthy and the cottage of the poor and lowly'.

loving radicals were in the distinct minority during the Crimean War and Palmerston's subsequent foreign policy adventures.

3. **Nonconformity and Religious Liberty**

Religious liberty was often a great unifying force for Radicals but there were major differences nonetheless. There were sharp divisions between Nonconformist militants like Edward Miall and secularists like **George Jacob Holyoake**. While both might have agreed on the disestablishment of the Church, Miall wished to see Temperance Reform (see page 100) whereas Holyoake concentrated on founding secular societies to counter the influence of religious institutions.

4. **Social Reform**

Traditional laissez-faire free traders such as Bright remained doubtful about the need for or desirability of government regulation of factories or even public health. Many Radicals, however, were becoming increasingly convinced of the need for such regulation, even to the extent of modifying rights to private property in the case of housing reforms. The differences on social reform diminished as more and more Radicals came to acknowledge the need for government intervention in relation to social issues.

KEY PEOPLE

George Jacob Holyoake 1817–1906 He founded the *Reasoner* magazine in 1846 questioning the value of religion and was a keen social reformer. Secularists believed that society had no need for religious belief: it was out of date and impeded modern progress. Moral standards should be developed without regard for the Divine or an after-life.

KEY EVENTS

American Civil War Fought between 1861 and 1865. The southern states in the Union wished to secede (leave) and the northern states wished to prevent them. Britain was officially neutral and opinion about who to sympathise with was divided at first. But as the war developed into a conflict about whether to retain slavery, support for the north grew, especially in more radical circles.

However, many divisions remained as acute as ever in the 1860s. For instance, there was disagreement on who to support, if anyone, in the **American Civil War.** Should it be the southern states struggling to be free of northern domination, or the slave-abolitionists in the north? Radical division on the point was shown for instance by Roebuck backing the South and Bright rooting for the North.

The social differences within the Radicals remained very wide. This meant many believed the establishment of a formal party would be extremely difficult. However, the coming-together of many different social groups to form a strong Liberal party by 1868 showed that it was not impossible. Between the formal formation of the Liberal Party in 1859 and their triumph at the 1868 election a number of factors promoted unity in a way they had not for an earlier generation of Radicals.

Leading Radicals

	Born	Background	Parliamentary Career	Particular interests	Died
John Bright	1811	Owned Mill in Rochdale	1847–57 Manchester, 1857–85 Birmingham	Free trade, parliamentary reform, administrative reform, Ireland	1889
Richard Cobden	1804	Moved to Lancashire when a child, manufacturer	1841–7 Oldham, 1847–65 Manchester	Free trade, international peace	1865
John Stuart Mill	1806	Londoner, classical education	1865–8 Westminster	Liberty and laissez-faire, votes for women	1873
Henry Fawcett	1833	Blinded in 1858, Cambridge professor in 1863	1865–84 Brighton	Parliamentary reform, votes for women	1884
Edward Miall	1809	Working-class Londoner, edited *The Nonconformist*, Congregational minister	1852–7 Rochdale, 1869–74 Bradford	Disestablishment, abolition of Church Rates, rights of Nonconformists, education	1881
John Roebuck	1802 (India)	Brought up in England and Canada	Bath 1832–47, Sheffield 1849–68, Sheffield 1874–9 (as Conservative)	Parliamentary reform, foreign affairs, education, free press	1879

HOW FAR DID THE LIBERALS COME TOGETHER BETWEEN 1859 AND 1865?

This was an important period in the formation of the Liberal Party:

- Free trade policies continued under Gladstone whose reputation was rising rapidly.
- Gladstone also became more liberal politically and a potential leader of a Liberal Party. Only the aged Palmerston, who continued to be sceptical of the need for immediate change, stood in the way of more substantial parliamentary reform.
- John Bright emerged as a prominent leader for the more radical Liberals.

- The more complex European situation meant the vigorous Palmerstonian foreign policy was less appropriate. In future, Liberal foreign policy would assume a distinctive character.

In addition:

- The middle-class provincial press was making a substantial impact on middle-class political opinion.
- The Liberals were also attracting the skilled working-class labour interest to a much greater extent than before.

Free trade

Gladstone continued his free trade policies in a more uninterrupted way during Palmerston's ministry of 1859–65 and for a further year under Russell.

- The 1860 Budget produced further major tariff reductions. Only 48 items were left on the tariff.
- By 1865 income tax had been reduced from **10d to 4d** in the pound.
- Government expenditure was less in 1866 than it was in 1860 (£70million down to £66 million).
- Sugar and tea duties were lowered in 1864 and 1865.
- The timber duty was abolished in 1866.

As technological change in the form of the railway and steamship cut costs, contemporaries saw free trade as key to prosperity and viewed this 'Liberal' policy as one they could support.

Gladstone and political reform

Gladstone, an economic champion of the liberal middle classes, was also becoming a political champion for a social group just below this: the skilled working class. During his second period as Chancellor he increasingly promoted their right to vote in elections. Deeply impressed with the way the Lancashire textile workers handled the cotton crisis of the American Civil War (see page 25), he made a speech in 1864 which created something of a sensation, implying that the working man had a moral right to vote. Gladstone protested in vain that his remarks did not necessarily mean this but the **People's William** had nevertheless emerged. Another factor in the development of this reputation was Gladstone's

KEY EVENTS

10d to 4d d was the symbol for (old) pennies. Two and a half old pennies make one new pence in current money.

KEY TERMS

The **People's William**
Popular nickname for Gladstone in the 1860s and beyond. First coined by the Daily Telegraph in the 1860s, then a Liberal paper edited by Thornton Hunt. Gladstone was seen as the senior politician most representative of the views of ordinary people. His role in the repeal of the Paper Duty in 1861 (see page 30) undoubtedly added to his reputation among journalists. (There is more on this term in Chapter 11.)

liking for long speeches in front of large audiences who were held spellbound by his oratory. Making good use of the modern railway he travelled all over the country and, like Palmerston, (see page 52) never patronised his audience, a fact they much appreciated: they sensed the sincerity of his beliefs. The increasingly popular provincial and national press reported Gladstone's speeches at length. Moreover, it had been Gladstone, with his repeal of newspaper taxes and paper duties when Chancellor (see page 30), who had made newspapers more affordable for the increasingly literate lower classes. Gladstone seemed the Liberal leader of the future and the days of the 'two dreadful old men' (Queen Victoria's name for Palmerston and Russell) seemed to be numbered. The Whigs had become merely a part of the Liberal Party, though the term Whig remained to describe particular political characteristics and individual politicians.

The emergence of Bright

John Bright (see page 24) (a famous Radical figure because of his role in the Anti-Corn Law League) **lost much popularity** after his criticism of the Crimean War. Never an out and out democrat and uncertain about female suffrage, he saw no reason why votes should not be extended to all male

KEY CONCEPTS

Bright's loss of popularity He was defeated at the election in Manchester in 1857 and suffered health problems. However, he was re-elected to Parliament to serve Birmingham later in the same year and by the early 1860s he turned his considerable speaking powers to the cause of parliamentary reform with renewed vigour.

Leading nineteenth century Radical: John Bright.

householders. His firm line on this question won over many Liberal MPs. The need for substantial parliamentary reform (even if there was still some disagreement on the details) became a uniting more than a dividing factor for Liberals.

Bright's long-standing colleague, Cobden, also played a significant Liberal role in the early 1860s and this would certainly have been greater but for his death in 1865. Though refusing Palmerston's offer of a cabinet post in 1859 he agreed to act as a government agent and negotiated an important Free Trade Treaty with France in 1860.

Changes in Foreign Policy

The emergence of a powerful Prussia (Northern Germany) under its Prime Minister Bismarck in the 1860s and the unification of Italy at a similar time made an aggressive **Palmerstonian-style policy** look more risky than before.

Significant change in foreign policy led to criticism. Conservatives accused the Liberals of being 'Little Englanders' and not sufficiently pro-Empire. Time was to show Liberal differences to exist in this area as well as others. However, broad agreement about the general principles outlined above made for a relative unity on foreign policy for an emerging Liberal Party, which would have been impossible before the late 1860s.

Death of Palmerston

Another major factor in terms of liberal unity was the death of Lord Palmerston in October 1865 shortly after his Liberal grouping had been successful in another election. Palmerston was aware his passing would bring changes. Suspecting Gladstone would succeed him he predicted that '*when he takes my place there will be strange doings*'. Palmerston's death led to Russell (now Earl Russell) succeeding him as prime minister, but Russell was 74 and only in moderate health. Gladstone would clearly be Liberal leader in the Commons and heir apparent to leader of the Party. The '*strange doings*' were about to begin (see page 32 and pages 63–68). This led to a period of great political excitement and drama between 1866 and 1868. It was only after these events had unfolded that Gladstone emerged as the clear leader of a strong and relatively united Liberal Party.

KEY CONCEPTS

The riskiness of a Palmerstonian-style foreign policy A foreign policy that became too actively involved with Europe seemed to be fraught with danger as large continental armies developed. Intervention would be too expensive and likely to disrupt the growth of the British economy – as had the Crimean War. Un-Christian in moral terms war was impossible to justify unless the weak were clearly being severely oppressed, because of the suffering and death of innocent parties.

The role of the press

During the 1850s and 1860s there was a substantial growth in the provincial middle-class press. Middle-class influence over public opinion in the industrial towns of Britain was substantial and that influence was frequently Liberal. The growth of the popularity of newspapers was aided by:

- the repeal of the Newspaper tax in 1854 and the repeal of advertising tax in 1855;
- Gladstone's repeal of the duty on paper in 1861;
- the technological improvements brought about by the steam press in the 1850s;
- the rapid increase in communication caused by the railway and the telegraph.

All these helped to make newspapers cheaply available everywhere and greatly encouraged the growth of more newspapers and their readers in the increasingly literate towns. Political knowledge and discussion was becoming less and less the preserve of the landed classes.

Liberal newspapers included:

- *Leeds Mercury* run by the Baines family, strong Nonconformist liberals;
- *Leicester Mercury* run by the vice-president of the Leicestershire Liberal Association;
- *Newcastle Chronicle* run by Liberal Joseph Cowan;
- *Sheffield Independent* run by the Leader family, also Liberals.

List taken from John Vincent: *The formation of the British Liberal party*, 1972

Working class involvement with the Liberals

In the 1840s working-class and middle-class political activity had tended to be separate. The radical demands of the Chartists were dominated by working people and middle-class radicalism was channelled into organisations like the Anti-Corn Law League. However, the Chartist movement faded rapidly after 1848. Even those who kept the Chartist flag flying were of the opinion by the 1860s progress was only likely to be achieved, in practice, by an alliance of all Radicals under a broader 'Liberal' umbrella.

George Odger 1820–77
A shoemaker, Odger was
an active trade unionist and
took part in the large and
widespread builders' strike
in 1859–60. Secretary of the
newly formed **London Trades
Council** (a group of leading
trade union secretaries) in
1869–72, he had a very radical
reputation in the 1850s and
early 1860s. From 1868
onwards he identified more
with advanced Liberals and
Radicals, giving broad support
to Gladstone.

In Birmingham, class conflict was traditionally less acute because its workshop (rather than large factory) base allowed more personal relations between employer and employee. Hence Bright was the city's acknowledged Radical leader for a wide social group. In London, men like **George Odger**, Secretary of the **London Trades Council,** were working-class leaders with a radical past who began to develop close links with the liberal middle-classes. Odger supported the middle-class John Stuart Mill's successful bid to be elected for Westminster in 1865 as an advanced Liberal. With no effective socialist movement in sight, many Liberals believed that an extension of the franchise into the skilled working-class would benefit them rather than the Conservatives. They believed they had nothing to fear from respectable and increasingly moderate trade unionists.

Others however wondered whether the average working man would vote for the same person as his employer and in some areas working-class and middle-class organisations remained distinct, with different demands. For instance: in 1864 there was the foundation of the middle and working-class Reform Union that campaigned for household suffrage, but it developed an almost exclusively middle-class membership. In 1865, those that wanted an exclusively working-class organisation with more radical demands set up the Reform League, which committed itself to manhood suffrage.

Survival of the Whigs

Because Lord Palmerston had died in October 1865, soon after constructing his **new government**, Russell, his successor, made few changes. This meant the Liberal Cabinet was still well stocked with aristocratic Whigs. Russell for instance, replaced himself as Foreign Secretary with the Earl of Clarendon. Six of the twelve members of the Cabinet were peers from Whig families, and posts in government such as Foreign Secretary and Lord Chancellor (the head of the English legal system) were still positions traditionally reserved for the landed classes.

As such the aristocratic Whigs (and Conservatives) were surviving remarkably well. Nonetheless, change was coming. At each election a new influx of Radical MPs from non-landed backgrounds emerged. This was particularly true of 1865, when Fawcett was elected for Brighton and Mill for Westminster.

**The new government of
1865** Looking more widely at
the composition of the House
of Commons generally the
aristocratic element had clearly
survived the granting of the
vote to the middle classes in
1832. Change was coming but
it was slow. Out of a total of
658 members there were:

Moreover, with Palmerston gone, the introduction of a parliamentary reform bill became much more likely. Over the next two years reform was to be the dominant issue, accelerating the transition from Whig to Liberal.

HOW DID THE TRANSITION FROM WHIG TO LIBERAL CONTINUE: 1866–8?

In 1866 the moderate parliamentary reform bill proposed by Russell's government (see page 63) was intended to continue the traditional Liberal/Conservative politics of the Palmerstonian period in which the Whigs could still play a major part in the now more united Liberal grouping in Parliament. However, the defeat of this Bill led to public protest (see page 65) which indicated the strength of Radical feeling on Reform and actually made the passing of a more Radical Bill more likely. It also produced the resignation of Russell, now the leading Whig after the death of Palmerston. Gladstone, already the dominant Liberal figure in the House of Commons, now emerged as the Liberal leader. Although it was, surprisingly, Disraeli and not Gladstone that now passed the more substantial Reform Bill (see pages 64–8), the effect was still to weaken the Whigs.

WHAT WAS THE IMPORTANCE OF THE 1868 ELECTION IN THE DECLINE OF THE WHIGS?

Another General Election was now seen as necessary even though one was not due for another four years, because it would give the new voters on the electoral register an early opportunity to cast their first vote. The focus of discussion at this election in the country at large was not so much the religious and political liberty beloved of the Whigs – this had now largely been achieved – but industrial and commercial questions, education, trade unions and the condition of the working classes. However, this change was partially disguised in the election's national debate by Gladstone's focus on the need to remove the Irish Church establishment, (see page 85) an issue on which the Whigs felt comfortable and which reminded them of their heyday in the 1830s.

The wider franchise would mean that the Liberal Party looked to acquire a wider social range with their new members of parliament: so one result of the election was

Wider group of Cabinet Ministers His cabinet included men such as Lowe (son of a clergyman), Cardwell (family of Liverpool merchants) and Bright (cotton spinning background) whose origins were middle class and non-Whig. Others such as Home Secretary Henry Bruce (from the minor Welsh gentry) were far removed from the great Whig landowners.

an increase in the number of MPs of middle-class origin to something like 250 out of 652. Moreover, Gladstone had never been a Whig and, though a great believer in the value of an aristocratic contribution to government, was more than prepared to look for a **wider social group of Cabinet Ministers** in his first Cabinet at the end of 1868.

CONCLUSION

By 1866 the Whig Party had largely been transformed into a Liberal Party in which Whigs were still prominent but the liberal-minded middle classes (and a few working class people) were also incorporated into a much wider social and political base. What were the main factors behind this transformation?

- The inability of the radical elements in Parliament to come together and formally develop a Party grouping completely separate from the Whigs.
- An agreement on the development of free trade policies.
- The emergence of Gladstone and Bright as champions of the Liberal interest in the 1860s and their clear commitment to political and administrative reform.
- Strong Nonconformist support from an increasingly powerful and politically literate middle class.
- The greater opportunities for a broader Liberal party afforded by the death of Palmerston in 1865. This opened the way to a greater chance of agreement on foreign policy and further parliamentary reform.

QUESTIONS TO CONSIDER

1. What was the relationship between Radicals and Whigs in the period 1846–59?
2. What were the main political issues that caused division in Radical ranks in the 1850s?
3. Why did the Liberal Party develop in the 1860s?
4. What was the importance of Gladstone in the emerging Liberal Party?

PERIOD STUDY EXAM-STYLE QUESTIONS

1. Assess the reasons why the Liberals had replaced the Whigs as the main opponents of the Conservatives by 1868?

CHAPTER 3

Why did the Conservatives find power elusive and temporary from 1846–68?

INTRODUCTION

In the mid-nineteenth century the Conservatives had the largest support of any single party in the country. But:

- The disastrous split in 1846 over the repeal of the Corn Laws brought a long-lasting division between Peelites and Protectionists that never fully healed.
- There were major problems concerning the leadership in the Commons of the main group of Protectionist Conservatives. These problems revolved around Disraeli's suitability as Conservative leader.
- The unstable political climate of the period did not help in the quest to establish more popular support for the party: it was not always clear what the Conservatives stood for. For many years they were seen to back the wrong horse – protection (see page 13).
- The electoral appeal of Lord Palmerston, a near conservative Whig, did not assist the cause of the Conservative Party.

This chapter will investigate the factors that kept them out of office for so long.

KEY ISSUES

The Peelites are important for **Key Issue 1** and the effects of the defeat of Peel are important for **Key Issue 3** (see page iv).

ORIGINS OF THE SPLIT

The Conservative Party recovered well from their heavy defeat by the Whigs after the passing of the 1832 Reform Bill. Under Peel, the Tories (often by that time referred to as Conservatives) had re-assumed office by 1841 with a strong and effective ministry. The recovery involved a change in direction. Conservatives had accepted parliamentary reform while the Whigs resisted. So the two issues which seemed to separate the parties were that:

- The Conservatives were the stronger defenders of the landed interest in general and the Corn Laws and protectionist principles in particular.
- The Conservatives were also keen not to undermine the position and privileges of the Church of England in any way.

The Maynooth Grant and the repeal of the Corn Laws

Peel, however, proceeded to take two decisions which seemed to undermine these basic principles. Both were linked to Ireland and while Peel believed he had acted in the national interest on both issues it was very damaging for the Conservatives as a Party:

- By increasing the **Maynooth Grant** in 1845 he offended many Conservatives who objected on principle to a measure which in their eyes undermined the established Church. Roman Catholicism was not generally looked upon sympathetically by the majority of the landed interest. No matter that the grant was merely being increased and used for general educational purposes, the objection was still strong.
- Peel's decision to **repeal the Corn Laws in 1846**, while partly inspired by strong humanitarian feeling, proved the breaking point for many Conservative landowners who saw this as a betrayal of their interests and principles. Agriculture was still perceived as the largest single industry and to fail to protect the farming community was seen to be undermining the economic strength of the country in an unacceptable way. A pledge, in 1841, to maintain the Laws in the next Parliament had been broken. Repeal was seen to be taking away the main form of protection for the landed interest.

The most eloquent and successful in attacking Peel was made by **Benjamin Disraeli** who, in a powerful performance in the Commons, accused Peel of betraying his party (see pages 39–40).

The repeal of the Corn Laws was passed by a majority of 97 in the Commons with Whig support; the influence of the Duke of Wellington (loyal to Peel) ensured it also passed through the House of Lords.

Maynooth Grant
Maynooth was a College near Dublin for training Irish Roman Catholic priests. It had received a government grant of £900 a year since 1795. It is said that some students attended without any inclination towards the priesthood in order to take advantage of general educational opportunities rarely found elsewhere. They would then leave before their final vows. In 1845, Peel proposed to treble the grant. Many Conservatives voted against the grant and Peel was embarrassingly forced to rely on Whig support to get the measure through.

Repeal of the Corn Laws
The serious famine that had begun in Ireland with the failure of the potato crop in 1845 demanded a reaction from government. Peel's response was to draw up a bill for the suspension of Corn Duties so that grain could flow more freely into the stricken country.

The voting figures in the Commons were:

For repeal: 339   112 Conservatives (Peelites)
                227 Whigs, Liberals and Radicals
Against: 242   all Protectionist Conservatives
Majority 97

This shows the serious nature of the Conservative split.

RESULTS OF THE SPLIT

The day after the repeal of the Corn Laws was passed by the Lords, Peel's government was defeated on a routine bill concerning law and order in Ireland. Protectionist Conservatives (see page 13) were bitter about what they regarded as Peel's betrayal.

Never before had Conservatives voted against an **Irish Coercion Act.** In doing so they ensured the political defeat of Peel and a spell of government for the Whigs and their Liberal allies. Peel and his loyal colleagues (Peelites, and prominent among them William Gladstone) disappeared into the political wilderness, refusing to attach themselves to either the Tory/Conservatives led by Lord Derby or the Whig/Liberals of Lord John Russell. But they cannot have imagined that, in the next twenty years, the Conservatives would have been the governing party for only two very short spells barely amounting to two years.

THE SPLIT CONTINUES 1846–52

Party problems: The Peelites

The minority of Conservatives who had supported repeal and stuck to the name Peelites claimed to be the true Conservatives and refused for the moment to link up with any other grouping. Senior politicians such as Peel's ex-Chancellor of the Exchequer, Henry Goulburn, were not likely to attach themselves to any other party and maintained, like all senior Peelites, a fierce loyalty to Peel. However, Peel's actions hardly helped the cause of reunion. He could not bring himself to realign with those who had failed to support him in his hour of need. It would, as

KEY PEOPLE

Benjamin Disraeli 1804–81 Born the son of a Jewish writer in London, Disraeli had a modest but not a poor upbringing and was educated privately. His father, who had lost his religious faith, had his children undergo Christian Baptism; Disraeli at the age of 13. He studied law, became a writer, especially of novels, and entered Parliament in 1837 by which time he was a Conservative. His early party allegiance had been uncertain. To his great disappointment he was not given office by Peel in 1841. His early reputation was as an elaborate speaker and fancy dresser with a fondness for gambling and society ladies. His speeches in 1846 against Peel secured his reputation overnight. See Chapters 7 and 8.

KEY TERMS

Irish Coercion Act
Coercion in general terms means force. In this context the Act was designed to remove the Rule of Law in Ireland and allow the authorities to arrest nationalists on mere suspicion of violent revolutionary activities. Such Acts were passed almost routinely in the early nineteenth century and were normally supported by the Conservatives without question.

he put it *'be inconsistent with my sense of honour'* even to discuss tactics with the Protectionists on how to organise opposition to Russell's Whig government. Since Peel would not stand down as leader either, the Conservatives remained an embarrassingly divided party.

This was particularly apparent in the General Election of 1847 when the chief Conservative agent, F.R. Bonham, used what few central funds the party had at that time in favour of Peelite candidates. Matters would have been even worse if Peelite and Protectionist Conservatives had frequently fought each other in the same constituency in the election. Fortunately for them this only happened on about ten occasions. Parliamentary constituencies were usually two member seats and in 1847 there was generally an arrangement whereby either a Peelite or a Protectionist would contest the seat, depending on who had the best chance of winning. Despite this, the result of the election was a definite victory for those who supported repeal (see table on page 45) and therefore free trade. True, Russell would only have a parliamentary majority if he could rely on the support of all the non-Conservative elements in parliament and it was not a strong government. It was the only one possible however, with Peel remaining aloof from all other groups. So, Russell's government continued and the Conservatives remained out of office.

PROBLEMS OF THE PROTECTIONIST LEADERSHIP: LORD DERBY

Who would lead the Protectionist Conservatives? In the nineteenth century parties not in government frequently had two leaders, one in the Commons and one in the Lords. Leadership in the Lords was a straightforward matter: Lord Stanley, who became the 14th Earl of Derby in 1851 (referred to in this text throughout as Derby) stood head and shoulders above all others. His speaking abilities, ministerial experience and strong support of both Protection and the Church of England made him the obvious candidate. He had spoken powerfully in favour of retaining the Corn Laws and had been the minister to resign from Peel's cabinet in December 1845 when repeal was first proposed. But Derby was reluctant to take on the full responsibilities of leadership. In the aristocratic tradition, he saw political service as an important duty to one's country but essentially a part-time occupation. Indeed, some of his other interests were more important to him. He enjoyed translating Classical Greek writers such as Homer and wrote a book of religious instruction for young children. Like one of his beloved horses faced with too large a jump, his reaction to being overall Party leader of the Protectionist Conservatives was to shy away. His reluctance to take over was increased by the fact that the outlook for the Conservatives seemed bleak.

One major problem was the lack of politicians who had previously been ministers. With the exception of Derby, those with experience and ability had stayed with Peel.

Leading Ministers who had stayed loyal to Peel	
Name	**Position in Peel's Government**
Aberdeen	Foreign Secretary
Graham	Home Secretary
Goulborn	Chancellor of the Exchequer
Herbert	War Secretary
Gladstone	President of the Board of Trade (then succeeded Stanley as Colonial Secretary)
Dalhousie	Succeeded Gladstone as President of the Board of Trade

These were all regarded as able administrators and, generally, capable speakers and without them the remaining Conservatives felt lost. More junior able ministers such as **Edward Cardwell** also stayed loyal to Peel. On the **back benches** Protectionist Tories were there in overwhelming numbers but lacked the experience, confidence or inclination to take a leading role.

HOW DID DISRAELI BECOME A PROMINENT CONSERVATIVE?

At first sight Disraeli seems an unlikely figure to become a leading Conservative. However, he was the party's leader in

KEY PEOPLE

Edward Cardwell 1813–86 Born in Liverpool. First became an MP in 1842 as a strong supporter of Peel. President of the Board of Trade 1852–5 in Aberdeen's Ministry; also served in Palmerston's and Russell's governments 1859–66; Secretary for War 1868–74, introducing important Army reforms.

KEY TERMS

Back benches In the British political system, government ministers are normally taken from the membership of the majority in the House of Commons (or Lords). They occupy the benches at the front of the chamber (House). Those MPs who support them occupy the benches behind them and are known as back benchers. (For front benches see page 89.)

the House of Commons in the 1850s and 1860s, eventually becoming overall leader of the party and Prime Minister in 1868. Despite losing his position as Prime Minister within a few months, he retained the party leadership for 13 years until his death in 1881 and was Prime Minister again for over six years, from the beginning of 1874 to the middle of 1880. How, then, did he rise to prominence?

He had not been selected for office by Peel in 1841 so remained both a back bencher and bitter towards Sir Robert. He was not initially seen as anything like leadership material. Others moved faster towards political promotion. For instance, William Gladstone was appointed Vice-President of the Board of Trade in 1841 and raised to President with Cabinet rank in 1843 but Disraeli was passed over again, a slight he chose not to forgive and which might help account for the tone of his attack on Peel later. Yet as his generally sympathetic biographer Robert Blake argued, Disraeli was not well connected and had apparently little to recommend him. Peel was never likely to have offered him office. Disraeli did make an effective speech over Maynooth in 1845 but remained a secondary, if not obscure figure until the parliamentary drama of 1846 when he launched his devastating attack on the Prime Minister. He led the Protectionist charge in the Commons against Peel with one particularly brilliant speech.

KEY ISSUES

The rise of Disraeli is important for **Key Issue 3** (see page iv).

Disraeli's speech attacking Peel over repeal of the Corn Laws

The speech involved personal attack. Peel was:

> 'No more a great statesman than the man who gets up behind a carriage is a great whip. Certainly both are disciples of progress. Perhaps both may get a good place. But how far the original momentum is indebted to their powers, and how far their guiding prudence applies the lash or regulates the reins, it is not necessary for me to notice.'

The speech declared that Peel had gone back on his principles and that he should resign:

> *'Let men stand by the principle by which they rise, right or wrong. I make no exception. If they be wrong, they must retire to that shade of private life with which our present rulers have so often threatened us.'*

The speech also announced that Peel had done great damage by splitting the Conservative party:

> *'Above all maintain the line of demarcation between parties, for it is only by maintaining the independence of party that you can maintain the integrity of public men, and the power and influence of Parliament itself.'*

(Extracts quoted from Robert Blake, *Disraeli* (1969 edition page 227)

In a moment Disraeli had emerged as a leading Conservative. His attack had been withering and most effective: no one else in the Conservative ranks in the Commons possessed a tenth of the eloquence or a quarter of the venom of Disraeli.

HOW DID DISRAELI RISE FURTHER TO BECOME THE CONSERVATIVE LEADER IN THE COMMONS?

Parliamentary fame was one thing, leadership quite another. The Conservative party remained primarily a landed one and Disraeli's background was not typical for a Tory MP, let alone a significant one. His Jewish background (though baptized a Christian he could hardly be described as a devout believer), debonair appearance, flamboyant speaking style, literary flair, unstable finances and racy private life made him an object of general suspicion. In particular, the personal nature of his attack on Peel in 1846 and his uneasy relationship with the Tory leader Lord Derby meant that many Conservative backbenchers did not want to see him in a position of authority. Yet this is what he achieved, becoming undisputed leader of the Party in the House of Commons by 1851 and (briefly) Chancellor of the Exchequer in the Conservative government in 1852.

What particularly helped Disraeli's rise in the Conservative Party was their lack of other good speakers in the Commons. Those with real talent in this direction such as Aberdeen, Graham, Gladstone and Lincoln had all taken Peel's side. The Conservatives' only remaining great speaker, Lord Stanley (Derby), was already in the Lords. The back bench Conservative Protectionists were numerous but not articulate. Disraeli was to supply the missing fizz. In this way he luckily, suddenly and unexpectedly became indispensable to Derby despite the suspicion in which he was held by many Tories. But Disraeli had helped to make his own luck:

- he had a clear grasp of the principal issues in debate;
- his oratory was quite outstanding;
- he was both quick-witted and not above self-promotion in debate.

All this meant that he had become a leading Conservative almost overnight.

However, many Tories continued to view him with suspicion. While his parliamentary abilities were widely acknowledged (he was easily the best debater the Conservative Protectionists possessed) other factors would count against him. While Disraeli's background was not as humble as he sometimes liked to imply, it was certainly not a landed aristocratic one. There were feelings that he was 'on the make', ambitious and not to be trusted. Protectionist Conservative **Chief Whip** William Beresford revealed his feelings about Disraeli in a letter to Lord Derby in 1847: '*As to D'Israeli I would not trust him any more than I would a convicted felon*' (criminal).

Yet in the absence of anyone else, Disraeli was able to maintain and indeed cement his rapidly acquired prominent position in the party in the Commons. While he had Derby's backing he was secure. Even so there was a reluctance to see him as the party's sole leader in the chamber. He would have to wait a little longer for the position. The result was that the Commons leader of the party between 1846 and 1848 was not Disraeli but **Lord George Bentinck**.

KEY TERMS

Chief Whip The politician who is responsible for trying to get party supporters to vote for his party's measures. It originates from hunting where the hounds had to be whipped into line. The whipping of the politicians was not quite so literal.

KEY PEOPLE

Lord George Bentinck 1802–48 Younger son of the Duke of Portland and therefore from a landed background. Suddenly took on a major political role when Peel proposed the repeal of the Corn Laws. Like Disraeli, Bentinck attacked Peel's 'betrayal' of the Party. Leader of the Protectionist Conservatives in the Commons 1846–8, and a passionate and somewhat ill-tempered man. Fond of horse racing, he sold many of his horses to finance his political activities. Soon after selling one of them it won the Derby: to own a Derby winner had been his lifetime's ambition.

Like Disraeli he had:

- risen to the top suddenly with stirring pro-Corn Law speeches;
- made severe attacks on Peel for letting down the party and the landed interest.

But he was not a success as leader. His fiery temperament was hardly what was required for healing wounds in the party. Moreover, while having passionate feelings about protecting the landed interest he did not feel so strongly about the Church. When he voted in favour of the removal of **Jewish Disabilites** at the end of 1847 he was criticised and decided to resign.

Disraeli was the obvious successor but the party as a whole could not stomach the idea. He too had supported the removal of Jewish disabilities (not surprisingly) so could hardly take over when Bentinck had resigned as he held identical views on this subject, out of line with the majority of the party.

Moreover, such was the continuing suspicion among Conservatives about Disraeli that Derby still hesitated to make him the leader of the party in the Commons. To Disraeli's open irritation the somewhat incompetent and ill-tempered Marquess of Granby initially took the post but resigned (feeling it beyond him) within a month. Yet still Disraeli was still not appointed leader. Bentinck's earlier resignation under different circumstances may have been temporary but barely 9 months after he suddenly and unexpectedly died. So the leadership position lay vacant – to Disraeli's even greater annoyance! By the end of January 1849 there was stalemate – the only man really capable of doing the job was Disraeli, but many did not want him. Derby's solution was to have three joint leaders, the Marquess of Granby, the elderly and ailing J.C. Herries (who had been a good financial administrator but had no leadership qualities) and Disraeli. Disraeli proved by far the most capable of the three. In fact the emerging **Spencer Walpole** and the new, young MP **Edward Stanley** were of more assistance to Disraeli in debates than Granby or Herries.

He entered the Commons as a very young man in 1848 before succeeding his father (the Conservative leader) in 1869 as 15th Earl of Derby and moving to the Lords. Both his ability and his connections propelled him to early prominence. He held junior office in his father's government in 1852. First Secretary of State for India 1858–9, then Foreign Secretary 1866–8 and 1874–8 when he resigned over Disraeli's pro-Turkish policy. A man of Liberal instincts, he frequently felt uneasy in his father's party. Switched parties and was Liberal Colonial Secretary under Gladstone 1882–5.

By 1851 it was clear Disraeli was finally the sole and undisputed Tory leader in the Commons. Russell's Whig government resigned and Derby attempted to form a government. The Tory forces were so weak that he gave up. Clearly, Disraeli was now his principal lieutenant. But his confidence had been severely knocked by all the opposition to his political rise. When Lord Palmerston was sacked by Russell in December 1851 and seemed briefly likely to join Derby, Disraeli indicated he would give up on the party leadership in the Commons if such a post would entice Palmerston to join them! Nothing, however, came of this and Disraeli remained number two in the Conservative Party.

Derby, however, remained very definitely the leader of the party as a whole for the next 18 years and it was never certain that Disraeli would replace him as leader until the last moment. His success in guiding through the second Reform Act in 1867 enabled Disraeli to succeed as Prime Minister in 1868 without a dispute. As late as 1872, however, some Conservatives were still plotting to remove him.

POLICY PROBLEMS: THE QUESTION OF PROTECTION AND FREE TRADE

The Conservatives were not helped by their doom and gloom predictions with regard to British agriculture after the repeal of the Corn Laws. As a result, Disraeli and Derby faced a major difficulty. Should they cling to the principle of protection? Or should the party accept the moves that had been made towards free trade, like Peel did on reform in the 1830s? Officially, up to 1852, the party remained a protectionist one and in theory aimed to re-impose the Corn Laws, which did not end suddenly in 1846 but gradually over a period of three years until 1849.

For a time it would be hard for them politically to admit that free trade had actually assisted English agriculture: yet farming showed greater signs of prosperity as early as 1850 and the next twenty years were seen as the 'Golden Age' of British agriculture. At first it seemed that many farmers would be forced to farm more efficiently or go under. In the event, soil drainage and increasing knowledge of fertilizers helped to prevent them from collapse.

Moreover, the landed interest benefited directly and indirectly from industrial development. They were aided by mechanical improvements including steam driven machinery. Some received income from mineral rights and others from urban development. The railway, initially regarded with suspicion by many landowners, was now cutting costs and widening their range of markets, with threshing machines and steam power also playing their part. With the landed community prospering it was difficult for the Conservatives to attract support and portray free trade policies as not being in the national interest.

The overall prosperity of the country was seen as intimately bound up with these developments. Free trade policies were increasingly seen as beneficial and these were more strongly associated with the Liberals and their allies. Although the Conservatives no longer officially supported protection after 1852, it was their Liberal opponents who benefited from their earlier commitment to the free trade cause.

The longer Russell stayed in office and the more other free trade measures were introduced, such as the repeal of the Navigation Laws in 1849 (see Chapter 2), the less likely it appeared that a reversion to Protection would occur. The electorate was now predominantly middle class. The growing prosperity of the country meant:

- more men were becoming £10 householders in the boroughs and so entitled to a vote;
- free trade was associated with prosperity and a re-imposition of protection looked like a vote loser.

Disraeli seems to have had doubts as to whether protection could be retained indefinitely. Not a member of the landed gentry, he was less committed to it emotionally and he was never a person to stay with a cause that was clearly lost. His attacks on Peel had been personal, accusing Sir Robert of deserting his Party's principles. He had not defended Protection rigidly as a matter of principle. The landed interest was entitled to special privileges to maintain their position in the English countryside but this did not necessarily have to be protection. Derby and his fellow Conservative peers might need more convincing but even Derby realised that they had no real alternative policy to the repeal of the Corn Laws to offer.

Election Results 1847–65

These figures are based on the estimates of Professor Rubenstein: without modern party discipline it is hard to be certain about exact numbers. There were 658 MPs, almost all loosely associated with one or other of the major groups.

Year	Protectionist Conservatives	Whigs/Liberals	Peelites
1847	225	330	100
1852	290	323	40
1857	281	348	26
1859	307	347	n/a
1865	298	360	n/a

The Peelites gradually faded out as a separate party. In the early days some returned to the Conservatives. Some remained independent until they died, like Aberdeen, but many of the more distinguished ones became Liberal supporters eventually.

LOST OPPORTUNITIES 1852–9

The resignation of the Russell ministry Russell's government was defeated in parliament when Palmerston, who had been sacked in 1851, combined with the Protectionist Conservatives to vote against it. The shifting political alliances and the importance of personal feelings in political fortunes are well illustrated by this event.

The Who? WHO? ministry 1852

With **the resignation of the Russell ministry** in February 1852 Derby formed the first Conservative administration since the split on repeal. However, the Peelites refused to join and the weaknesses of the Conservatives without them were now exposed even more clearly. Without the Peelites they lacked sufficient people of the right calibre and experience to take senior office. As the names of Derby's ministers were read out in the House of Lords the increasingly aged and deaf Duke of Wellington shouted out after each name: 'Who? WHO?'. The nickname stuck for the ministry: only three members had previous experience of government.

The government was a minority one and Derby felt he must call an election in the summer of 1852 to try to establish a majority. The result was not entirely discouraging for the Conservatives, since a few Peelites returned to the fold, but this did not include the most prominent ones, and other parties still outnumbered the Protectionists (see table on page 45). The question was did they still believe in Protection? Derby was rumoured to be keener on having a Corn Duty than Disraeli who began to speak of the benefits of free trade. Even before the days of a **parliamentary mandate** it was a strangely uncertain position for the Party to be in.

Disraeli as Chancellor

Disraeli felt somewhat out of his depth as Chancellor of the Exchequer. When he protested to Derby about his unsuitability for the post, his chief replied '*They* [the Civil Servants] *give you the figures*'. It was Disraeli's budget that brought the brief ministry to a close. Though not intending to reimpose the Corn Laws he did take measures to aid the landed interest:

- The **Malt Tax** and taxes on sugar were reduced.
- To make up for this, income tax was extended to cover those on lower incomes than before.

Disraeli called this '*compensation instead of protection*' since the lower middle-class was effectively paying more to make up for the tax reductions for the landed interest.

Speaking for the opposition of Whigs and Peelites, Gladstone weighed in with a comprehensive demolition of the economics behind Disraeli's budget. Comparing Disraeli unfavourably with Peel, he cast doubt upon Disraeli's figures and theories and convinced the House to vote against the budget by a majority of 19 votes and Derby resigned. The Conservatives were to remain in opposition until 1858.

The tense relations between Gladstone and Disraeli date from this time. Gladstone's attack was personal as well as political: Disraeli, asserted Gladstone, '*has not yet learned the limits of discretion, of moderation and forbearance that ought to restrain the conduct and language of every member of this House*'. Gladstone's oratory did much for his reputation in liberal quarters, but it ensured the coolest of relations between the two men. There was an unseemly and somewhat childish row about which of them should pay for alterations to the Chancellor of the Exchequer's house, which resulted in Disraeli retaining the Chancellor's robes, refusing to pass them on to Gladstone when he succeeded him in the post shortly afterwards. From this time on it was very unlikely the two men could ever serve in the same government, a factor of some significance in party manoeuvring for years to come.

The Whig-Peelite coalition 1852–5
Since it seemed no government could now be formed without the Peelites, a Whig-Peelite coalition was formed with:

- a Peelite Prime Minister in Aberdeen;
- a Peelite Chancellor in Gladstone;
- a Whig Home Secretary in Palmerston;
- a Whig Foreign Secretary in Lord John Russell.

It seemed that though a few Peelites had returned to the Conservative fold, the most important seemed to be identifying with the other side. This weakened the Conservative position further. Whigs and Peelites shared positions equally in the Cabinet, with one Radical member, Sir William Molesworth.

The effects of the Crimean War
It could be thought that the disasters of the Crimean War (see Chapter 2), which brought down the government at the end of January 1855, might have brought the Conservatives back to office. For a very short time this appeared likely. The Queen asked Derby to form a ministry but he declined to do so. He suspected, probably rightly, that public opinion was clamouring for Lord Palmerston to be given the post. Palmerston had resigned from the previous government complaining they had not taken a sufficiently strong line against the Russians before the outbreak of the war; now he seemed to be vindicated. Only Palmerston, it was believed, had the experience, expertise and will to bring the War to a successful conclusion.

The Charge of the Light Brigade at the Battle of Balaclava during the Crimean War, October 1854.

Derby's refusal of office was therefore shrewd, if timid. He correctly saw in Palmerston a person who, though in many ways an old-fashioned politician of a past generation (he was 70 and had first held government office back in 1809) was very modern in one crucial way: now that politicians had to take into account an expanding electorate, Palmerston had the personality, policies and willingness to appeal to and exploit public opinion. His vigorously anti-Russian policy was well received by a middle class public who saw the maintenance of a Turkish Empire freed from Russian influence as vital to British trading interests in India and the Far East. What Derby could hardly have foreseen was that Palmerston was not a stop-gap Prime Minister who would quit office at the end of the war: he would be Prime Minister for most of the next ten years and only allow the Conservatives a brief period of government in that time.

- There was a dispute over the seizure by China of a Chinese-owned vessel, *The Arrow*, dubiously flying the British flag in the Canton river adjacent to Hong Kong.
- It was almost certainly involved in smuggling and piracy but no proof was found.
- Though the Chinese released the crew who had been arrested they refused to apologise and so a squadron of the Royal Navy shelled Canton causing many casualties.
- Palmerston, though he had not known about the bombardment, expressed his full approval.
- This action brought condemnation in Parliament and Cobden's vote of censure (condemnation) was carried by 263 votes to 247.

KEY ISSUES

The role and influence of Palmerston is important for **Key Issue 1** (see page iv).

The continuing popularity of Palmerston

Palmerston's aggressive foreign policy was not confined to the Crimean War. For this he counted on a good deal of support in Parliament and from the electorate. If he overstepped the mark with MPs he could appeal to the voters. In 1857 his aggressive tactics in **the Arrow incident** went too far for many tastes. It united Gladstone and Disraeli against him.

Palmerston, however was not to be undone. He decided on a dissolution of Parliament, and the election of 1857 (see table on page 45) was a triumph for his supporters.

Palmerston's views

Now it was apparent that Palmerston was likely to remain in office for longer than anyone had expected and this was bad news for the Conservatives. Indeed, Palmerston was the most cautious of Whigs and had been a moderate Tory in his younger days in office before 1830. It is true that some Whigs and Radicals disliked him and that some of the big names in Parliament opposed some of his activities in foreign policy as the *Arrow* incident in China demonstrated. Yet he could muster support from a wide range of MPs. His foreign policy appealed to:

- his fellow Whigs, such as Russell;
- quite a number of Conservatives such as Lord Malmesbury;
- some of the Radicals such as Roebuck (though not Cobden and Bright);
- the liberally-minded middle-classes who liked his general image of championing British interests and standing up to despots (dictators) abroad.

In short, Palmerston was all things to all people. As Home Secretary in the Aberdeen Whig-Peelite Coalition he had shown himself capable of Liberal reform: he abolished transportation of prisoners abroad and introduced special institutions to deal with young offenders. He was also seen as someone the Conservatives would find hard to oppose. This was because:

- His support for parliamentary reform was lukewarm.
- He refused many of the demands for change after the Crimean War such as the administrative reform of the Civil Service.

- Many were impressed with his handling of the **Indian Mutiny** in 1857/8.
- Though not a particularly religious man he showed no sign of attacking the position of the Church of England.

For his **prime ministerial ecclesiastical appointments** he relied on the advice of his son-in-law Lord Shaftesbury who recommended **evangelical** clergymen who would not be sympathetic to Roman Catholicism.

Even the Royal Family liked Palmerston. Victoria and Albert had earlier disapproved of what they saw as his **low moral tone**. They had found his conduct of foreign policy high-handed and Victoria and Albert were responsible for his sacking in 1851, vowing he would never be Foreign Secretary again (he wasn't: he became prime minister!). In this respect the Conservatives were not seen as any better. Derby's racing companions excited suspicion and Disraeli's reputation with the Queen was not yet established. Prince Albert had been appalled by the tone of his attack on Peel.

The mid-Victorian political situation

The attitude of the monarch to the leaders of the different parties was not as significant in gaining office as it had been and was soon to become of little importance at all. But between 1846 and 1866 when party loyalties were fluid, it enjoyed a final opportunity to exert influence. With the parties evenly balanced and party allegiance muddled and variable, Queen Victoria had a deal of discretion in choosing the man she could invite to form the next government – though whether he would necessarily accept was another matter.

This fluidity and uncertainty certainly counted against the Conservatives. Though they dropped the policy of protection after the 1852 election the Whig/Peelite/Liberal/Radical/Irish grouping continued to work against them. True, it was not a united group and the more nationalist Irish members doubted Palmerston's willingness to repair the ravages of the country caused by the famine of 1846. (Peel's gesture in repealing the Corn Laws had not averted disaster.) This meant that though the Conservatives were generally the largest single group in Parliament they could never command

KEY EVENTS

Indian Mutiny 1857/8
An Indian uprising protesting against British Imperial control. Both sides were guilty of brutality at first but though Palmerston acted firmly he powerfully backed the Governor General of India, Lord Canning, whom some had accused of following a relatively lenient policy towards the rebels (see also page 136).

KEY TERMS

Prime ministerial ecclesiastical appointments By the mid-nineteenth century the prime minister rather than the monarch had the greater say in Church appointments such as bishops (see also page 125).

Evangelicals A group within the Church of England who stressed the importance of individual faith and the authority of the Bible and preaching, rather than the Catholic emphasis on the authority of the Church as a body and the importance of sacraments.

Low moral tone Victoria and Albert set high standards of morality for personal conduct. They took a dislike to Palmerston's occasionally flippant manner and less than serious conversation. In particular, Palmerston was a well-known ladies' man. He never satisfactorily explained why, when staying in Windsor Castle in 1839 as the guest of the Queen, he was found one night entering the bedroom of one of the Queen's Ladies-in-Waiting.

The Orsini Affair Orsini was an Italian nationalist who attempted unsuccessfully to assassinate the French Emperor Napoleon III in 1858. The plot was hatched in England and Napoleon III complained that no existing English law could restrain such an activity. Palmerston then brought in a Conspiracy to Murder Bill. This was defeated in Parliament. For once, Palmerston stood accused of giving in to foreign interference in British affairs.

a clear majority in this period. This difficulty is shown in their next brief period of office in 1858–59. Palmerston was again defeated in Parliament (thought strangely, this time for not being nationalistic enough) in **the Orsini Affair.** Palmerston did not feel he could ask for another dissolution and so Derby and Disraeli had another opportunity to form a Conservative government. It lasted just 15 months and was destined to be another minority administration.

THE CONSERVATIVE GOVERNMENT OF 1858–9

The formation of a Conservative government proved almost as difficult as in 1852. Such was the uncertainty of party allegiance (not least among the remaining Peelites) and the continued absence of talent in the Conservative ranks, that Derby invited Gladstone to join his government. Gladstone, however, declined. It was clear that dislike of the Conservatives by other groups was still strong and above all, Disraeli was still regarded with a good deal of suspicion. Gladstone could not bring himself to be in the same government as Disraeli.

Disraeli and Reform

The feeling that Disraeli was motivated by power rather than principle was enhanced by his introduction of a Reform Bill in 1859. Although Prime Minister Derby was in favour, it met considerable resistance: this was not merely from the opposition but also from his own side where distaste of *any* parliamentary reform was still strong. In the short term at least it was not a success. The terms of the Bill which included a redistribution of seats (see Chapter 4) was seen as an attempt to gain political advantage for his own side. In the Commons Disraeli was strongly opposed even by those traditionally associated with reform such as Russell. As a result it was Russell's motion opposing the Bill that was carried by 39 votes.

The downfall of Derby's government

This defeat greatly weakened Derby's government but it was an issue of foreign policy which confirmed its downfall. Outside Conservative ranks Palmerston was at his strongest and most popular when he supported Liberal causes in foreign policy and support for the Italian nationalists struggling to be free of the rigid rule of the Austrians was one such example (see page 13). It was this that produced the meeting at Willis's rooms in

June 1859, as Whigs, Peelites and Radicals agreed to a 'Liberal' coalition to defeat Derby. A motion of no confidence was passed by 13 votes. Although the Conservatives made up some ground at the ensuing election, the more united nature of the opposition meant that Palmerston was able to form another government. The Conservatives would have to wait just as long as before for their next opportunity (over six years) and even then they formed yet another minority administration.

WHY DID PALMERSTON REMAIN SO POPULAR UNTIL HIS DEATH IN 1865?

Many contemporaries regarded Palmerston as finished politically after his defeat in 1858, so how did he manage to regain office and hold it for six more years, keeping the Conservatives out of power? Moreover, had he not died soon after being re-elected in 1865 it would have almost certainly been longer.

He seemed to hail from an earlier pre-Victorian period (he was well over 50 before Victoria ascended the throne). However, Palmerston was attuned to the age:

- He read middle-class public opinion very accurately – his foreign policy showed Britain's position in the world to advantage and the degree of reform at home was moderate and cautious.

- Though his religious beliefs verged on the **nominal** he never attacked the church and as Prime Minister used his power of ecclesiastical patronage to promote low churchmen. He sensed the predominantly Protestant views of the nation.
- He adapted to the railway age and frequently travelled to the industrial towns and cities to present political speeches at which he never patronised his middle class audiences, but paid them the compliment of engaging in serious political talk. He praised the leading townsmen of Manchester and Liverpool on the way they had handled local independence – so much better he said than on the continent where, he asserted, government was heavily centralised.
- It proved difficult to attack him from any political direction. Many Tory MPs said they gave an 'independent support' to Lord Palmerston. Knighthoods (though not peerages) were offered to those of middle

class and Nonconformist background and Palmerston even toyed with the idea of appointing life peers! His raffish instincts and racy private life were well known in general though the details were not. It only seemed to make him more popular.

- Politically he disarmed Radicals by offering them cabinet office, such as **Milner Gibson** in 1859.
- He regularly received visits from representatives of the working class and treated them more politely than did the more radical Russell.
- Clearly he benefited from holding office at a time of considerable economic prosperity.

The result was that in the early 1860s Conservative prospects for office looked no better than ten years previously:

- Derby was in despair about the likelihood of forming a strong Conservative administration.
- Many Conservatives found Palmerston's cautious policies at home very much to their liking.
- Disraeli was still regarded with suspicion both inside and outside the party as an unprincipled opportunist.
- The newly found Liberal unity looked as if it was going to last.

The Peelite grouping had steadily declined and while a few had gone back to the Conservatives, many men of talent such as Gladstone (see below) had now moved over to the Liberal side.

ECONOMIC PROSPERITY BENEFITS PALMERSTON AND THE LIBERALS

Just as the Liberals had benefited from being the free trade party in the early 1850s so this advantage continued into the 1860s. Palmerston laid great stress on economic stability and he saw this as linked to his foreign policy. When a railway chairman complained of high taxation, Palmerston, in a speech at the opening of a new line, asserted '*it is the public revenue which produces that security at home through which the great developments of the railway industry have been made profitable*'. He was aware that an industrial economy with strong overseas links was more vulnerable to disruption

KEY PEOPLE

Thomas Milner Gibson 1806–84 Left the Conservatives in 1839 because of his free trade convictions and was active in the Anti-Corn Law League. Liberal MP 1841–68. Vice-President of the Board of Trade, 1846. Opposed the Crimean War and Palmerston's foreign policy generally but accepted Cabinet office in his government, 1859, and soon became President of the Board of Trade until 1866. Successfully campaigned for the Free Trade Treaty with France (1859) and the Abolition of the Paper Duties (1861).

by large scale war. Free trade and security were related – a strong navy would certainly be an advantage.

Indeed, the general mood of economic confidence in the country between 1848 and 1866 (punctured only momentarily with a brief crisis in 1857) had tended to favour the fortunes of whichever government was in office and this was rarely the Conservatives. Some significant features of the prosperity related to the increasing fortunes of the Liberal middle-classes which derived from a variety of developments:

- the prosperous manufacturing sectors of textiles, coal and iron and (in the 1850s) steel;
- the **invisible exports** of merchant shipping, international banking and insurance;
- large scale **capital investment** abroad;
- the development of prosperous new industries such as rubber and Portland Cement along with considerable growth in metal trades and engineering;
- the continued growth of the railway network.

KEY TERMS

Invisible exports The provision of services to a foreign country rather than selling of actual goods which can be seen.

Capital investment British money put into developments overseas. The profit then returned to its British owners in this country.

Liberals continued to possess a greater awareness than many Conservatives that Britain was being transformed from an agricultural and rural society into an industrialised and urban one. The prosperity of the period contributed to the Liberal political domination of it. The prominent values of this new society fitted in well with the Liberal approach to political issues with its laissez-faire approach and emphasis on state retrenchment.

This was recognised in Parliament in the 1850s and 1860s in terms of policy – Peel had also appreciated it with his policies in the Budgets of 1842 and 1845 as well as the Corn Law repeal of 1846 which had been an early indicator of the way economic policy was going. It was Palmerston and the Liberals, however, who ultimately benefited politically. The Tory association with Protection in the crucial period of the late 1840s and early 1850s meant that the free-trading (and now voting) middle classes increasingly identified with the Liberals and not them.

However, it was a Peelite, Gladstone, who became most associated with free trade. As late as 1859 Gladstone's political allegiance had remained uncertain. He had supported Derby's government the no confidence vote in June 1859 but was persuaded to join the Palmerston government of 1859–65 where he proved a very successful Chancellor of the Exchequer. He was able to pick up the threads of his free trade policy from the early 1850s (see Chapter 2) and this time there was no Crimean War to interrupt him. The obvious achievement of Gladstone as a *Liberal* Chancellor was another blow to the Conservatives.

The end of Palmerston

When Palmerston's Liberal coalition increased their majority in the General Election of 1865 it seemed the Conservatives would be out of power for even longer, but Palmerston was over 80 and he was mortal. When he died in October 1865 he was replaced by Lord John (later Earl) Russell. Without Palmerston, the issue of parliamentary reform was likely to rear its head once again.

WHY DID DISRAELI BECOME THE CONSERVATIVES' LEADER IN 1868?

Although Disraeli had become a prominent Conservative back in 1846, after his dramatic attack on Peel, suspicions of him remained in the higher ranks of the party. He had therefore shown considerable political ability and skill to stay near the top but even so relied on the protection and patronage of the leader, Derby. As late as 1866 when Derby became prime minister for the third time – and with Disraeli again his Chancellor of the Exchequer – it was still by no means certain that Disraeli would succeed him as leader.

It was the events of 1867 and Disraeli's role in the passing of that year's Reform Act that propelled him to the position where he was seen as **Derby's natural successor**. In February 1868 medical opinion told Derby he would remain ill unless he relinquished his responsibilities: he immediately resigned. Without the Monarch asking for his advice (the normal procedure) Derby took the initiative and wrote to the Queen telling her that Disraeli should succeed him as the only person who could command the general support of the Conservative Party. There was no formal position of leader, let alone the kind of leadership election we might have today, but by inviting Disraeli to form a Conservative government, the Queen was effectively making him party leader.

Conclusion

- The Conservative Party had been the largest single party in the House of Commons during the mid-century period.
- They had two men of great talent in Derby and Disraeli.
- On the two occasions when they had been briefly in government they had improved their performance at the subsequent General Election.
- They had shown they could govern and managed to drop the embarrassing issue of Protection.
- Derby was the leader of the party throughout this period but Disraeli, despite resistance from some Conservatives, soon became the chief spokesman of the party in the Commons.

However:

- The split over repeal had been a damaging and long lasting one: many Peelites moved eventually to the Whig/Liberal side, and the Conservatives lacked experience and talent with few exceptions.
- Derby was very wary about taking office as a minority government and refused the chance of government in 1855.
- Disraeli was viewed with great suspicion both by his own side and by opponents such as Gladstone.
- Palmerston adopted such a moderate but non-Conservative position between 1855 and 1865 that it was difficult to oppose him effectively. He was extremely well-attuned to middle class public opinion.
- The economic prosperity of the period confirmed the triumph of free trade and the need to govern more in the interest of the middle classes. The Liberals seemed best equipped to do this.

QUESTIONS TO CONSIDER

1. Why was the split of 1846 so damaging to the Conservative Party?
2. What was the role of Palmerston in keeping the Conservatives out of office in this period?
3. What role did the Peelites play in this period?

PERIOD STUDY EXAM-STYLE QUESTIONS

1. Assess the reasons why Palmerston was able to stay in power as Prime Minister for most of the period 1855–65?

CHAPTER 4

What was the significance of parliamentary reform for the Liberal and Conservative parties?

INTRODUCTION

After the 1832 Reform Act, further reform of parliament was not really a matter of controversy until the 1850s. The Act had:

- given the franchise (the right to vote) to the £10 borough householder. It had ensured that some of Britain's largest towns and cities such as Birmingham and Manchester had separate representation. This attempt to make parliamentary seats of less unequal size was known as redistribution;
- tried to ensure that only the increasingly prosperous and respectable middle-class received the vote.

In 1832 the Whigs had been the party of cautious parliamentary reform while the Tories had strongly opposed change. Once Peel had accepted that reform had come to stay in the mid-1830s, however, it no longer seemed an issue to divide the parties. Both were united in their desire to oppose Chartist demands (1838–48) and resist universal male suffrage, equality of electoral districts, payment of MPs and the secret ballot (see page 16). Whigs were as adamant as the Conservatives. Lord John Russell called the 1832 Reform Act a final adjustment to a well-nigh perfect British Constitution (see page 11).

THE 1850s: REFORM BECOMES AN ISSUE AGAIN

By 1850, however, Russell had changed his mind: the franchise might be extended further quite safely. Though it was not to become a *central* issue again until the late 1860s the different party attitudes towards it now had to be reconsidered. Why?

- The near collapse of the Chartists and the absence of revolution in Britain in 1848 – in contrast to the 1848 revolutions abroad (see page 22) – suggested that extension of the vote lower down the social scale would be safe. As early as 1848 and the failure of the Chartist movement, Russell spoke about the possibility of further reform, initially without a lot of support.
- More men were acquiring the vote anyway: the **growth in population** and greater prosperity of the skilled working classes had produced an increase in the electorate from 717,000 in 1833 to 1,364,000 on the eve of the next Reform Bill in 1866.
- To grant the franchise to the skilled working-class man just below the £10 limit would be safer than continuing to stop them voting and possibly driving them into the arms of extreme Radicals.
- Given therefore that further reform might come anyway, politicians felt that their party could gain an electoral advantage by being the ones to introduce such a change.

The 'respectability' of the skilled working man

The economic boom which lasted almost uninterrupted from about 1843 to 1873 benefited the literate and skilled worker who was now thought 'respectable' by the middle class and whose revolutionary mood earlier in the century was now much less evident. The suitability of this skilled male worker for the franchise was becoming generally accepted.

For this group, wages generally rose while prices remained steady or fell, employment was regular and there was more incentive to accept the norms of the society in which they lived. Many were becoming literate and joined increasingly influential and expanding trade unions such as those that got together to form the **Amalgamated Union of Engineers** in 1851. The skilled working-classes appeared patriotic, often applauding Palmerston's foreign policy, religious (if not always Anglican) and loyal to the monarchy. To political leaders they appeared generally sober, sensible and **thrifty**, forming Friendly Societies (see page 116) and putting away savings for old age or a time when work might not be so abundant. Many had become

(see page 22)
(see page 116)

Growth in population The population of England and Wales grew from 14 million in 1831 to nearly 23 million in 1871. In the UK as a whole the increase was 25 million to 31.5 million. Ireland's population *dropped* as a result of the famine in 1846 through both death and emigration.

Amalgamated Union of Engineers Union founded by William Allen of Crewe and William Newton of London. They brought together the different engineering groups that had developed in the early nineteenth century as a result of the industrial revolution. Like other large unions of skilled workers at the time, it demanded high subscriptions from its members but provided generous sickness and funeral benefits.

Victorian thrift To be *thrifty* is to look after your money very carefully and spend it cautiously and effectively, not on gambling and drink for instance. In an era when the financial resources of many were adequate but limited, thrift was seen as a major virtue. In the Victorian age, prices did not rise significantly and saving limited resources was seen as particularly wise and prudent: the kind of quality seen as one which helped the working class to deserve the vote.

This is part of the painting *Work* by Ford Maddox Brown, painted in 1863. The painting shows a mid-nineteenth-century artist's rose-coloured view of working life: but the skilled working classes were becoming more prosperous.

£10 Householders and appeared to have used the privilege of the vote with care and thought. Surely, more such men could be safely admitted to the franchise.

In contrast, contemporaries made a sharp distinction between the upper and *lower* working class. The unskilled working class did not share in this prosperity and were not seen as fit for the 'privilege' of voting. Even Radicals such as John Bright spoke of a 'residuum' that would be fit to vote.

REFORM PROPOSALS

The introduction of a serious attempt at a reform bill by Derby, Disraeli and the Conservatives in 1859 emphasised the lack of party differences on the question by this time. It indicated that Conservatives were no longer totally opposed to parliamentary reform of any kind. Indeed, both Gladstone and the Liberals opposed this Bill. This was hardly surprising, however. The 'Fancy Franchises Bill', (see below) as it became popularly known, was no radical measure: rather, it reflected Disraeli's attitude to reform as a Conservative. He was essentially looking for possible party advantage. This was not for the first time, according to Disraeli, who felt that the Whigs had constructed a bill in their own interest back in 1832 and the Conservatives were now entitled to do the same. Gladstone's long speech opposing the proposals struck a more generally anti-reform stance than the Liberals (see Chapter 5). Yet as we will see, Gladstone's views on the vote soon underwent a remarkable transformation. Other Liberal reformers opposed the Bill because they thought it had been specially constructed to benefit the Tories.

Disraeli's proposals in 1859

- The £10 borough franchise limit was to be extended to the counties.
- **The extension of borough boundaries** in order to include more rural voters.
- A £20 **lodger vote** for both county and borough seats.
- A second vote was to be given to those who owned at least £60 in a savings bank and had an income of at least £10 a year from investments in government funds or a pension from the government of at least £20 a year.
- A limited redistribution of seats: the smaller boroughs would lose seventy, most of which (fifty-two) would be given to the more populous counties and the remainder to larger boroughs.

This Bill would clearly favour the Conservatives by increasing their supporters in county seats and was therefore opposed by Liberals. Bright, sarcastically gave the name 'fancy franchises' to the idea of extra votes targeted at the respectable and thrifty working classes. In fact the idea was not Disraeli's but came from one of Russell's earlier efforts

KEY ISSUES

Disraeli's support for constitutional reform is important for **Key Issue 3** (see page iv).

KEY CONCEPTS

The extension of borough boundaries
Boundaries would be re-drawn so as to take in the surrounding countryside. Disraeli's idea was that the predominance of the independent-minded urban £10 householder (usually Liberal) would be counterbalanced by more Conservatively-minded rural voters.

KEY TERMS

Lodger vote Voting in boroughs was based on occupancy not ownership of a house. Lodgers in a house, especially common in the larger cities, were not qualified to vote at all.

at reform. The Bill was defeated when Russell proposed a resolution calling for an extension to the borough vote which passed the House of Commons by 330 votes to 291: Derby resigned. Because of their resolution, Palmerston and Russell were now honour bound to bring forward soon afterwards (see also page 52) their own reform proposals. They duly did this in 1860, suggesting a lowering of the borough franchise to £10: their hearts, however, were not in it. Faced with hostility and apathy in the country they soon dropped the idea. In truth, Palmerston had never liked it and there was little apparent demand in the country at large for it.

FACTORS FAVOURING REFORM IN THE 1860s

The advances of the skilled urban working class

Though the issue faded for a few years, parliamentary reform was now established as something that could be introduced at any time. No longer were working men considered necessarily unworthy of the vote. They were rapidly developing the education, political knowledge, experience and economic stability to do justice to the 'gift' of the vote. Their efforts had made Britain the 'workshop of the world' and the leading industrial nation. Had they not earned the franchise?

The continued increase in the political knowledge of the nation can be explained by:

- The spread of education to the skilled working-classes.
- The cheaper press encouraged by the abolition of the Stamp Duty in 1855 and the Paper Duty in 1861 (see page 30).
- The greater visibility of national politicians who used the Railway to travel around the country.

Palmerston, for instance, felt obliged to move with the times. Though unconvinced of the immediate need for reform, he was aware of the need to court the electorate. It was whilst he was on his travels around the country that he noticed an increasing desire for an extension to the franchise. Visiting Bradford in 1864 he was surprised to find the advanced

Liberal MP W.E. Forster criticising him for not having made more effort to introduce parliamentary reform. This stirred up considerable local political excitement.

Gladstone supports reform

Gladstone was another political figure who made use of the increased opportunities for travelling and public speaking. But unlike Palmerston, whose visits could have a mixed reception, he was nearly always well received. He was impressed with the advances of the working people and particularly so with the Lancashire cotton-workers. Between 1861 and 1865 it would have been in their self-interest to condemn the northern states in the American Civil War for blockading southern ports. This prevented raw cotton leaving for Lancashire and thus ruined the workers' livelihood. However, their support for the northern states on the principle of opposing slavery made a deep impression on Gladstone, doubly so because of his family's historical involvement in the slave trade. Gladstone created quite a stir in a speech in Parliament in May 1864 which was reported to suggest that all working men had a **'moral right'** to a vote (see margin). He had actually qualified his remarks quite considerably but this was ignored in the ensuing excitement. Prime Minister Palmerston was taken aback. Back in 1859 Gladstone had seemed sceptical about further reform. Now things had changed dramatically, and Palmerston predicted that if Gladstone succeeded him there would be *'strange doings'*. There were. When Palmerston died in October 1865 and the aging Russell became Prime Minister, Gladstone, in the House of Commons, was seen as the vital figure in the government. Reformist hopes were raised.

Other effects of the American Civil War

It was not only Gladstone on whom the American Civil War had a significant effect. Reformers saw the triumph of the North as a victory for freedom and democracy. It could act as a spur for reform in Britain. The eloquence of supporters of reform such as John Bright (listened to with renewed respect after the Crimean War and the recovery of his health) also raised the profile of the issue. According to Bright, the victory of the North in the Civil War was *'the event of our age and future ages will confess it'*.

KEY EVENTS

Gladstone's speech in 1864: the moral right to vote.

Gladstone was the victim of his own long-windedness (even by the standards of his time) and also of a press summary of his speech that was misleading and headline-seeking; a not unknown occurrence today. What he actually said was:

'Every man who is not presumably incapacitated by some consideration of personal unfitness or of political danger is morally entitled to come within the pale (limit) of the Constitution'.

He went on to assure the House of Commons that he was still against *'sudden violent excessive or intoxicating change'* but the damage had been done.

Guiseppe Garibaldi 1808–82 Italian nationalist and soldier born in Nice. After early revolutionary activity in Italy and South America he played a central role in the 1848 revolutions in central Italy. In 1860 he undertook a sensationally successful military campaign through southern Italy which was crucial to the unification of the country. Refusing all powers, reward and honours he retired to his farm and became a romantic liberal and nationalist hero.

Visit of Garibaldi

Nor was America the only place to find democratic heroes. The Italian **Garibaldi**, on his visit to England in 1864, was treated as such (if somewhat inaccurately). His visit caused such excitement in Radical circles that Palmerston's government cut short his speaking tour lest it stirred too much agitation for reform. Garibaldi unexpectedly went home early but his impact continued. A protest committee which was formed to complain about his early departure developed into a permanent organisation campaigning for manhood suffrage – the Reform League.

Role of the Trade Unions: economic problems

One area of support for the League was from the trade unions, now busy passing reform resolutions at their meetings. Their demands for change were soon to become more insistent. This was because of:

- the unexpected collapse of a major finance company (Overend and Gurney) in May 1866;
- a poor harvest after a wet summer;
- cattle plague epidemic;
- a major cholera outbreak;
- a temporary depression and unemployment in the winter of 1866/7.

THE REFORM BILL OF 1866

All this meant that the introduction of what might have been regarded as another routine effort at reform in 1866 produced more excitement than the last few attempts put together. It was not surprising that Russell, freed from Palmerston's influence, should introduce a bill. Its terms were mild:

- A lowering of the borough franchise from £10 to £7.
- An extension in the counties to those paying an overall rent of £14 or more.
- A Fancy Franchise for those with over £50 in a savings bank deposit.
- Very modest redistribution, grouping small boroughs into large constituencies rather than abolishing them altogether.

But the changed circumstances in the country had resulted in two major differences:

- There was vigorous opposition to the Bill, partly from the Liberal side.
- The reaction in the country when the Bill was defeated was far more extreme.

Robert Lowe, Liberal MP for Calne in Wiltshire, made an especially powerful speech against the Bill. Time spent in Australia had convinced him of the perils of democracy and he spoke passionately against working class involvement in the political process. In one passage he argued that such inclusion would bring **'venality'**, 'drunkenness' and 'violent feeling'. His speech achieved two things:

- It persuaded enough Liberal members to reject the measure and ultimately cause the Government's resignation.
- It also inflamed working class opinion and produced meetings of protest, organised by the Reform League.

John Bright's eloquence in favour of reform matched Lowe's against it. Speaking in large cities such as Birmingham and Manchester, Bright attacked those who had opposed this modest reform as *'out of touch'*. They had retreated into a political *'Cave of Adullam'*. Ironically, Lowe's attitude had stirred up the supporters of and increased the pressure for reform. Reformers were dismayed at the resignation of the Russell government and the coming to power of yet another Derby/Disraeli government whose supporters had helped to reject the recent Bill. Would reform now be lost? By no means.

Why did Disraeli decide on reform?

Russell's Liberal Government was replaced by a **minority administration** of the Conservatives. It may seem strange that this new government should introduce and eventually carry through a substantial reform bill when they had helped Lowe's Adullamites to reject a more modest one. The new Prime Minister Lord Derby would probably not have done so had he been acting alone; but he was elderly and in fading health and the real power lay with Disraeli in the Commons.

Venality Being prepared to sell ideas, goods or secrets (in this case applied to the vote) for financial reward.

Cave of Adullam: Adullamites A cave in an Old Testament Biblical story (First Book of Samuel) where the followers of King David retreated and hid away from their Philistine opponents. Bright's speeches were full of Biblical references such as these: the comparison of David's followers with that of Lowe's was particularly apt as the opponents of even moderate reform were indeed *'distressed and discontented'*.

Minority administration A government that did not have majority support in the House of Commons. Since the Conservatives won no election between 1841 and 1874, the three brief administrations of Lord Derby in 1852, 1858–9 and 1866–8 were all minority ones.

What influenced Disraeli?

- He was anxious to score political points off Gladstone and reach a successful settlement of the reform question where the Liberals had failed.
- A major bill could provide electoral advantage, especially if the Conservatives could determine the terms and also the details of the redistribution of seats.
- By granting a large franchise extension, Disraeli could satisfy the Radicals demanding change such as the Reform League. Although he was not prepared to meet their demand for manhood suffrage, he was prepared to consider Household Suffrage, with safeguards. This would, he hoped quieten down agitation.

KEY PLACES

Hyde Park The largest London park (138 hectares) in the Kensington area, west of Oxford Street. Of medieval origins, it has been a public park since the seventeenth century. Used for many different purposes including large political meetings. Its north-west corner is traditionally the home of public speakers on all topics asserting the absolute right to free speech.

This last point was not a trivial one. On the rejection of Russell and Gladstone's Bill in June 1866 there were angry protests that Parliament appeared to be rejecting even modest reform. In July, the Reform League planned a major demonstration in **Hyde Park**. When the new Home Secretary, the Conservative Spencer Walpole tried to ban it, he was unsuccessful. Although the gates of the Park were locked, the force of the large crowd was so great that the railings collapsed and thousands surged in and held their meeting anyway. Nor was this an isolated incident. John Bright and other Radical speakers were drawing large crowds in the north of England at reform rallies. Later, when Disraeli's Bill was debated, a further demonstration was held in the Park in May 1867.

Disraeli, reform and the Conservative Party

How did Disraeli persuade naturally anti-reformist Conservatives to pass the Bill? He seems to have convinced them of both the advantages and necessity of reform. The Liberals were dominant in the borough seats. By granting the vote to all borough householders it would in effect give the vote to the skilled working-class man in the towns. These might not vote for the same candidates as their (frequently) Liberal employers. Moreover, Disraeli sold the package of Household Suffrage to them because it included many safeguards:

- Personal payment of rates: this would exclude a substantial number of **compound householders**.
- A two-year residence qualification before being registered to vote. It was believed this would exclude large numbers of workmen who travelled from job to job.
- Fancy Franchises: such as for those with at least £50 in a savings account.

These safeguards, combined with the kind of **electoral influence** that was possible with an open ballot, seemed to convince many of the doubtful Conservatives. Derby was a convert if not a very enthusiastic one. He called it a *'Leap in the dark'*. Significantly, it was a leap he persuaded many of his fellow peers to make later when the Bill, having passed through the Commons, came to the Lords.

Another factor that helped Disraeli was the ineffectiveness of the Conservative opponents. Though there were quite a number, they resisted from their own individual positions rather than form an Adullamite-like grouping. They included three Cabinet members; Lord Carnarvon, General Jonathan Peel (brother of the former prime minister Sir Robert) and Lord Cranbourne, the future **Marquess of Salisbury**. Cranbourne was the most formidable of the opponents but even he did not stoop to organising a concerted opposition to the Bill's terms. Like the other two, he contented himself with resigning. But Disraeli simply replaced the three men and continued. The contrast with the previous Liberal collapse is considerable, and testimony to Disraeli's powers of persuasion and political skill.

Amendments to the Bill

Things did not turn out quite as Disraeli had anticipated. His original proposals were subject to a number of important amendments which passed the Commons:

- The two year residence qualification was reduced to one despite Disraeli's opposition.
- A £10 lodger franchise undermined the household only principle. This time Disraeli accepted the change without a vote.
- He also accepted **Hodgkinson's amendment** which effectively gave the vote to the compound householder.
- The 'fancy franchises' were removed.

KEY TERMS

Compound householders
Householders (around 400,000 of them) who paid their rent to their landlord and then added on (compounded) their rate – local tax. In effect it was the householder who contributed the rate but technically it was counted as the landlord as it was him who passed it on to the council. Thus, compounders did not qualify for the vote as they did not pay rates personally, one of Disraeli's supposed conditions for voting. In practice many ex-compounders were still prevented from voting before legal cases and subsequent legislation established their right beyond doubt.

Electoral influence
Landowners and (sometimes) factory owners felt it was quite legitimate to influence how their workforce should vote if they were enfranchised. This could be a mild hint, outright bribery or a threat that a wrongly directed vote could lead to the end of their employment. By the 1860s this 'influence' was becoming more and more morally unacceptable.

Hodgkinson's amendment Grosvenor Hodgkinson, the otherwise largely unknown MP for Newark, came up with the simple but clever idea of abolishing the compounding of rates with rent to the landlord. Thus they would have to pay their rates personally and so qualify for voting.

Robert Cecil, 3rd Marquess of Salisbury 1830–1903 Youngest son of 2nd Marquess, but his elder brother died and he became Lord Cranbourne in 1865 and third Marquess in 1869. Became an MP in 1853. Secretary of State for India 1866–7 and 1874–8. Foreign Secretary 1879–80. Prime Minister 1885–6, 1886–92, 1895–1902. His own Foreign Secretary 1887–92 and 1895–1900. A strong opponent of parliamentary reform, though reluctantly accepting its necessity in 1884. A firm defender of landed interest and the Church of England. Like Gladstone, a strong personal religious faith. Always pessimistic about the way British society was going. A formidable political operator.

Why did Disraeli accept most of these changes that altered the nature of the Bill?

- Party advantage: Disraeli opposed all amendments coming from Gladstone and his supporters but accepted ones from Liberals (often more Radical) who were not close to Gladstone.
- A desire to settle the reform question with a substantial bill and so put a stop to the growing public agitation such as the Hyde Park protests.

Party advantage?

Did Disraeli gain the political initiative he was seeking for the Conservatives at the expense of Gladstone's Liberals? In the short term yes, but not for long. Gladstone was outmanoeuvred over the Bill itself. Disraeli had the pleasure of seeing Radical Liberals such as Henry Fawcett revolt against Gladstone's authority in a protest originating in the House of Commons tea room. Fawcett and his colleagues would vote for or against each amendment on its merits: this generally meant supporting the more radical ones. Moreover, Disraeli's success in getting the Bill through the Commons (and out-manoeuvring Gladstone) finally ensured that he would be Derby's successor as Conservative leader. This was not to be a long wait, since Derby was already a sick man. In February 1868 he finally retired and Disraeli became prime minister.

However, this was to be a very brief spell. If Disraeli thought Liberal disunity would last long enough for the Conservatives to triumph over the Liberals in the first election under the new franchise in 1868, he was to be disappointed. Gladstone had also replaced the similarly ailing Russell as Liberal leader and soon brought about rapid Liberal recovery from the embarrassments of their confusion over Disraeli's Reform Bill. The result was a comfortable majority for Gladstone's Liberals over Disraeli's Conservatives in the general election of December 1868 (see pages 84–5.)

Disraeli resigned without meeting parliament as a result of his defeat, now a normal procedure once an election result is known but unheard of then. It showed that the more definite party system emerging as a result of the

1867 Act was already having an effect. Almost every MP's allegiance (normally Liberal or Conservative) was now known.

THE EFFECTS OF THE 1867 REFORM ACT

Bribery and Corruption

The 1867 Reform Act helped to bring in what we would recognise as the modern British political system in a number of ways. Firstly, the old system, often dominated by bribery and corruption took a severe blow. What had been the main features of this system?

- Many voters were prepared to accept money for casting their vote.
- If voting decisions *were* more personal they were based more on one's position in society than on one's personal political opinions.
- Landed influence over voting was seen as a legitimate use of privilege.
- Many seats were left uncontested: partly because of deals done by parties in **two member seats** to avoid their excessive expense.
- Elections were often unruly and drunken, even violent affairs.

With the increase in the electorate of about one million people, the attempts to continue these features led to ruinous expense, violent conduct and extensive corruption in 1868 with election petitions at record levels. Gladstone's Liberal Government after 1868 therefore decided on the introduction of a secret ballot for voting in 1872; it had been a longstanding demand of the Radicals. Perhaps the Liberals felt this move would aid them as they saw the landed interest in the Conservative party as having most to lose by this restriction. In fact, influence, **treating** and outright bribery were at their worst in small boroughs, many of them Liberal. Even after the 1867 Act there were a number of small boroughs with just over 10,000 people where corruption was rife. Nor did the Act have a sudden or dramatic effect: bribery continued in other ways such as offering money to supporters of one side to abstain from voting. In any event the move did not

KEY ISSUES

The aims and significance of the 1867 Reform Act is important for **Key Issue 3** (see page iv).

KEY TERMS

Two member seats
Before 1885 many, though not all parliamentary seats were represented by two MPs. Quite often a close and potentially expensive contest could be avoided by an agreement for each side to share the representation.

Treating The giving of generous amounts of free food and drink by prospective candidates to potential voters shortly before an election.

benefit the Liberals directly in 1874 as the Conservatives won the election that year.

When the Liberals returned to power in 1880 there were demands for further legislation, especially after a Royal Commission on election petitions found abundant evidence of bribery, corruption and violence. In the election in Gloucester in 1880 it was established that over half the borough's 5,000 voters had accepted bribes. There was also serious violence in Leamington and wholesale corruption in Macclesfield and Worcester. The Corrupt Practices Act of 1883 was even more significant in clearing up elections:

- It defined unlawful practices very clearly and made legal action against them more straightforward. The new measures included legislating against impersonation, undue influence, bribery, treating, payment for conveyances to the polls, assault, abduction and perjury (lying under oath).
- In addition, financial restrictions were placed on candidates' **election expenses**.
- **Party Agents** would have to account for their expenses very precisely.
- Election workers were paid a fee for their services to lessen their chances of accepting a bribe.

KEY TERMS

Election expenses In borough seats with over 200 electors, candidates could spend £380 plus £30 for every extra 1000 people: in counties the equivalent figures were £710 and £60.

KEY PEOPLE

Party Agent The person who was employed to assist a parliamentary candidate win their election. Agents were responsible for organising the finances of the campaign and until 1883 possessed considerable freedom of action.

Corruption and violence: Nineteenth-century electioneering. This cartoon appeared in *Punch* in March 1853.

THE VOTE AUCTION !

Party Organisation

Because of the gradually changing nature of political activity and the growing numbers of voters, both Liberals and Conservatives were forced to change their approaches. They would now need to seek support from the wider electorate on the merit of their policies, and organise themselves to project these more effectively. The Liberals were first to do this. In the 1868 election campaign, Bright appeared in widely separated places in the British Isles speaking at Limerick, Edinburgh and Birmingham. Gladstone made a series of speeches in Lancashire industrial towns; by all accounts some of his very finest. In contrast, Disraeli made only one speech, at Aylesbury in his Buckinghamshire constituency midway through the campaign (voting was still spread over several weeks) and otherwise merely wrote a letter outlining his ideas to the same constituents.

By 1874, however, the Conservatives had made up for lost ground in party organisation. Thanks to the work of **John Gorst** they were now, like the Liberals, establishing a party presence all over the country. In sharp contrast to 1868, Disraeli issued a manifesto outlining Conservative ideas although it tended to be a general promise to defend the major institutions of the country and concentrated on attacking the *'mistaken'* policies of Gladstone's government. Gladstone for his part promised the electorate the abolition of the income tax if the Liberals were elected. This was his long-cherished ambition, but never before had it been dangled as a carrot to the voters. Gladstone lost the election and so his promise was never put to the test. All of this, however, suggest a recognisably modern era of party politics.

How did the Parties go about trying to win mass support?

* National Party institutions were established. The National Union of Conservative Associations was set up in 1869 to co-ordinate activities and helped to make up some of the ground lost to the Liberals. Gorst was the first to see that the new middle classes in the **suburbs** were potentially Conservative and he wanted to work on getting support from **'Villa Tories'.** After their defeat in 1874 the Liberals set up the National Liberal

KEY PEOPLE

John Gorst 1835–1916
A barrister, who became an MP and Conservative Party organiser. Having lost his seat in 1868 he was asked to help with party organisation in the post 1867 reform era, a task he accomplished with great success. When re-elected in 1875 he directed his efforts to his own political career and also fell out with the Chief Whip Sir William Hart-Dyke. He was disappointed to see his successors lose many of the advantages he had established over the Liberals.

KEY TERMS

Villa Tories in the suburbs The railways were making it possible for the middle classes to live away from their place of work in the city centres. The suburb was born and the first commuters came into existence. The Conservatives, especially Gorst and then Salisbury, saw potential Conservative voters in these people, the wealthiest of whom lived in relatively grand accommodation, sometimes termed 'villas'.

Federation in 1877 (see below) which went even further in organising support for the Party.

- Local constituency associations also developed. These would enrol members, look for funding, and try to maximise the vote at both national and local election times – for elections to the municipal corporations (councils) were becoming more party political. Many had begun in the years before 1868 but they now met more regularly and encouraged a wider social range of members.
- Linked to these associations were clubs, Conservative and Liberal, of a more social nature where a drink and a game of billiards could be enjoyed in pleasant surroundings with like-minded friends and where occasionally more serious political discussions and meetings could take place. Some of these had already developed in the 1850s and 1860s but there was now was a rapid growth.

Despite this central interest, however, the emphasis on the local area to organise its own affairs and supply their own candidates was still strong. With the Conservatives, professional and regional agents that linked the local and national organisations more effectively were not to develop until after 1885 with the appointment of a new Chief Agent 'Captain' Middleton (see page 202). Liberals, however, had gone further.

National Liberal Federation

By the late 1870s the Liberal organisations had rapidly made up for the lost ground of the earlier part of the decade, when Gorst had been so active for the Conservatives. One of the terms of the 1867 Act encouraged further organisation. For the large cities of Birmingham, Manchester, Glasgow and Liverpool a third MP had been created, but the qualified electorate still only had two votes.

- Of these cities only **Liverpool** was likely to return a **Conservative.** The Conservative idea behind the insertion of this clause in the Act was that in the other cities with this arrangement the third candidate elected was likely to be the top Conservative. This would give the Tories valuable minority representation.

KEY THEMES

Liverpool Conservatism
Alone among the large English or Scottish cities in the mid-nineteenth century, Liverpool regularly returned Conservative candidates to Parliament. Roman Catholic Irish immigration was not popular in the city and the firm Protestantism of the majority of the inhabitants resulted in support for the party seen as stricter in maintaining the Protestant institutions of the country.

- The Liberals countered this idea by developing a particular approach to voting in these areas. Supporters in different parts of the town would be told to vote for a different pair of candidates, with the idea being that all three Liberals would then get enough votes to be elected and continue to exclude the Conservatives. But of course this involved a great deal of organisation, not to say compulsion. This was one of the tasks of the National Liberal Federation (NLF)

The NLF was set up in 1877 and originated in Birmingham in the time of **Joseph Chamberlain**. In that year almost 50 Liberal Associations in different boroughs affiliated to the NLF. Members would elect a General Council which would make decisions about party organisation and tactics. Conservatives (and often the remaining Whigs in the Liberal Party) complained about this development. It was seen as dictatorial and at worst (and inaccurately) as similar to the American **Caucus**:

- It gave ordinary Liberal members a say in electing management committees.
- In a city such as Birmingham, members of these management committees or 'councils' were often skilled working men, actively involved in the political process for the first time.

KEY PEOPLE

Joseph Chamberlain 1836–1914 Made his fortune as a Birmingham screw manufacturer. A Radical Liberal until 1886. Made Lord Mayor of Birmingham in 1876, introducing many social reforms including improvements in public health and housing. President of the Board of Trade 1880–5. Split with Gladstone over Home Rule in 1886 and became a Liberal Unionist. Colonial Secretary 1895–1903 when he split the Conservative party by arguing for the abandonment of free trade.

KEY TERMS

Caucus Originally one who advises or encourages. In Britain the caucus tried to co-ordinate political activity and decision-making in a constituency, whereas in the United States it was (and still can be) a preliminary meeting of members of a party to select candidates for office.

Conservative city: nineteenth-century Liverpool. This photograph was taken in 1890.

Parties in 1846:
Whigs, Liberals, Radicals,
Peelites: Protectionist
Conservatives

Parties in 1868:
Liberals, Conservatives

KEY PEOPLE

Sir Stafford Northcote
1818–87 Became a Baronet
1851. Helped draw up the
Civil Service Report 1853.
Conservative MP from 1855.
Held office under Lord Derby.
Chancellor of the Exchequer
under Disraeli 1874–80.
Leader of the Party in the
Commons 1880–5. Created
Earl of Iddesleigh 1885.
Foreign Secretary 1886.

KEY THEMES

**Queen Victoria's
detestation of Gladstone**
The Queen and Gladstone
never got on very easily
together. Victoria found
his manner awkward and
pompous: *'Mr Gladstone
addresses me as if I were a
public meeting'* she once
complained. Unlike Disraeli
he was not prepared to
flatter her. After 1870 the
relationship deteriorated
further. When he was in
opposition Victoria greatly
disliked Gladstone's *'stump
oratory'* as she put it, stirring
up public excitement over
Disraeli's foreign policy, and
she also mistrusted some of his
radical domestic policy when
he was Prime Minister.

- It helped the Liberals in their election performance in 1880 and 1885.

The two party system and political personalities

One important effect of the 1867 Act had been to end the rather confused party state of the 1850s and early 1860s. Liberal and Conservative were now the two clearly established groupings. Peelites had either died, like Aberdeen, Goulburn, Graham, and Sidney Herbert, or, like Gladstone and Cardwell, eventually drifted over to the Liberals. Radicals were less independent than before and generally associated themselves with Liberal policy. Conservatives now accepted free trade and the bitter days of division were long behind them. There could now be more confidence about the precise party allegiance of most MPs, as 'Independent' was now rarely a name they gave themselves. At the elections of 1868, 1874, 1880 and 1885 the electorate had a clear choice: only the Irish grouping remained partly (and increasingly) separate.

For the first time voters might wish to consider party policies as a whole when casting their vote, a far cry from the local and sometimes corrupt factors that dominated nineteenth century elections so frequently. Moreover, it was also clear who was to become prime minister if his chosen party was successful in 1868, 1874 or 1880: Gladstone if the Liberals succeeded or Disraeli if the Conservatives were triumphant. Only after Disraeli died in 1881 was there uncertainty about a future Conservative prime minister: Salisbury from the Lords or **Sir Stafford Northcote** from the Commons, soon resolved in favour of Salisbury. It was also clear that **Queen Victoria**, however much she **detested Gladstone**, would eventually agree to ask him to form an administration if, as in 1880, he was electorally successful. In 1880 she asked Lord Hartington to be Premier but he declined and she had to ask Gladstone. A semi-democratic kind of political activity was starting to emerge.

CONCLUSION

- After the political uncertainty of the mid-century years, parliamentary reform had again become both a major national question and a party political issue in the 1860s. Disraeli played a significant part in showing that reform could come from Conservatives as well as Liberals, although Salisbury continued to oppose it at least until 1885.

- The Act of 1867 heralded a political era which could be termed modern in that a clearer two-party system emerged and Gladstone and Disraeli became well-known personalities who received national coverage to an extent previously unknown.
- After 1868, electoral corruption declined with the larger electorate, thanks to changing public attitudes and the Secret Ballot and Corrupt Practices Acts.
- Improved party organisation was essential to recruit and maintain the support of the new electorate, and at different times, and in slightly different ways, both parties set about the task.

QUESTIONS TO CONSIDER

1. Why did parliamentary reform become such a prominent issue in the mid-1860s?
2. Why did the Conservative Disraeli pass such a substantial Reform Act?
3. What were the main political effects of the 1867 Reform Act?

PERIOD STUDY EXAM-STYLE QUESTIONS

1. Assess the extent to which the 1867 Reform Act was due to Disraeli's political skills?

CHAPTER 5

What was Gladstonian Liberalism?

KEY ISSUES

This whole chapter is important for **Key Issue 2** (see page iv).

Gladstone - Timeline

1809	Born in Liverpool
1832	First entered parliament
1841	Served in Peel's Government
1843	Promoted to the Cabinet as President of the Board of Trade
1845	Resigned over the Maynooth Grant (Jan.)
1845	Back in Cabinet as Colonial Secretary (Dec.)
1846	Supported Peel over repeal of the Corn Laws
1852–5	Chancellor of the Exchequer under Lord Aberdeen
1859–66	Chancellor under Palmerston (and Russell 1865–6)
1865	Leader of the Liberals in the Commons
1866	Introduced unsuccessful reform bill
1868–74	Prime Minister – first ministry
1874–6	Retired from Liberal leadership
1876	Returns to political life over the Eastern Question
1879	Midlothian Campaign
1880–5	Prime Minister – second ministry
1884	Third Reform Act passed
1886	Prime Minister. Formed his third ministry but Irish Home Rule Bill is defeated
1892–4	Prime Minister – fourth ministry
1894	Resigned
1898	Died

INTRODUCTION

The Liberal Party emerged by the 1860s from the Reformers, Whigs and Radicals of the 1840s. It was to be led by someone from a different background from most of them. William Ewart Gladstone began political life as a young Tory in 1832 yet by middle age was so wrapped up in the leadership and overall philosophy of the Liberal Party that he was able to give his name to the ideas and the policies implemented by the Liberal Governments in the second half of the century. Indeed, the Liberals tended to be a disparate (widely varied) group with a great variety of ideas and policies, arguably only held together by the charisma and force of the personality of the great man whose popularity as the 'people's William' (see page 27) aided the popularity of the party as a whole. Gladstonian Liberalism is a complex phenomenon but can be simplified into a number of parts: economic; religious; political and humanitarian. However, these ideas developed at different times, at different speeds and to varying degrees.

1. GLADSTONE THE YOUNG CONSERVATIVE 1832–41

Gladstone was first elected to parliament for the borough of Newark in 1832 at the time of his 23rd birthday. His Tory **patron** the Duke of Newcastle was looking for a young figure with traditional views: someone who would oppose

KEY TERMS

Patron One who supports a cause, often with money. In this case the Duke used his control of the parliamentary seat to benefit his chosen candidate, Gladstone.

The young Gladstone at the start of his political career in the 1830s. Compare this image with the one on page 184.

parliamentary reform and champion the cause of the Church of England. Gladstone seemed the most suitable candidate. Throughout the 1830s he largely retained Conservative views and became increasingly attached to the Church of England as an institution, even writing a book to defend it. He was certainly not liberal-minded at this point. His speaking and administrative abilities were soon noticed and he held junior office in the Conservative government under Peel, first in 1834–5 and then as Vice-President of the Board of Trade in 1841. The latter post began to change his outlook.

2. FREE TRADE AND YOUNG ENGLAND: ECONOMIC LIBERALISM BEGINS 1841–5

Gladstone's interest and ability in financial matters quickly became apparent. His liberal side emerged as he became convinced, as Peel was, that the encouragement of free trade by a lowering of tariffs was the key to economic success. Gladstone became a strong supporter of the Budgets Chancellor of the Exchequer Henry Goulburn essentially inspired by Peel, such as the ones in 1842 and 1845 which removed tariffs on many duties. Gladstone was not without achievements himself, piloting the complex Railway Act of 1844 through the Commons.

3. GLADSTONE: THE PEELITE AND RELIGIOUS LIBERAL 1843–7

Increasingly believing in a liberal approach to economic policy, Gladstone also began to modify his view about the privileged position of the Church of England. Though he remained totally committed to it personally, he began to realise that there were many Christians in the country (Nonconformist and Roman Catholic) who did not accept Anglican authority and who could not reasonably be denied office because of this. His views therefore became more liberal. He accepted the need to increase the grant of government money to the Roman Catholic College in Maynooth in 1845 (see page 35), and supported the attempt to remove the regulations preventing Jews (as non-Christians) from becoming MPs in 1847.

4. GLADSTONE THE HUMANITARIAN LIBERAL 1844–52

Gladstone had supported Peel's repeal of the Corn Laws primarily because of his Liberal belief in free trade, but also because he was genuinely concerned about the fate of the Irish peasantry if they did not receive cheap corn. However, a more central event in the development of Gladstone's liberal thought was his visit to **Ferdinand II's Kingdom of Naples** in the winter of 1850–1. The corrupt legal system, lack of free speech or any prospect of a parliamentary system appalled him: he called it *'the negation of God erected into a system of government'*. The overcrowded prisons and the dreadful treatment of its inmates made a deep impression on him and confirmed the increasingly liberal direction of his thinking. Gladstonian Liberalism was beginning to take shape.

5. GLADSTONE THE FREE TRADE CHANCELLOR 1852–5 AND 1859–66

Gladstone's economic policy continued to mature. Supporting free trade in March 1848, his speech defending the general direction of Peel's policy in this area since the Budget of 1842 was impressive and marked him out as a possible Chancellor of the Exchequer in a future government, though whether this would be a Conservative or Liberal one it was hard to tell. Gladstone's liberalism was not fully formed and the Conservatives appeared to be accepting the need for free trade. In 1849 he supported the Russell Government's repeal of the Navigation Laws, another important free trade measure. Perhaps Gladstone would return to the Conservative fold if they could completely swallow the free-trade pill. Lacking financial talent of their own, they certainly needed him, and as early as 1848 tentative enquiries were made to see if he would rejoin his other colleagues.

Gladstone had the opportunity to focus on putting his liberal economic ideas into practice when appointed Chancellor in Aberdeen's Whig-Peelite coalition, formed in December 1852. This period of office coincided with a growing economic confidence in the country halted only by the British involvement in the Crimean War in March 1854. Gladstone seized his chance in style:

Ferdinand II's Kingdom of Naples Until the late nineteenth century Italy was divided into many different states. The largest in area was the Kingdom of Naples which occupied approximately the southern half of the peninsula. It was the poorest and most backward area in the region. King Ferdinand II (1830–59) was regarded as a particularly cruel and dictatorial ruler. The British nicknamed him King Bomba.

- Because of growing economic confidence, he had the opportunity to plan a progressive reduction in income tax.
- His mastery of detail and intimate understanding of tax schedules and intricate financial detail was unmatched.
- After his impressively delivered budget in 1853, he found he had raised the status of the office of Chancellor to a place where, apart from the Prime Minister, only the Foreign Secretary was of equal status.

However, the war and other political complexities kept Gladstone out of office between 1855 and 1859 (see pages 11–12). Later he was able to resume his work on reducing tariffs, planning for a phased reduction and eventual abolition of the income tax. In 1859 he played a crucial role in persuading the Radical Richard Cobden to go to Paris on behalf of the government and negotiate the details of a **Free Trade Treaty with France.** In the House of Commons he continued to explain eloquently (if sometimes long-windedly) how the increasing prosperity of the country could allow both tariff and tax reductions yet still produce a surplus. When he delivered his budget speech in 1860 the Commons sat tantalized, as Gladstone, with a total mastery of the subject, outlined several possible other budgets more or less generous than the one he actually went on to propose. His achievement was great. He had, to use his own words '*set free the general course of trade*'.

KEY EVENTS

Free Trade Treaty with France 1860 In 1860 the Palmerston government asked Richard Cobden to travel to Paris (as a private citizen) and inquire into the possibility of a Free Trade Treaty between Britain and France. He met the French Minister Chevalier and together they negotiated an agreement later incorporated by Gladstone into his Budget of 1860. British duties were lowered on French silks and on wines and spirits. French duties were lowered on coal and many manufactured goods to a maximum of 30% and later 24%.

6. GLADSTONE: THE POLITICALLY UNCERTAIN MAN 1855–60

Gladstone continued, however, to remain unsure as to which party he really belonged. Having accepted office at the start of Palmerston's ministry in February 1855 he resigned within a few weeks when the government announced an enquiry into the government's handling of the Crimean War. Gladstone, as a member of that government did not feel he could remain in the new one. In truth, Palmerston was the Whig-Liberal that Gladstone was most reluctant to serve under, disliking what he saw as his rude and aggressive foreign policy and casual moral tone. Now that it was clear that the Conservatives had abandoned protection there was always the possibility that Gladstone, still regarded as the most Conservative of the leading Peelites, might rejoin them. The full extent of his religious liberalism was not yet apparent and on parliamentary reform his views still appeared Conservative.

However, during this period his views on foreign policy were clear. Right from his dislike of Palmerston's aggression in the Don Pacifico affair in 1850 (see page 136) Gladstone had distanced himself from what he saw as an aggressive and blustering foreign policy. Gladstone was frequently to take an international rather than very nationalistic view of foreign affairs. He had misgivings about Palmerston's aggressive policy in China (see pages 138–139). Though there was little scope for him to develop these views while Palmerston was alive, his ideas are seen in aspects of his foreign policy when Prime Minister between 1868 and 1874 (see Chapter 7).

By 1860 Gladstone was clearly still moving in a Liberal direction but politically he remained cautious. His long speech opposing the modest parliamentary reform proposals of 1860 struck an anti-reform stance: he defended the **rotten and pocket boroughs** that had helped to put great men into Parliament in the past. It sounded more like an old-fashioned Tory speech defending the pre-1832 system of election! Given these views it can be seen how Gladstone could accept office (again reluctantly) under Palmerston in 1859. Both were Liberal on free trade and (partly in Gladstone's case) religious policies yet both were still sceptical on the question of parliamentary reform. Moreover, for once they were in agreement over foreign policy. The major foreign question of the day was Italian Unity (see Chapter 2). Given his previous attitude towards the Kingdom of Naples, Gladstone could not be anything but pleased to see its position undermined and eventually destroyed.

7. GLADSTONE: THE POLITICAL REFORMER 1864–8

In the early 1860s, while serving as Palmerston's Chancellor, Gladstone's views on parliamentary reform underwent a remarkable transformation and hastened his move towards Liberalism. By 1864 he was in the position to make his remarkable 'pale of the Constitution' speech (see page 62) that clearly represented a shift from his earlier views, however much it was misinterpreted as democratic. He was full of admiration for the stoical way the average Lancashire cotton

Rotten and pocket boroughs Rotten boroughs were very small or deserted towns and villages which still returned two members to parliament who were effectively nominated by the local landowner, since there were hardly any voters. Pocket boroughs might be larger, but the landlord's control was still the predominant factor. He had the borough in his pocket (under his control). Both types of borough had been severely reduced in number by the Reform Act of 1832, but some pocket boroughs in particular still remained until at least 1867.

worker had endured the hardships caused by the cotton famine (see Chapter 4). They had shown a *'willingness to suffer patiently'*, he told the working men of Chester at the end of 1862, which should be *'instructive to us all'*. *'Cotton is but the instrument in the hand of God'*. Gladstone was now coming to believe that, thanks partly to his own efforts as Chancellor, the working man's growing prosperity, independence and loyalty to established authority were preparing him for the privilege of the franchise. Many of the better-off working men returned the compliment and saw Gladstone as the 'People's William' whose mastery of the economic complexities of the time had aided their growing prosperity. The working class began to admire him, just as the middle class had a decade earlier.

So, by the end of 1865, with Palmerston dead and Prime Minister Russell in the Lords, it was Gladstone who was the logical choice to introduce the 1866 Reform Bill in the Commons. By its £6 limit he proposed a modest extension of the franchise to just that class of person now deemed fit to receive the privilege. That the Bill failed and that Gladstone was politically out-manoeuvred by Disraeli does not take away the fact that Gladstone (though clearly not a democrat) was now committed to further parliamentary reform.

WHAT WAS GLADSTONIAN LIBERALISM?

A distinctive type of Liberalism (Gladstonian Liberalism) had become apparent. This comprised:

- **Economic Liberalism**: The extension and development of free trade policies to all sectors of the British economy. Gladstone's first ministry continued the policies he had developed as Chancellor. It is significant that he appointed Robert Lowe to this position. This was despite all the trouble Lowe had caused Gladstone when the former's speeches helped to wreck Gladstone's Reform Bill in 1866. Lowe was a very strong believer in economic **laissez-faire.**
- **Political Liberalism**: Not democracy or votes for women but an extension of the franchise to those men who were seen to be sufficiently educated and financially independent enough to cast their vote freely for the good of the country rather than just themselves. This was clearly felt to be a higher proportion of the population than when

Gladstone first entered Parliament at the end of 1832.

- **Religious liberalism**: the idea that there should be equality of opportunity for all, regardless of precise religious belief. Gladstone, though a strong believer in the importance of the Church of England had come to accept that those of other religious persuasions should not be discriminated against in society because of their different views.

- **Humanitarian Liberalism**: Gladstone believed that everyone should always be treated humanely. He wished to remove privileges in Church or State which he felt could not be justified. He applied this belief to institutions such as the Civil Service, Army and to the whole question of English rule over Ireland (see the following chapters).

- **A Liberal Foreign policy:** Gladstone sought international co-operation and understanding. Talking was always preferable to fighting.

- **Administrative reform and efficiency**: This developed greatly after Gladstone became prime minister. He saw the opportunity in his first ministry to improve government efficiency, clarify laws, and address problems in these areas, some of which had been apparent since the Crimean War of the mid 1850s. His belief in keeping down government spending was longstanding from his time a Chancellor.

However, the political circumstances of the time meant that Gladstone would have to adjust his ideas and beliefs to bring about reform in his first ministry (see Chapter 6). Thus, a major Reform Act was unlikely since the Conservatives had just passed one. Other issues pressed for attention: the education question was brought to the fore by the 1867 Reform Act. Events in Ireland as Gladstone assumed power made it likely the policies for this area of the country would also loom larger than planned and result in some legislation not seen as Liberal. This was also true of Gladstone having to rely on Nonconformist support – resulting in the illiberal Licensing Act of 1872. Also, **trade union** problems made legislation in this area highly desirable. Moreover, Gladstone's personal interest in reforming legislation varied from one measure to another. Nevertheless, the years 1869–72 saw more reforms and legislation than at any time since 1846. Why was this?

The distinctive strand common to all of Gladstone's policies at this time was the removal of unjustified privilege.

Gladstone was not a Democrat and described himself as '*an out and out inequalitarian*' but he had come to believe that privileges had to be justified to be defended. Gradually he came to defend fewer and fewer of them. To Gladstone, a glaring example of a privilege that could not be justified was the Anglican Church's establishment in Ireland (see page 89). Here he had moved clearly away from his previously rigid views on Church establishment. The statistics of membership did not warrant this particular privilege of the Church. The removal of the Church's privileges in Ireland proved a useful rallying cry (starting point) for putting Gladstonian Liberalism into practice.

Thus the Gladstonian Liberalism that was so apparent in his 1868–74 ministry had been many years in the making. It had its political, religious, economic and humanitarian sides. Gladstone also developed the concept of administrative efficiency to add to his other beliefs.

Liberal appeal to different social groups

At the time Gladstone became Prime Minister in 1868 the appeal of Liberalism to the middle classes was at its height. They were in tune with the removal of unjustified privilege which they felt had enabled the landed classes to hold on to political power at Westminster despite being in a minority, electorally speaking, since 1832. The middle classes were keen to see the major institutions of the country such as the Universities, the Civil Service, the Army and the Church open their doors to all, not just Anglican, Oxbridge-educated men from the upper reaches of society. Many were not Anglican but Nonconformist and had made their money through trade and manufacturing, not through land. So they would not normally feel they could identify with the landowning Anglican image of the Conservatives. They also strongly favoured the continuation of free trade.

However, the Liberals gained working class support as well. Gladstone was seen as the man behind the idea of the extension of the franchise in 1867, even if it was Disraeli's tactical skill which actually achieved it. The skilled artisans in the towns were the main social group that had benefited from the extension of the franchise in 1867. They were now literate and self-sufficient, acquiring property of their own and a growing sense of responsibility, finding the Liberal philosophy of self-help and personal effort an attractive one. Many were joining trade unions in the late 1860s and were anxious for a government that would confirm the legal status of these bodies. As yet there was no separate working man's party to turn to.

This dual support from different social classes was not to last. As the century progressed, more middle-class voters moved to the Conservatives and by the end of the century a separate political party (the Labour Party) was being set up to represent the interests of working people. But back in 1868 the Liberals were highly favoured by both groups. This helps explain why Gladstone's Liberals rather than Disraeli's Conservatives won the election in 1868.

How did Gladstone and the Liberals achieve success?

The Liberals won the election in 1868 because:

- The middle class manufacturers and businessmen (and they were still *men*) tended to identify more often with Liberal candidates than Conservative ones for historical reasons, seeing the Conservatives as the party of the landed classes.
- The new urban voter did not (as Disraeli hoped) vote in very large numbers for the Conservatives but more frequently preferred the Liberals. It was acknowledged that, though not always successful, historically **the Liberals were the party of reform.**
- The Liberals adjusted to the new trends in electioneering quicker than the Tories. The effectiveness of party organization at election time was a significant factor in the election result. In the 1868 election Gladstone and Bright toured the country on speaking tours for the Liberals. In contrast, Disraeli spent much of the time at his home in Buckinghamshire (see page 70).
- The Liberals gained substantial extra support in Scotland and Wales winning 74 seats to the Conservatives' 16 in these two counties (though their majority in England over the Conservatives was only 26, the same as in 1865).
- The Liberals had been steadily coalescing as a party since 1859 and by 1868 were as united a party as they ever would be.

The Liberal victory in 1868 was not that sensational – after all they had been successful in the previous elections in

KEY CONCEPTS

The Liberals as the party of reform Right back to 1832, the Liberals had tended to make the running in the past when the question of votes for working people had been considered. It was frequently Liberal (if not Gladstonian) amendments in 1867 that transformed Disraeli's Reform Bill. Advanced Liberals had ensured that the proposed adult male suffrage for all borough householders would be a more radical bill, by removing many of the Conservative-placed safeguards. Trade Union supporters were hopeful of a Liberal Bill to confirm their legal status (and they were not disappointed, see pages 94–5).

1859 and 1865 when Liberal majorities had been 40 and 62 respectively. But the increase in the majority to 112 was partly due to the way that social classes who were new to voting perceived the parties.

In 1868 Liberal recovery had been greatly aided with a Gladstonian master stroke to re-capture his party's lost unity over Reform. In March he had successfully introduced **Resolutions into the Commons**, calling for the disestablishment of the Anglican Church in Ireland. Gladstone had been particularly effective at uniting Liberals in a common and popular cause. This move particularly appealed to the increasingly strong Nonconformists who saw the Conservatives as the party of the Church of England and its privileges. A Liberalism clearly moving in the direction of religious liberty (even if it was led by a strong Anglican, Gladstone!) was particularly appealing to many of the middle classes and the skilled working-class.

THE SIGNIFICANCE OF THE ELECTION

The 1868 election was in some ways the last traditional election before the full impact of parliamentary reform. Voting was still open and bribery common. Violence was still not unknown. Landlords still felt entitled to use their 'influence' with their tenants. In addition, boroughs such as Gloucester, Reigate, Barnstaple, Beverly and about twenty others were still extensively corrupt.

However, in other ways the 1868 election was the first modern one. This was because the number of voters, nearly 2 million, was almost a doubling of the previous number and forced party campaigners to argue their case to the voting masses rather than just rely on corruption or the standing of candidates in their local community. The politics of opinion began to triumph over the politics of interest. Moreover, it was the first election when there were two very clear parties to choose from. For an increasing number of voters the policies of the different parties were often of greater significance than the personality of the actual candidates. For instance even Gladstone could not get elected in south west Lancashire because the area was strongly Conservative. Gladstone was not the People's William here.

CONCLUSION

Gladstonian Liberalism was evident in the views of the developing Liberal Party. Political, religious and economic liberalism were all prominent, held together with a belief in the removal of unjustified privilege. Gladstone himself played a major role in influencing the developments which came to bear his name.

Gladstone's political views underwent a great deal of change in the 1840s, 1850s and early 1860s:

- Gladstone had begun his political life as a keen young Conservative.
- He gradually moved to a more Liberal position, starting with a belief in free trade as a result of his experiences in Peel's Government 1841–6.
- His visit to the illiberal Kingdom of Naples in 1850 cemented and extended his Liberal views.
- By the 1860s this Liberalism now encompassed religious equality and a belief in parliamentary reform.

However,

- Gladstone remained a committed member of the Church of England: his religious beliefs were central to all his political activity.
- Though possessing increased respect for the 'respectable' working man, Gladstone never became a Democrat and continued to oppose women's suffrage.

QUESTIONS TO CONSIDER

1. What do you understand by 'Gladstonian Liberalism'?
2. What were the main causes of Gladstone's changes in political thinking up to 1868?
3. How far was Gladstone personally responsible for the Liberal success in the election of 1868?

PERIOD STUDY EXAM-STYLE QUESTIONS

1. Assess how far Gladstone was personally responsible for the Liberal Party's success in the election of 1868.

CHAPTER 6

How successful was Gladstone's first ministry 1868–74?

KEY ISSUES

This entire chapter is important for **Key Issue 2** (see page iv).

INTRODUCTION

Gladstone held office as Liberal Prime Minister for the first time for a period of just over five years: December 1868 – February 1874. During this time Ireland came to dominate English politics in a way that it had not since the Famine of 1845–6 and Gladstone devoted a good deal of attention to it. *'My mission is to pacify Ireland'* he had remarked in December 1868 on hearing that the Queen had asked him to form a ministry.

The greatest run of reform came in the first three and a half years of the ministry. This period produced a major series of changes concerning not only Ireland and the introduction of the secret ballot, but also education, social reform, public houses, and legislation concerning prominent institutions in the country such as the Army, the Law, the Universities, the Civil Service, Local Government and Trade Unions. How far did all this reflect the Liberal ideas that had been developing in Gladstone's mind in previous years?

WHY WAS 1869–72 SUCH AN IMPORTANT TIME FOR REFORMS?

Some of Gladstone's reforms such as in education (partly) and the secret ballot (largely) could be seen as a natural result of the 1867 Reform Act. Action over Trade Unions could be attributed to a specific legal difficulty over the safety of their funds which arose in 1866. However, the need for change in many of these areas had been apparent for some time.

- The Crimean War in the 1850s revealed a number of inefficiencies in the Army and in the Civil Service. Bodies such as the Administrative Reform Association, set up in 1855, called for greater openness in appointments in these areas.

- Palmerston, however, deflected many of these requests for changes by using his popularity in other areas, especially foreign policy: by the mid 1860s many reformers felt it better to delay further new measures until after his retirement or death.
- Although lip service was still paid to laissez-faire, the greater complexities of an increasingly urban society meant that state intervention in social questions such as public health and the problem of alcoholism was seen as increasingly justified.
- Nonconformists, on whose vote the Liberals relied, were an increasingly numerous and powerful element in society and putting heavy pressure for changes not only for regulating sales of alcohol but also regarding admission to, and privileges at, **Oxford and Cambridge Universities**. Having failed to raise sufficient funds to finance many of their own schools, they had come to the conclusion by the late 1860s that state financing of non-denominational schools was the answer.
- The need for action on Ireland had been highlighted by Irish nationalist **Fenian** activity in 1867. Their activities were linked to attempts to get Fenian prisoners released including an attempt to seize Chester Castle in February (see page 161), the killing of a police officer in Manchester in September (for which three Fenians were hanged) and an explosion at Clerkenwell Jail, London in December.

Why was Gladstone's government able to deal with these issues?

With Gladstone's ministry of 1868–74 the Liberal party was stronger and more united than it had ever been. It had:

- A comfortable majority in Parliament.
- A forceful leader; Gladstone, who had the Liberals united around his leadership, with divisions over the 1867 Reform Bill largely forgotten.
- A definite sense of direction: to remove unjustified privilege, reform a number of existing institutions and to open up opportunities to a wider range of people within society.

(see page 161)

KEY PLACES

Oxford and Cambridge Universities The only two ancient English Universities. Long seen as the preserve of the Anglican aristocracy and without rivals. In the 1830s collegiate universities had begun in Durham and London: Oxbridge was raising its academic standard by the middle of the century.

KEY TERMS

Fenian Brotherhood An Irish nationalist group of American origin, founded in 1858. They sought a military solution to the problem of English control of Ireland. Some saw service in the American Civil War, and when this ended in 1865 many returned well supplied with money.

Front bench The benches
at the front of the House of
Commons on either side of
which sit senior government
ministers and the leading
figures of the main opposition
party (for back benches see
page 38.)

By 1872, however, the reforming impulse had blown
itself out or, as Disraeli remarked, the Liberal **front
bench** reminded him of a *'range of exhausted volcanoes'*.
Nonetheless, the catalogue of achievement was considerable
and the character of nineteenth-century Liberalism is
clearly shown in the various issues tackled.

IRELAND: THE DISESTABLISHMENT OF THE ANGLICAN CHURCH IN IRELAND 1869

Background
After the comparative confusion in Liberal ranks in 1867 as
a result of Disraeli's passing of the Reform Bill, the Liberals
recovered swiftly. This was due to Gladstone's shrewd choice
of a subject that could bring the Party back together. Since
Russell had, like the Conservative Derby, now retired from
active politics, Gladstone was free to select the debating
ground that he wanted. He chose the Irish Church. This
had proved effective because:

**Religious belief in
Ireland** About 78% of
the Irish population were
Roman Catholic. Most of the
remainder were Presbyterians,
mainly in the northern
province of Ulster. In some
Church of Ireland parishes
in the remote rural areas
there were no members at
all. The Irish Anglicans came
disproportionally from the
wealthier sections of society.

- Religious Liberalism united the party more firmly than
  most other issues. Almost every Liberal had voted for
  Gladstone's Resolutions on the subject early in 1868 (see
  page 82).
- The Irish Church was an establishment that was difficult
  to defend. Only 12% of the population of the country
  were Anglican by **religious belief.**
- As champions of the established Church, the Conservatives
  would feel obliged to defend the institution.

After the success of the Resolutions, Disraeli's days were
numbered and another election inevitable, especially since
the newly enfranchised voters would be anxious to exercise
their freshly acquired privilege. Once Gladstone was
installed in office the disestablishment of the Irish Church
was likely to be his first undertaking.

Disestablished and
Disendowed This meant
that the Church was no
longer legally established by
Parliament and would govern
itself. It would be deprived
of some of its property
(endowments) and so lose its
income from property which
would now be redistributed
for educational purposes and
public works.

The terms and the passing of the Act
In 1869 the Church was **disestablished** and partially
disendowed. The measure was opposed by the Conservatives.
Disraeli argued that it *'licensed confiscation'* but it passed
by the comfortable majority of 118, unusually large for a
controversial measure. The Commons accepted Gladstone's

argument that the Irish Church establishment was one that could not be justified. Its passage through the House of Lords was more difficult but the Irish Church had never been the most popular part of the Anglican establishment and few were prepared to fight to the last ditch to defend it when a newly elected government had been so clearly committed to the proposed change. It passed by a majority of thirty-three.

Effects

This was the most successful piece of Gladstone's Irish legislation in that it removed a major Irish grievance and extended the principle of religious liberalism to Ireland. It did not lead to the disestablishment of the Church in England, as many of its opponents feared, though it did encourage the strong Welsh Nonconformists to undertake a similar campaign later in the century. However, Gladstone was less successful when he moved on to tackle the land question in Ireland.

1870 IRISH LAND ACT

Background

After an exhaustive study of the intricate legal problem of **Irish land tenure** Gladstone produced his **Irish Land Bill** to reform the landlord/tenant relationship. The central complaint had been the relative ease of eviction of tenants by their landlords. Tenants frequently had to pay for their own improvements on their holdings. In Ulster, but rarely elsewhere, it had been the custom to pay compensation for these improvements when the tenant quitted the holding. With the property value enhanced, landlords could now charge a higher rent to the incoming tenant.

Main proposal for the Irish Land Bill

- Compensation to tenants for eviction other than for non-payment of rent.
- Limitation on the landlord's power of eviction for non-payment of rent if the Courts judged the rent to be excessively high.
- Extension and formalisation of the custom of compensation for improvements. In the northern

province of Ulster it was traditional for the landlord to pay compensation to a departing tenant for the expense of any improvements to the property that the tenant had made.

The passing of the Act and its effects

The result was less satisfactory than the Disestablishment Act. The Lords were very sensitive to property rights: would not true Liberalism uphold them? So the Upper House made it far less likely that the Courts would indeed judge that rent was pitched too high by amending 'excessive' rent to 'exorbitant'. The land system arguably required complete overhaul but Gladstone had done his best to reform it. Within a few years it was seen that his best was not good enough. Despite their Lordship's complaints, Gladstone's policy had again been liberal (the wholesale raising of rent and failure to compensate for improvements was an abuse of privilege) but Irish nationalists did not see it as radical enough: they wished to do away with the English landlords altogether.

Nineteenth-century Ireland: rural poverty. This photograph, taken in Co. Donegal in 1885, shows a tenant and his family being evicted for failing to pay rent. Their furniture was removed and the thatch roof destroyed to prevent it from being re-tenanted.

1873 IRISH UNIVERSITIES BILL

Background

Another example of Gladstone's policy failing to win over the strong-minded on either side was his proposal for a new University in Ireland. Along with the English established Church and a foreign absentee landowning system, Gladstone saw Irish educational grievances as fundamental to solving the problem of poor relations between the two countries. **Trinity College, Dublin** was a university of high repute but its whole atmosphere was Protestant and Catholics could not hold official positions there so few attended.

The failure of the Bill

Gladstone proposed to set up a new university for Roman Catholics. But here, religious Liberalism was tricky to implement. In his anxiety to cater for all viewpoints, Gladstone introduced aspects of the Bill which pleased no one. For example, three controversial subjects (theology, philosophy and modern history) would not be taught. This was hardly a Liberal approach to learning and pleased neither the Catholic bishops nor more secular reformers. The Bill was defeated by nine votes in the Commons and Gladstone offered to resign and let Disraeli form a government of his own. Disraeli, however, shrewdly refused and let what he correctly saw to be an increasingly weakening government stagger on for a little longer.

EDUCATION ACT 1870

Background

Gladstone was not only concerned with *Irish* education. One of his ministry's first priorities was schools in England and Wales. This is hardly surprising given Robert Lowe's sour comment *'we must educate our masters'*. Greater numbers in society now had the opportunity to exercise political choice, and this meant that educational reforms needed to be carefully considered. But the impact of the 1867 Reform Act was only the immediate cause of the change. Barely half the 5-13 age group were attending school with any degree of regularity. Nonconformist Ministers aided by Birmingham politician Joseph Chamberlain had formed a National Education League which demanded state-aided **non-denominational education.**

KEY PLACES

Trinity College, Dublin
University founded in 1591. Trinity was to be the first of a number of Colleges for a University of Dublin but it turned out to be the only one. It had (and still has) a high academic reputation.

KEY TERMS

Non-denominational education Education that did not teach the views of one religious denomination (such as the views of the Church of England) to the exclusion of others.

The struggle to pass the Bill

Concern over the religious clauses in the Bill was the greatest challenge for **W.E. Forster,** the Vice-President of the Board of Education, whose demanding job it was to pilot the Bill through the House of Commons. The struggle illustrates the central and still controversial role that religion played in domestic politics. Forster had to please both Nonconformists and Anglicans. The established Church was anxious to keep the educational initiative: it already controlled about 80% of the **existing elementary schools of religious foundation**, which in turn formed about 80% of all elementary schools. But Nonconformists were almost as numerous as Anglicans in the country as a whole. So they were determined to stop a similar Anglican domination in the new schools. What would religious education consist of in these schools? The question was 'solved' by an amendment put forward by a Liberal MP, William Cowper-Temple, who proposed that religious teaching should not be 'distinctive of any denomination'.

Quaker background, involved in Radical politics in Bradford, becoming its MP in 1861, a strong supporter of further parliamentary reform and the North in the American Civil War. Vice-President of the Council in Gladstone's government, 1868 with special responsibility for education. Guided the Education Act of 1870 through the Commons – a very difficult and complex enterprise. Chief Secretary for Ireland 1880–2 when he resigned in protest at the release of Parnell from Kilmainham Jail (see Chapter 9).

Main terms of the Education Act

Existing Elementary Schools of religious foundation Historically the Church of England was the main educational organiser in England and Wales. In the early nineteenth century it was joined by Nonconformist and Roman Catholic schools. However, only a proportion of children could ever be educated in this way. The Churches did not have the resources to cope with the concept of universal education for children.

- All children between five and thirteen were to be given the opportunity to attend an elementary school.
- Where Church schools and other voluntary schools (those funded by voluntary contributions) existed they would remain, but in areas where Church provision was not sufficient, a School Board would be established.
- This board, elected by ratepayers, male and female would raise money locally and organise the supply of buildings, equipment and teachers.
- The Boards had discretion to excuse fees for children of poor parents or make attendance compulsory. The fees were on average about £1.50 per year, per child.
- Religious teaching was not to be distinctively in favour of one church, and parents could ask for their children to be withdrawn from scripture lessons.

Effects

Largely literate generation In 1891 one survey showed a literacy rate of 94% for school leavers. Before 1870 literacy rates among the working classes varied widely depending on the availability of local schooling. The importance of the Act was in ensuring a local elementary school was available everywhere.

The Act passed was immensely significant: it led to the mass elementary education of the English and Welsh populations. In fact, the long term importance of this Act would be hard to exaggerate:

- By the end of the century this had produced a **largely literate generation**.

- It therefore encouraged the development of a popular press and, subsequently, led to widespread media power and influence.
- Before the Act only 20% of children between 10 and 12 till attended school. This Act would transform this figure in a generation.
- It vastly increased educational opportunities for girls (and therefore the prospect of female franchise), who soon proceeded to learn to read and write at the same level (or better) than boys.
- Although the Act seemed purely educational and administrative, later educational developments widened the state role to encompass the physical well-being of the children, with school meals and medical inspections introduced shortly after the turn of the century. Moreover, the central Liberal principle of equality of opportunity would mean little without the education to enable people to take full advantage of those opportunities.

Given the difficulties and complexities of the subject this had been a valiant attempt by the government to tackle a growingly important and vital issue.

TRADE UNION ACT 1871

Background
The action on education was not the only one clearly influenced by the events surrounding the period 1866–7. As well as the Reform Act there was a severe economic recession in the winter of 1866–7. This led to difficulties between Trade Unions and the law. There were doubts about their legal status suggested by the verdict in the Courts in 1866 in the case of Hornby versus Close. Close was the Treasurer of the Boilermakers Union who had run off with £24 of Union funds. The Union officials thought that their legal status had protected them from such a loss. However, a judge ruled that Trade Unions were technically illegal organisations, being **'in restraint of trade'** and so could not recover the money.

Terms and Effects
The new Act made it clear that actions 'in restraint of trade' would be lawful and funds secure. Legal recognition was secure providing that Trade Unions officially registered their funds.

KEY TERMS

Action in restraint of trade Any activity that prevented normal business or production in a firm but normally referring in legal terms to a strike by workers.

Peaceful picketing An
attempt by organisers of a
strike to draw attention to
it by assembling outside the
relevant place of work and
informing all workers of
the reason for the dispute.
Peaceful persuasion would be
used to attempt to prevent
employees from continuing to
enter the factory or relevant
building while the strike
continued.

**Compulsory Church
rates** The rate or tax that
the Church of England was
entitled to impose upon
property within a parish.
They used the money to
meet Church expenses. It
was a major grievance to the
Nonconformists who resented
having to pay when they had
their own church expenses to
meet. However, by 1868 few
clergy insisted on their legal
right to collect money from all
their parishioners.

KEY CONCEPTS

Religious Equality At the
start of the nineteenth century
not being a member of the
established Church of England
meant restrictions in terms of
education (no entry to Oxford
and Cambridge) and political
opportunity, such as becoming
an MP. Other denominations
had freedom of worship and
so were tolerated but there was
not complete equality. These
restrictions were gradually
removed between the 1820s
and the 1880s. Religious
equality was to the nineteenth
century what racial and sexual
equality were to the twentieth.

Significantly, the legislation benefited precisely the class
given the vote in 1867, the skilled male urban working-
class. Was Gladstone trying to win their support? If so,
one aspect of the new legislation did not help. The new
Act involved a restatement of the 1825 Criminal Law
Amendment Act which outlawed **peaceful picketing**.
Unions felt that the size and nature of their activities meant
that some form of picketing was essential if strikes were to
be effective. This was one of Gladstone's less liberal moves
and Trade Unions campaigned for change; Disraeli was later
to oblige them (see page 120).

Gladstone's government had granted the Trade Unions
what were seen as justified privileges. However, in the
case of other institutions, some of their privileges were
seen as unjustified and in need of modification. This had
influenced the Irish legislation and was now also to be
applied in England and Wales.

RELIGIOUS EQUALITY AND THE UNIVERSITY TESTS ACT 1871

Background

Issues of religious equality of opportunity are apparent in
a significant reform of Gladstone's ministry and one with
which he was personally involved. The Prime Minister's
strong Christian faith was not diminished, but his view of
Nonconformists had become more tolerant. No longer did
he believe, as in his younger days, that the state had a duty
to distinguish in precise terms between truth and error
in religious belief. In 1868 he had not only successfully
moved the Irish Church resolutions but also steered
through Parliament the abolition of **compulsory Church
rates**. Now he turned his attention to one of the few
remaining grievances of Nonconformists that prevented
them from feeling that true **religious equality,** rather
than mere toleration, had been achieved. After reforms
in 1854 and 1856 non-Anglicans could attend Oxford
and Cambridge without having to promise to uphold the
faith of the Church of England. However they still could
not hold any official position in those Universities or be
Fellows of any College.

Terms and effects of the Act

Gladstone's Act meant that all academic appointments at Oxford and Cambridge (except for a few theological positions) were now open to those of any religious belief or none. So, for example a Nonconformist could now become a professor or a master (in charge) of a college. This was a significant change, all the more so coming from the devoutly Anglican Gladstone who had been opposed to it only a few years previously, and so was a truly Liberal measure. It did not have a dramatic or immediate effect although some colleges such as Queen's College, Oxford did take more students from the north of England including quite a number of Nonconformists. However, the general atmosphere at the universities remained Anglican for some years yet.

ARMY REFORMS

The Army Reforms of **Edward Cardwell** in 1869–71 bring out clearly the humanitarian side of Gladstonian Liberalism as well as its concern for administrative and operational efficiency and, once again, for the removal of unjustified privilege.

Background: personnel

Recruits into the ranks of the army (common soldiers) had traditionally been regarded as coming from the 'lower' sectors of society and army officers believed that severe discipline such as flogging was the only language they understood. However, by 1870 this attitude was beginning to diminish, particularly against severe corporal punishment.

Officers in the Army were originally commissioned (authorised) by the monarch and had to purchase their commission. This preserved a useful outlet for the landed classes (like the Church and the Law) for younger sons who would not inherit family property and meant that those without money could not become Officers. By 1870, however, ideas concerning promotion on merit and equality of opportunity made this far less acceptable. The purchase of commissions was no longer seen as justified.

Background: administrative

No changes of any substance had been made since the Crimean War. The Army was in need of a simplified organisation and more up-to-date equipment. The success of the slick and well-organised Prussian troops against the French in 1870–1 did not cause the reforms but certainly hastened them.

Terms of the reforms

- **Humanitarian**: the abolition of peace-time flogging in the Army.
- **Administrative and operational efficiency**: infantry regiments were reorganised on a territorial basis so that 69 new county areas each contained two battalions of the old regulars. The battalions took it in turn to serve abroad which meant that recruits could be properly trained at home.
- The staff structure of the army was completely reformed.
- The twelve year minimum period of service in the forces was reduced to six with six further years in the reserves.
- The infantry was re-armed with the breech-loading Henry Martini rifles used by the Prussians in 1870–1.
- **Removal of unjustified privilege**: This involved the radical and controversial abolition of the purchase of commissions. Although originally included as part of the Army Enlistment Act of 1871 it was opposed by the House of Lords and had to become law by a special Royal Warrant from the Queen which had the authority to override the rejection of the Bill by the House of Lords.

Effects

Though controversial at the time, the changes were soon accepted and in 1880 all flogging of troops was abolished. The reforms made possible rapid and large scale campaigns such as the one in Egypt in 1882 (see page 154–5). The improved reputation of the British Army after the reforms gave strength to Foreign Secretaries and other officials who had to conduct diplomatic negotiations.

CIVIL SERVICE ACT 1870

Background

Another institution whose shortcomings had been apparent in the Crimean War was the **Civil Service**. Ironically, a report advocating its reform had been produced just before Britain entered the War, in 1854. The calling of the inquiry in the first place indicated a feeling that civil servants were too often

KEY TERMS

Civil Service Encompassed all direct employees of the Government apart from the *armed* services. After a reduction in numbers earlier in the century to reduce corruption, the service was now expanding steadily in the 19th century as government intervention in social life increased. As a result of the Northcote/Trevelyan Report, a Civil Service Commission was set up in 1855 to unify the departments and make it possible to move from one to another.

lazy, inefficient and lacking in initiative. The report, produced by Sir Charles Trevelyan (Assistant Secretary to the Treasury) and Sir Stafford Northcote MP, recommended amongst other administrative changes, the introduction of competitive examinations for appointments to the service and indeed suggested that the Civil Service was the resting place for those *whose abilities* [would not] *succeed in the open professions*'. But Palmerston did not act on the Committee's recommendations for changes in the method of appointment.

Terms of the Act

- Taking a competitive exam to enter the Civil Service was open to all who wished to sit it.
- The Foreign Office was exempted from these conditions. Gladstone, despite his love of efficiency which the reform illustrated, was a sufficient admirer of the aristocracy to feel they would be the social class most suitable for the diplomatic dealings a post in this department might involve.

The controversy over its passing

- The reform was strongly opposed by the upper classes because the Civil Service had been seen as an opportunity for the poorly qualified younger sons of the landed classes to join a well paid profession.
- Because it was thought unlikely that the House of Lords would agree to the measure, an **Order in Council** was required to make it law.

Main effects of the Act

- The change began the development of a Civil Service which was more efficient and for which staff were appointed on merit.
- There was great competition from the well educated to gain a position in it.

KEY TERMS

Order in Council
The Council was the Queen's Privy Council which was, historically, an important body advising the monarch. Though it had been largely replaced by parliament in terms of enacting laws it still possessed the authority to authorise changes to the administration, such as the civil service reforms.

POLITICAL REFORM

The Liberal Party of Gladstone clearly stood for political reform but the changes of Gladstone's first ministry were more restricted in this area. The Ballot Act of 1872 (see page 190) was the major piece of legislation in this ministry but it needed the more substantial Corrupt Practices Act of 1883 (see page 190) to make it effective: a further extension of the franchise at parliamentary level, or a re-distribution of seats, was unlikely after Disraeli's achievement in 1867. Developments in this area again had to wait for the 1880s.

Background

A more likely possibility for reform was local government. Powers of local authorities had been growing steadily since the **Municipal Corporations** had been established in 1834, taking on numerous responsibilities in the fields of sewerage, water supply, street paving and lighting. The argument that *all* ratepayers should have a say in how their money was spent had grown ever stronger.

Terms of the reforms

- In1869 female householders were granted the vote in Municipal elections, the first time that women had been allowed to vote in any kind of election
- A Local Government Board was set up to co-ordinate poor relief and public health measures (though it was some way from a modern Department of Health) The President of the Board was a senior politician who was usually a Cabinet Minister.

Significance of the reforms

- The Act of 1869 began the political involvement of women in local government which was to lead to campaigns for the right of women to vote at a Parliamentary level.
- As frequently occurred in Gladstone's local government changes, re-organisation rather than innovation was a principal theme. The Local Government Board's business was dominated by the Poor Law and the Board was not regarded as working very effectively.

SOCIAL REFORM

Introduction

Unlike Disraeli later in the decade, the Liberals did not have a reputation for wide-ranging social reform. It was supposed to offend their laissez-faire principles and was not seen as Liberal. However, the temper of the times frequently demanded measures in this area, as even the cautious Palmerston had earlier acknowledged in measures such as his liberalising

KEY TERMS

Municipal Corporations
A Royal Charter had granted the right of local self-government to particular boroughs run by a Mayor and local worthies who came together (were incorporated) to organise services in their local town (or municipality). The range of their responsibilities was increasing rapidly in the mid to late nineteenth century.

Divorce Act of 1857. When Gladstone's measures ran directly counter to the enabling of freedom, they tended to be ineffective, and led to Disraeli having to develop the legislation further (see pages 121–2). Alternatively, they caused offence. The best example of this would be the Licensing Act of 1872.

Background to the Licensing Act

Alcoholism was seen as a major social problem, a destroyer of families and a major cause of poverty, crime and violence. In the country there was a strong teetotal movement spearheaded by the **temperance organisation** – the **United Kingdom Alliance.** The first attempt to limit drinking hours had initially been brought before Parliament in 1871 but this Bill was so unpopular that it was withdrawn.

Controversial Passage and Terms of the Act

In a genuine attempt to deal with these issues Home Secretary Bruce's Bill proposed to restrict the opening hours of Public Houses but ran into opposition. The debate aroused strong passions on both sides. *An England free, better than an England sober'* cried Bishop Magee of Peterborough in one of the House of Lords debates on the subject. He reflected a commonly-held opinion. Perhaps Gladstone had run into trouble because this was not Liberal legislation. In his desire to please his Nonconformist supporters, from whose ranks many of the teetotallers were drawn, the Government had produced an untypical and illiberal measure. It provided for:

- licensed hours determined by local authorities;
- penalties against tampering with the contents of the beer;
- enforcement by police.

Effects

Opening hours of many Public Houses were restricted to lunch time and evenings only and a movement grew for local choice, where boroughs or counties could choose to become dry altogether or at least ban sales on Sundays. These ideas had considerable support and some success in Wales, with a number of counties opting to remain dry.

Gladstone's ministry did address some other social issues such as pollution, merchant shipping and public health (see Chapter 7). Yet the Prime Minister's parting shot in the 1874

Temperance organisations: The United Kingdom Alliance
Temperance is moderation in general and in particular in alcohol consumption. After temperance reformers early in the nineteenth century encouraged a move from drinking gin to beer, later nineteenth-century temperance organisations often urged total abstinence; they developed in reaction to the liberalising of the Licensing Laws in 1828 and the 1830 Beer House Act. The United Kingdom Alliance was founded in 1853 and eventually became the largest of these organisations. They campaigned for the re-imposition of strict licensing laws.

This cartoon by Sir John Tennie depicts a Victorian pub scene. The downcast woman suggests the devastating impact on families of excessive drinking.

election campaign (the proposal to abolish the income tax in the next parliament) hardly suggests someone planning major state-funded intervention in subsequent years.

JUDICATURE ACT 1873

Background

This was the last major piece of legislation in Gladstone's increasingly weak first ministry. The slowness, complexities and cost of English law had long been complained of and satirised by writers such as Charles Dickens. When he was a government legal officer in the 1860s, Roundell Palmer had spoken in favour of simplifying and consolidating centuries of complicated and contradictory laws. Gladstone appointed Lord Selbourne (Palmer) as **Lord Chancellor** in 1872: he then produced a simplification of the law which was praised on all sides and passed without difficulty.

Terms
- **Common Law and Equity were fused**.
- The complex court system was re-organised so that there was just one Supreme Court of Judicature.
- The appeals system was transformed and a final Court of Appeal established.

Effects

This act represented a considerable administrative achievement. Further reorganisation of the Court system followed in 1880 but the Act of 1873 still forms the basis of much of the legal system of England and Wales to this day. Initially, a final appeal to the House of Lords was removed but was reintroduced by amendment in 1876.

CONCLUSION

Gladstone's first ministry was one of substantial reform which in many ways established a new outlook and direction for governments yet to come. It:

- Removed a good deal of what Gladstone and others considered to be unjustified privilege.
- Completed the programme of religious liberalism that gave non-Anglicans virtually full legal equality.
- Set a radical new direction in education.
- Began the process of cleaning up the corrupt electoral system.
- Reformed some of the country's major institutions such as the Army, Civil Service and universities, and set Trade Unions on a secure legal footing.
- Tackled the problems in Ireland with the utmost seriousness and thoroughness.

Why did the Liberals lose the election of 1874?

In view of the considerable achievements of Gladstone's ministry it may seem surprising that his government was not re-elected. Yet Gladstone had offended many powerful interests in the country with his reforms. Their very success had hurt those already in well-established positions in society like those who automatically thought they could buy an army commission, push their 'dull' child into the Civil Service or not treat trade unions as legal bodies. In addition Gladstone's Irish policy was not popular among the English as opposed to (the much less numerous) Scottish and Welsh voters; moreover, apart from the Disestablishment measure the policy had not succeeded in dealing with Irish grievances.

Many, not only drinkers, had been offended by his Licensing Act. It seemed to go against the Englishman's idea of liberty.

Gladstone, when analysing his defeat, claimed that he had been '*borne down in a torrent of gin and beer*'. While this was clearly an exaggeration, public houses in both the 1874 and 1880 elections often allowed Conservative candidates to hold meetings on their premises but not Liberal ones. Also, some Liberal supporters felt Gladstone was paying too much attention to the Nonconformist interest in order to gain their support. Yet the Nonconformists themselves were not completely happy. On the sensitive subject of education they felt the Liberals' compromises (see page 93) had conceded too much to the Established Church interest.

By 1873 the Liberals seem to have run out of steam. Disagreements about future priorities appeared, especially on Irish policy as reflected in the defeat of the Irish Universities Bill (see page 92). The economy showed an uncharacteristic downturn in that year and the Chancellor Robert Lowe was involved in some relatively minor maladministration at the Exchequer and had to resign. Disraeli's jibe that the Liberal front bench '*resembled a range of exhausted volcanoes*' struck home. Gladstone first offered his resignation to the Queen as early as March 1873 but Disraeli shrewdly refused to take office, correctly sensing that if the Liberals staggered on a little longer the situation would only improve for the Conservatives: and so it proved. Gladstone's final throw of the dice was to dissolve Parliament in January 1874 and promise the abolition of the income tax in the next parliament if the Liberals were re-elected. It was a bold move but does not appear to have been believed by the electorate.

QUESTIONS TO CONSIDER

1. What were Gladstone's most important achievements in his first ministry, 1868–74?

PERIOD STUDY EXAM-STYLE QUESTIONS

1. Assess how far the successes of Gladstone's first ministry were due to Gladstonian Liberalism.
2. Assess the view that Gladstone's Liberalism was the dominant force behind the domestic legislation of his first ministry, 1868–74.

CHAPTER 7

What was Disraelian Conservatism?

Disraeli Timeline

1804	Born London
1813	Baptised into the Church of England
1837	First became an MP
1846	Made the crucial speech attacking Peel over Corn Law repeal
1849	Became leader of the Conservatives in the House of Commons under Lord Derby
1852	Chancellor of the Exchequer in Derby's first ministry
1858/9	Chancellor in Derby's second ministry
1858	Supported removal of Jewish Disabilities
1866–8	Chancellor in Derby's third ministry
1867	Piloted second Reform Bill through Parliament
1868 (Feb – Dec)	Became Prime Minister when Derby resigned through ill health. His first ministry
1868–74	Leader of the Conservative opposition to Gladstone's Liberal Government
1872	Major speeches in Manchester and the Crystal Palace, London
1874–80	General Election victory: became Prime Minister – second ministry
1876	Created Earl of Beaconsfield
1881	Died

EARLY POLITICAL VIEWS OF DISRAELI

Benjamin Disraeli was of Jewish background. As a young, ambitious man he apparently held quite radical opinions. He had decided of his own initiative, and certainly with no hint of an invitation, to contest the Buckinghamshire Borough of Wycombe. This was an area where his father had recently bought a modest country house. He stood as a Radical against Whig candidates – '*Toryism is **worn out** and I cannot condescend to be a Whig*' – but he came bottom of the poll. Only after several more attempts was Disraeli elected to the Commons.

Worn out Tories After the passing of the 1832 Reform bill against their wishes and their heavy election defeat later in the year, Disraeli saw Toryism as 'worn out'. It seemed doomed to extinction in the new industrial age. However, Peel's Tamworth Manifesto accepted the spirit as well as the letter of the Reform Act in 1834. The subsequent recovery of the party as the Conservative Party gave Disraeli fresh faith in its future, albeit not in the same way as Peel saw it.

Thirty-five years later Disraeli and Gladstone, already political opponents for some years, were to alternate as Prime Minister for some thirteen years, a rivalry ended only by Disraeli's death in 1881. Yet it was Disraeli as Conservative Prime Minister who was seen as the less radical of the two. How had this situation developed?

It had not taken long for their political differences to narrow somewhat. When Disraeli was finally elected to parliament in 1837, his fifth attempt in five years, he was standing in the Conservative interest, though his motives for doing so were certainly not identical to Gladstone's. One consistency in Disraeli's beliefs that can be detected is an anti-Whig one. But when he realised that the Conservatives (rather than the Tories) were not 'worn out' he was happy enough to attach himself to them. In 1837 he was elected for Maidstone but this time *defeating* a Radical candidate.

Benjamin Disraeli: just as Disraeli's political career was like no other at the time, his personal appearance was just as individual.

Dislike of all Whigs

Disraeli's early dismissal of the Whigs as a possible party to support brings out a consistent strand in his thinking. What was the nature of this dislike?

- Though they were clearly aristocratic he saw them as a rather narrow clique inclined to accept a lessening of the influence and privileges of the Church.
- Even more, his principal objection was to their acceptance of the centralising tendencies of reformers such as Jeremy Bentham whose views had inspired the changes to the Poor Law in the 1830s and their inclination to accept **bureaucratic** and centrally driven solutions to social problems rather than more sensitive local ones.

Disraeli's views in the 1840s can be examined by looking at his novels of the period. In the first of a trilogy, *Coningsby* (1844), a survey of political attitudes of the day, he emphasises his anti-Whig opinions seeing them as wishing to exclude all other groups from power, such as the monarchy, the Crown and the ordinary people of England (for it was *England* that most interested Disraeli). His political heroes were **Lord Bolingbroke** and **William Pitt**, whose Chancellor's robes he had managed to retain (see page 47). Pitt, he argued, had provided truly national leadership with sound principles.

Dislike of some Tories

However, Disraeli was also critical of many Tories. He viewed those who opposed all change and reform as unwise, unrealistic and 'worn out'. Yet this did not mean that Disraeli approved of Peel's attempt to reform the Conservatives in the 1830s. Disraeli felt the Tamworth Manifesto (see page 3) was an attempt to construct a *'party without principles'*. Disraeli wished to develop Conservatism in a different direction. Dislike of Peel also became personal. Disraeli had hoped for office under Peel in 1841 but was offered nothing – an imagined slight that he chose not to forgive. Without office, he attached himself to a group known as Young England in 1843. This was led by two younger ex-Cambridge graduates from aristocratic backgrounds, George Smythe and Lord John Manners:

KEY TERMS

Bureaucratic Emphasises the importance of detailed and precise government regulation (often central government) with an emphasis on general procedures rather than judgment of individual cases.

KEY PEOPLE

Henry St John Viscount Bolingbroke 1678–1751 and **William Pitt 1759–1806**, were both regarded as leading political thinkers at either end of the eighteenth century. Bolingbroke only held office briefly whereas Pitt was Prime Minister for almost 20 years of his short life.

- They protested against the party discipline imposed by Peel, and his tendency to legislate in the interests of the middle class economy.
- They stood for a romantic view of England where aristocratic tradition and influence could complement the true working classes.
- They wished to outflank the Whigs who they saw as narrow-minded and heartless and imposing a cruel Poor Law on the country.
- Only with the defeat of the Whigs, they believed, could proper concern be shown for the social welfare of the ordinary people.

Disraeli and One-Nation Conservatism: The Ideas
Disraeli had a high regard for the institutions of the country – Aristocracy, Monarchy, Church, and as such was always a potential Tory. He combined these traditional views however, with a concern for the poorer classes and a dislike of some of the effects of industrialisation and what he saw as the grasping nature of the new urban middle class. They were not seen as treating their workers well. Urbanisation (and the responses to it) was, he felt, threatening to undermine those traditional institutions. While not supporting the detailed demands of the Chartist movement (at its height between 1838 and 1848) Disraeli sympathised with their complaints about the treatment of ordinary hard-working people in the new industrial towns and cities both at work and at home. Particularly alarmed by the lack of contact between the employers and employees in those areas, he felt there was a danger of creating two nations: the rich and the poor; the haves and have-nots. He was always open to the idea of moderate parliamentary reform.

He saw the traditional paternalistic (father-like) values of the landed gentry as more likely to bring stability and harmony in a rapidly changing society. His vision was of one nation united, not in a classless way, but by the upper classes showing genuine concern for the lower classes: deference (respect to those considered your social superiors) would still be shown by the poorer to the richer.

What Disraeli seemed to want, was a third way in contrast to Whig and traditional Tory ideas: to use the powers and influence of the traditional institutions of the country, the

Church, Parliament including the House of Lords, the monarchy and the landed interest generally to ally with the ordinary people and improve their conditions. In another revealing novel, *Sybil* (1845) Disraeli's most famous passage bewails the two nations of rich and poor (see below): the solution as he saw it was a revival of the monarchy and the traditional landed interest who would care for the social welfare of the ordinary people. The Church would also have a role in raising the aspirations of the people as Disraeli also indicated in his writings, not least in the third of his trilogy *Tancred* (1847) which also has a Jewish theme.

An extract from Disraeli's *Sybil*

'Well, society may be in its infancy' said Egremont... but...our Queen reigns over the greatest nation that ever existed'.

'Which nation?' asked the younger stranger 'for she reigns over two...two nations between whom there is no intercourse and no sympathy; who are as ignorant of each other's habits, thoughts, and feelings as if they were dwellers in different zones, or inhabitants of different planets; who are formed by a different breeding, are fed by a different food, are ordered by different manners, and are not governed by the same laws.'

You speak of? said Egremont, hesitatingly.

'THE RICH AND THE POOR'

(Benjamin Disraeli, *Sybil* World Classics Edition 1981 pages 65/6)

One-Nation Conservatism: religion and class

Disraeli had identified two nations: could they become one? How one-nation Conservatism would work out in terms of hard political policy was not always clear. Indeed, the phrase only came into common use much later and was not generally applied directly to some Tories until the early twentieth century. For instance, although Disraeli was a

**Disraeli's Sceptical
Father** Isaac D'Israeli (his
son Benjamin dropped the
apostrophe) was a substantial
man of letters in his own
right. He had fallen out
with members of his Jewish
Synagogue in London, lost
his religious faith and had his
children baptized as Christians
so they could get on in the
world.

Chartist pressures
The Chartist petitions of
1839, 1842 and 1848 were
signed by several million
people. The accompanying
demonstrations, excitement
and (occasionally) violence
surrounding them made
governments feel they could
not give in to any of their
demands, as it would appear
to be weakly giving in to
threats.

Reactionary In general
political terms someone
who reacts against change
and wants to return to how
the system used to be. Since
1789 many Tory politicians
had reacted against the
French Revolution and all it
stood for. So, partly on these
grounds, they had opposed
parliamentary reform and
many other changes in the
previous fifty years.

strong supporter of the established position of the Church
of England he never showed the religious intensity of
Gladstone. Baptized at thirteen by a **sceptical father** who
had lost his Jewish faith, Disraeli's regard for the Church
was always in a very broad context. It was seen as a central
plank in the maintenance of the English way of life upheld
by a disinterested and paternalistic aristocracy, rather than
what Disraeli saw as the narrow-minded, money-grabbing
middle classes to whom the Whig Party paid far too
much attention. It was part of the glue that held society
together and, as such should be supported. This was a
more pragmatic view of the institution than the religious
certainties of a youthful Gladstone.

One-Nation Conservatism: social and political views

Here, Disraeli's ideas could be seen as romantic, pining
for the happy days of good old rural England before
grasping industrialists and greedy Whig lawyers came
along. Unfortunately circumstances did not favour the
implementation of this policy. **Chartist pressures** made
it impossible to put forward a further extension of the
franchise so that the alliance with the people could be
cemented. Worse still, in 1846, political circumstances
forced Disraeli into an alliance with the more **reactionary**
sort of Tory in opposing Peel's repeal of the Corn Laws,
Young England permanently disbanded and the Tories
remained largely out of office for over twenty years.

Disraeli's interest in parliamentary reform can be seen in
his Bill of 1859 and the Act of 1867 and his concern for
the welfare of the people in his social legislation of the mid
1870s. His strong nationalistic feeling can be seen in his
development of imperial ideas from about 1872.

Disraeli and protection after 1846

With the political upheaval of 1846 Disraeli found
himself in the largest single group in Parliament – the
Protectionists, but one where his parliamentary skills and
especially his speaking ability would be much in need. The
prejudices that had been evident against him ever since
members of Parliament laughed at his **maiden speech**
back in 1837 did not disappear, but he was too valuable an
asset to be ignored. Disraeli struggled with the possibility

that, despite his efforts in 1846, protection might have to be abandoned as a policy. This issue first became apparent in 1848 with the resignation and subsequent death of the protectionist leader in the Commons Lord George Bentinck. Although Derby was not prepared to make Disraeli the official party leader in the Commons this is what he effectively became (see page 42). In 1849 when Derby made a strong protectionist speech in the Lords, Disraeli was less enthusiastic in the Commons. He was reproved by Derby for a speech in which he suggested that repeal could remain if farmers could be compensated in other ways. After the sudden death of Peel in 1850 Disraeli was keener than ever for the Tories to accept free trade but the time had not yet come.

In his Budget of 1852 Disraeli was attempting to compensate farmers for the loss of the Corn Laws by measures like the Malt Tax reduction but this was subjected to an attack by Gladstone which really marks the start of the intense rivalry between the two figures (see page 46).

Disraeli and parliamentary reform

Disraeli's early approach to the Chartists (see page 109) indicates that his mind was never closed to the possibility of parliamentary reform. In 1859 he had introduced a Reform Act into the House of Commons (see page 60) where it was opposed by the emerging Liberal, Gladstone. The Fancy Franchises Bill, as it became popularly known, was no Radical measure and reflected Disraeli's attitude to reform which was essentially pragmatic, looking for possible party advantage.

Disraeli's views on parliamentary reform were 'purely opportunistic' (Robert Blake) throughout this period; there was no reason why the Conservatives could not support the moderate Reform Bill of 1866 and so prevent the likelihood of anything more radical coming along for some time. So how did such a radical bill come to pass?

- Like Disraeli, Derby was not totally opposed to reform on principle – he had been a strong supporter of it in 1832.
- Seeing the possibility of a split in the Liberal ranks, Disraeli urged Derby to oppose the Liberal Bill of

Disraeli's maiden speech
Disraeli's first speech in parliament, on the subject of corruption at Irish elections, was a disaster. He spoke awkwardly and was subject to what his biographer describes as 'hisses, hoots, laughter and catcalls'. But he ended with a prediction that he fulfilled. 'I will sit down now but the time will come when you will hear me'.

1866 which, with the aid of the Adullamite opposition, brought down the government and put Derby and Disraeli into office with the chance of settling the reform question on their own terms.

- Disraeli's handling of the situation was initially impressive. He persuaded the majority of his party of the need for reform, overriding the opposition in his own party and the resignation of three Cabinet colleagues: Cranbourne, Peel and Carnarvon. This contrasted with the severe splits in the Liberal Party that had occurred over the same reform issues.
- But his touch deserted him somewhat when a combination of public agitation, uncertainty over the finer detail of the terms and a desire to get one over Gladstone at almost any cost resulted in his acceptance of amendments so radical that some contemporaries could hardly believe what was happening.

Perhaps Disraeli took some satisfaction from the fact that working men were now enfranchised in sufficient numbers to outvote the middle classes in some areas. This seemed to tie in with his traditional view of an alliance between the landed classes and the working people of England as being a more satisfactory arrangement for government than the rule of a middle class of limited vision and hard-nosed laissez-faire individualism.

Tory democracy

Did Disraeli's radical second Reform Bill show Tory democracy in action? Hardly. As with one-nation Conservatism, this is a phrase that tended to be used a little later in the century by **Lord Randolph Churchill** in the 1880s, just after Disraeli's death. Back in the 1860s things were different. One historian has described Disraeli in his efforts on reform in 1867 as being 'the great improviser'. He had a complex mixture of motives and aimed to settle the question, quell any agitation and embarrass Gladstone and many of his fellow Liberals politically. He only succeeded in the short term. Household suffrage in the boroughs was indeed a major advance but did not settle the reform issue and would soon lead to demands for a similar franchise in the counties. Gladstone was outmanoeuvred in 1867 but was to triumph in the elections a year later. Lord Derby's influence in getting the 1867 Bill through the Lords (and so avoid the chaos of 1831/2) smacked of the old aristocratic politics not democracy. Public disturbances were indeed quelled but were to resume in 1884, though admittedly on a smaller scale.

However, one major feature of a democratic state now seemed to be established; the necessity of public support for political actions. To regain office after the defeat of 1868 Disraeli (and others) appreciated the need to improve party organisation and appeal to the new voters. He felt policies such as imperialism and social reform would attract them, while the institutions of the country in state and Church would be maintained. Over five years of opposition gave the Conservatives an opportunity to develop these ideas.

Disraeli as Tory leader

After his defeat in 1868 there had been moves to depose Disraeli as leader, but he held on to make two significant public speeches which were to influence the future direction of Conservatism, in 1872 at the **Free Trade Hall** in Manchester in April and at the **Crystal Palace** in South London in June. Both outlined his interpretation of Conservatism.

At Manchester in a long address fortified by brandy (special white brandy so it would look like water) he promised to:

- be proud of Britain and to uphold the institutions of the country such as the monarchy; and the Church and the landed aristocracy, and to maintain the British constitution;
- stand up for British interests abroad (with a side-swipe at what he saw as a weak Liberal foreign policy, see also page 144);
- act on the need for sanitary reform (this was only a tiny fraction of the speech but has been made much of since, in view of his later reforms).

At the Crystal Palace he emphasised similar themes:

- the Conservatives were the '*National Party*' rejecting the '*continental*' ideas of the Liberals. They were the party to appeal to all classes and unite the nation;

KEY PLACES

Free Trade Hall, Manchester: The Free Trade Hall was built in Manchester in 1847 as a celebration of the victory of the principle of Free trade with the repeal of the Corn Laws in 1846. Possibly the only building named after a proposition rather than a person or a place (see image on page 17).

Crystal Palace, South London The Crystal Palace was a huge glass building which was designed and built for the Great Exhibition in Hyde Park in 1851 to show off the world's (but especially Britain's) industrial advances. Moved to a permanent site in South London, it burnt down in 1936 (see image on page 19).

Imperial Until Disraeli's
speech when he used this
word, it had been regarded as
a continental term referring
to foreign emperors such as
the French or Russian rulers.
Disraeli's opponents criticised
him for using it, especially as
he had attacked the Liberals
for being too continental.
They sarcastically referred to
his 'imperialism' as a term of
insult. However, the word
stuck and became used for
those who gloried in the size
and strength of the British
Empire.

Irish Home Rule The idea
of giving Ireland their own
Parliament back (abolished
in 1800) and making them
responsible for running their
own domestic affairs. Defence
and foreign policy would
be left in the hands of the
Westminster government.
(See Chapter 10 for the Irish
Home Rule Party.)

- the working classes would be proud to belong to an '*imperial*' country (see examples of Disraeli's policy on pages 145 and 150);
- social reform rather than political reform was now required (again, this was actually a minor part of the speech).

Disraeli was certainly aware of the much enlarged working class electorate from his own reform in 1867 and sensed they would be attracted by a firmly nationalistic policy. Disraeli realised that a new European situation was developing with the rise of Prussia (soon to be Germany) and Italy. In these changing circumstances he sensed the need for a more assertive British foreign policy (see Chapter 9). This would be in addition to improvements to their own quality life at home. To simplify his message considerably, the Conservatives would stand for tradition, imperialism and social reform. This did indeed prove popular though not always to the people Disraeli intended.

Disraeli had first become Prime Minister in February 1868 when Lord Derby had resigned on grounds of ill health. '*At last I have reached to the top of the greasy pole*' he remarked. Indeed he was soon to slither down as Gladstone's Liberals comfortably won the election of 1868. However, this election result was reversed in 1874 when the Conservative majority was 105 over the Liberals and 48 overall when the **Irish Home Rule** Party supporters were taken into account: Disraeli had finally achieved real power. The fact that there was a comfortable Conservative victory at all was significant. It was the first time this had occurred since Peel's triumph in 1841.

CONCLUSION

- Disraeli's early political beliefs were formed without party attachment but by the 1840s he had developed a clear Tory philosophy.
- These ideas later became known as One-Nation Conservatism. He was concerned by the poor social conditions resulting from rapid industrial development and the consequent lack of communication between the different social classes in the country.

- His rise to prominence in the Conservative Party was sudden, with his devastating attacks on Peel's proposals to repeal the Corn Laws in 1846.
- However, his unusual social background for a Conservative leader resulted in some delay before he assumed undisputed leadership of the Conservatives in the House of Commons.
- Suspicion remained in some circles and it was uncertain for many years whether he would follow Lord Derby as Conservative leader.
- Only with the successful passing of the second Reform Act in 1867, when Disraeli was seen to have achieved a tactical triumph, was his succession to the leadership of the Conservative Party assured.

QUESTIONS TO CONSIDER

1. Why, despite his background, did Disraeli maintain his position as a prominent Conservative between 1846 and 1874?
2. What were the main ideas behind One Nation Conservatism?

PERIOD STUDY EXAM-STYLE QUESTIONS

1. Assess the view that Disraeli had assumed a prominent position in the Conservative Party by the end of 1852.

CHAPTER 8

How successful was Disraeli's ministry 1874–80?

KEY ISSUES

This entire chapter is important for **Key Issue 5** (see page iv).

WHY DID DISRAELI WIN THE 1874 ELECTION?

The Liberals lost the 1874 election (see end of previous chapter) as much as the Conservatives won it. Nonetheless there were some very positive features in the Tory victory under Disraeli. Conservative organisation had now caught up and surpassed that of the Liberals (see page 70–71). Though administered in a more top down way than the equivalent Liberal organisations, the National Union of Conservative Association had started to become an effective organisation, attracting the middle-class support the Conservatives needed if they were to rid themselves of the image of being a purely landed party. As a result, the well-off middle classes increasingly saw the Conservatives as their party, maintaining the status quo out of which they had done so well. The growing professional classes, doctors, architects, lawyers and academics, as well as businessmen, were frequently if not invariably sympathetic to the Tories and added a wider social range of support to the landed and church interest of the previous generation. Even so, landed support was still valuable to the Conservatives who won 145/172 of the County seats in 1874. The secret ballot (see page 190) was not immediately effective in stamping out bribery until coupled with the more effective Corrupt Practices Act of 1883 (see page 69).

To a lesser extent there was a developing Conservative working-class vote, especially in England. Popular Conservative support in Lancashire was very strong – going back to the 1830s when Conservatives had supported factory reform against the wishes of many Whigs. They patriotically supported maintaining firm control over Ireland, Irish immigration into Lancashire merely re-enforcing the existing Conservative support. Working people were also starting in similar vein to become attracted to the new Imperial ideas that the Conservatives, rather than the Liberals, were adopting (see also page 144). At this stage of the electoral system the growing Home Rule Party in Ireland, who won 59 seats at the election, were having little effect on Conservative support but were eating into the Liberal vote.

WHAT WERE THE POLITICAL AND SOCIAL ISSUES OF DISRAELI'S GOVERNMENT 1874–80?

How dominant were the ideas of Disraelian Conservatism in his major period of office between 1874 and 1880? Would Disraeli be able to take full advantage of his opportunity? He was seventy years old and by his own admission lacked the drive and energy he had possessed just a few years previously. '*It has come too late*' he admitted when he was congratulated on becoming Prime Minister again. In truth he had never possessed the forcefulness and zest of a man like Gladstone and had a much hazier idea than the Liberal Prime Minister of what policies he would introduce. In these last years of his life (he died in 1881) he suffered apparently from asthma, gout, bronchitis and towards the end, kidney disease.

Background to Disraeli's social reform

The frenzy of legislative activity in Gladstone's first ministry was not repeated in Disraeli's second. Nevertheless, the ministry was very active in the field of social reform. In an era where national politics, national issues and national parties were all developing, national solutions were demanded. It is true to say that Gladstone's government had tackled these issues but, as Disraeli had sensed in his speeches, public opinion was looking for further action in certain areas:

Firstly, areas Gladstone's government had not addressed:

- **Housing**: poor quality, ill-ventilated and cramped housing in the larger industrial towns was a major handicap to a satisfactory quality of life for many working people. There had been a Housing Act proposed by a Liberal MP which became law in Disraeli's first ministry in 1868 but it had not been effective.
- **Merchant Shipping**: there had been an increase in shipping disasters due to overloading with cargo.
- The growth of **Friendly Societies** required regulation. This *had* been recognised by the Liberals who had set up a Royal Commission to investigate the issue in 1870 but there had been no legislation.

Secondly, where Gladstone's changes had not been seen to settle the question:

Public health legislation from the 1840s The most important measure was the 1848 Public Health Act which set up a Central Board of Health, but the provisions were not compulsory for local authorities to take up. After 1854 it was disbanded and its functions taken over by another government department, the Home Office.

KEY CONCEPTS

Maximum number of hours worked The first effective restrictions on the hours worked in textile factories by women and children were passed in 1833. There had been further restrictions on hours in 1844 and 1847 and a widening of the provisions to workshops in 1867.

KEY PEOPLE

Richard Cross 1823–1914 Cross came from a wealthy Lancashire manufacturing family. He was the only middle-class politician in Disraeli's very aristocratic Cabinet and was a fine administrator who was regarded as a 'safe pair of hands'. Because of Cross's Lancashire background, Disraeli may have selected him to please Lord Derby who owned great estates in the county.

- **Food adulteration**: as an increasingly urban society grew less and less food for themselves and bought more and more, issues of hygiene and inaccurate labelling had become a major issue. Some supposed medical remedies were very dubious. A Liberal Act of 1872 had been seen as ineffective in this area.
- **Labour Relations**: Trade Unions had objected to Gladstone's ban on peaceful picketing and also complained that the law punished workers who broke their contract more severely than employers who did the same.
- **Licensing of Public Houses**: where Gladstone's restrictions were regarded as too severe.

Thirdly, where previous legislation needed to be consolidated and/or developed:

- **Public Health**, where there been a mass of **legislation from the 1840s** to the Liberal Act of 1872. Regulations were now increasingly complex and contradictory. River pollution was now a serious concern.
- **Factories**: administrative complexity was again an issue and public opinion now favoured a further reduction in the **maximum number of hours worked**. This had been recommended by a Liberal enquiry which had reported in 1873.
- Educational provision was to be amended from the trail-blazing Act of 1870.

Though Disraeli was not a good administrator himself, a strong group of Ministers in his Cabinet was able to produce substantial reforms in these areas. The most active figures were the Home Secretary, **Richard Cross** and the President of the Local Government Board, George Sclater-Booth.

As a result of their efforts, eleven major Acts of Social Reform were passed in the years 1875 and 1876. Though Disraeli rarely took a personal interest in their detail the philosophy behind many of them was not inconsistent with his earlier ideas: many would prevent the grasping businessman from taking short-cuts and risking working people's health and safety for their own profit.

THE LEGISLATION

Title	**Artisans Dwelling Act 1875**
Minister Responsible	Cross
Main Terms	Local authorities, if they wished, could purchase slum property and organise the building of new, cheap properties to be let at favourable rents to urban workers.
Significance	The first ever substantial piece of legislation with regard to housing and prepared to interfere with property rights in exceptional cases with the idea of compulsory purchase.
Effects	Considerable in Birmingham where Joseph Chamberlain used the Act to transform the city's housing. Overall, however, because the Act was **permissive** and not compulsory, many authorities, shy of expense, did little. Only ten authorities had taken advantage of it by the end of the 1870s though later, Liverpool and London were more active in its implementation. In London, it could even create a housing problem as properties of the very poor were demolished without being replaced with dwellings these people could afford.
Title	**Merchant Shipping Act 1876**
Minister Responsible	Viscount Adderley (President of the Board of Trade)
Main terms	Shipowners were made to draw a line around the vessel to indicate the maximum load that could be taken.

KEY TERMS

Artisan Originally, anyone practising an industrial art. It had become a word for the skilled working class.

KEY CONCEPTS

Permissive legislation A law passed by the Westminster Parliament giving local authorities permission to exercise specific tasks if they wished to do so.

Significance	Backbench pressure: the Act owed its existence to Samuel Plimsoll, Liberal MP for Derby, who had made a scene in the House of Commons the previous year when an earlier bill had been dropped. It was a compulsory Act and one of a number that increased state regulation.
Effects	Not totally effective since the line could be drawn by the owners of the vessels themselves, but an important step towards greater regulation.
Title	**Friendly Societies Act 1875**
Minister Responsible	Sir Stafford Northcote (Chancellor of the Exchequer)
Main terms	A degree of regulation of the Societies was introduced. The Societies could be given **actuarial advice** by the government and their funds would be safeguarded.
Significance	The idea was to ensure the societies could continue their work even more effectively in providing insurance for the better-off working class.
Effects	Friendly Society funds continued to grow. By 1891 they had 4.2 million people investing a total of £22.7 million in them. By 1901 the equivalent figures were 6.2 million and £48.2 million.
Title	**Sale of Food and Drugs Act 1875**
Minister Responsible	Sclater-Booth
Main terms	Ingredients harmful to health were forbidden in foods. Certain drugs were forbidden from general sale.

KEY TERMS

Actuarial advice An Actuary is an official in an insurance office who estimates the best rates of premium to charge for insurance based on rates of probability.

Significance	Another major step in state regulation and the main piece of legislation in this field until 1928.
Effects	Fairly successful but limited to the prohibition of harmful substances. Thus, adding salt to beer or water to milk was not covered.
Title	**Conspiracy and Protection of Property Act 1875**
Minister responsible	Cross
Main terms	Legalised peaceful picketing.
Significance	Pleased the Trade Union leaders and removed a major grievance.
Effects	Ensured the moderate and peaceful development of the Trade Union movement.
Title	**Employers and Workmen Act 1876**
Minister Responsible	Cross
Main Terms	Replaced the **Master and Servant Act** with more sensitive names implying greater equality. Before the Act employ*ees* could be sued in the Criminal Courts as well as the Civil Courts, but this did not apply to employers. All cases regarding conditions of employment and possible breach of contract would now be dealt with in the Civil Courts.
Significance	The law would now treat all classes equally.
Effects	Disraeli now felt all major problems regarding the relations between labour and capital had been settled. The Secretary of the **Trades Union Congress**, George Howell, also expressed himself satisfied.

KEY TERMS

Master and Servant Act
In the 1860s, particularly in Scotland, magistrates could still threaten strikers with prison for breach of contract when a strike began. After 1867 'aggravated cases' could still result in a criminal prosecution.

KEY TERMS

Trades Union Congress
An annual meeting of Trade Union representatives first held in 1868. It co-ordinated Trade Union activities and discussed matters of common interest.

Title	**Licensing Act 1874**
Minister Responsible	Cross
Main terms	Amended Bruce's Licensing Act. Drinking time was increased by 30 minutes, police rights to search were reduced and **magistrates**' discretion on interfering with hours of opening were removed.
Significance	A good example of Disraeli's Government amending an unpopular Gladstone Act to gain popular support.

THE GOOD LITTLE "VITLER."

GRANDMAMMA CROSS. "GRANDMA' BRUCE SENT YOU TO BED AT TWELVE O'CLOCK, BUT AS YOU WERE A VERY GOOD BOY LAST ELECTION, GRANDMA' CROSS WILL LET YOU STOP UP TILL HALF-PAST!!"

[*Intense Delight of the good little Vitler.*

A cartoon from Punch November 1874 on the Licensing Act. This clever piece of legislation was not untypical of Disraeli's government when amending Gladstone's legislation. It gained popularity at the expense of Gladstone with only a very small concession. The 'lady' depicted is actually Richard Cross, the home secretary.

Effects	Government intervention in this area had become accepted. Some publicans favoured the Conservatives as a result, though this may be exaggerated.
Title	**Public Health Act 1875**
Minister Responsible	Sclater-Booth
Main terms	Consolidatory measure (bringing together and simplifying a mass of different and possibly contradictory laws on one subject). In 1872 the Liberals had put into practice the recommendations of a Sanitary Commission report set up when Disraeli was first Prime Minister in 1868. **Medical officers of Health** had been set up in large towns and sanitary authorities had been established. What Sclater-Booth's Act did was to consolidate the measure and define the powers of the new authorities more clearly.
Significance	Seen as a triumph for administrative efficiency and as more effective than the Liberal legislation of 1872.
Effects	Coupled with the Pollution of Rivers Act of 1874, it remained the basis of Public Health Law until the 1920s.
Title	**Factory Acts of 1874 and 1878**
Minister Responsible	Cross
Main terms	1874: hours in textile factories reduced from 60 hours a week to 56 and a half for women and young people. The age limit for half-time employment for children was raised to 10 years and full-time to 14.
	1878: consolidated all previous legislation and abolished the distinction between factories and workshops (smaller

	than factories and generally employing less than a few dozen workers).
Significance	A great achievement for Cross whose praises were literally sung to the words: '*For he's a jolly good fellow, whatever the radicals think, for he has shortened the hours of work and lengthened the hours of drink*'.
Effects	Reducing the working hours of women and children often meant hours were effectively reduced for adult men as well. Laissez-faire beliefs were hanging on sufficiently tenaciously to make direct restrictions on adult male labour more difficult to pass.
Title	**Education Act 1876**
Minister Responsible	Viscount Sandon (Vice-President of the Committee of the Council for Education)
Main Terms	Children between 10 and 14 could only leave school if they had a certificate indicating minimum levels of attainment. Parliamentary grants of money for voluntary schools could exceed what the schools themselves had raised.
Significance	Conservatives hoped to encourage more voluntary (usually Anglican) schools as these seemed to be expanding at a slower rate than the newly established board schools.
Effects	Elementary education up to the age of ten was now effectively compulsory as long as local authorities were prepared to enforce attendance. Moreover, more and more of them were exempting the poorer families from school fees.

Disraeli's ministry is remembered especially for its social reforms but the Prime Minister's high regard for the great institutions of the country, the monarchy, the landed interest and the Church, featured prominently in his activities. Moreover, in Disraeli's time the Empire came to be added to this important list.

DISRAELI AND THE QUEEN

One of the revealing developments of Disraeli's second ministry was the partial return to public life of Queen Victoria. Widowed with the death of Prince Albert at the end of 1861 she had become something of a recluse, only rarely seen in public and spending a good deal of time either at her Scottish retreat Balmoral or at Osborne on the Isle of Wight. Disraeli, generally at ease in women's company, handled her more sensitively than Gladstone. '*Mr Gladstone addresses me as if I were a public meeting,*' complained the Queen, whereas Disraeli knew how to flatter her. Although **Disraeli's skill with the pen** was much greater than the Queen's he was tactful enough to make comments such as '*we authors Ma'am*'. Nor were Gladstone's letters as enjoyable as Disraeli's, who could, as the Queen's Secretary remarked, write '*in an amusing tone while seizing the points of an argument*'.

The Widower and the Widowed

When Disraeli's wife Mary Anne died in 1872, Victoria's condolences were profound, sincere and doubtless made with her own widowhood in mind. They may have been a comfort to each other, but while Victoria helped Disraeli overcome his loss on a purely personal basis, Disraeli's aid to the Queen had wider consequences. The Monarchy had become unpopular around 1870 because of the Queen's reluctance to show herself in public since Albert's death, and the behaviour of the Prince of Wales: a known womaniser and gambler. However, after the Prince almost died of typhoid fever (the illness which had killed his father ten years before) at the end of 1871, public sympathies changed.

Disraeli's encouragement of the Queen to appear more often in public was an important element in the recovery of her popularity. Moreover, the contrast in her relations with Gladstone was marked. This did not mean, however, that

KEY TERMS

Disraeli's skill with the pen Disraeli wrote novels on and off throughout his life. Two, *Coningsby* and *Sybil*, written in the 1840s, are still highly regarded today. Coningsby provides an insight into the political activities of the day and *Sybil* is famous for its portrayal of social problems including the idea of the 'Two Nations' of rich and poor (see page 108).

Royal Constitutional Duty Although the monarch theoretically invited someone of their own choice to form a Government, in practice it was understood by the mid-nineteenth century that the person would normally be the leader of the majority party in Parliament – though there might be two leaders, one in the Commons and one in the Lords.

Edward, Prince of Wales 1841–1910 The eldest son of Victoria and Albert. Reacted against his strict upbringing and worried his parents with his tastes for fine food, women, gambling and shooting parties. Only his severe illness at the end of 1871 brought an end to growing Republican feelings.

Expanding Russian Empire Russia was expanding its borders to the south and east in the mid to late nineteenth century so that by the 1870s only Afghanistan stood between it and the British Empire in India (see page 133).

Church Appointments Senior clergy were officially appointed by the Queen, but by this time the Prime Minister was also consulted. Sometimes there was quite a battle between Victoria and Disraeli over this. In 1868 she persuaded him to accept her own choice for Archbishop of Canterbury, Archibald Tait, whose Liberal leanings were distrusted by Disraeli.

the Queen overstepped the mark in terms of exercising her power. When Disraeli lost the election in 1880 she knew that she would have to **perform her royal constitutional duty** which meant accepting his resignation and asking the Liberals to form a Ministry.

Empress of India

After a visit to India in 1875/6 by **Edward, Prince of Wales** the Queen let it be known to Disraeli that she would like to add to her royal titles and become Empress of India. It appears to have been her own idea: Disraeli may not have approved. Certainly, he did not feel the timing was right but he went along with the suggestion and a Royal Titles Bill was introduced in 1876. Opposition was considerable, with the leading Liberal peer Lord Granville speaking strongly against it in the House of Lords. The Prince of Wales returned from India annoyed that he had not been informed of the development. Disraeli had two main justifications for the Bill:

- It would emphasise that British authority in India *was* much more welcome than at the time of the Indian Mutiny in 1857.
- It would indicate to the Russians that an **expansion of the Russian Empire** near India would *not* be welcomed.

Once passed it was clear that the monarchy was assuming the role of Head of the British Empire and not just the British Isles. The whole incident associated the Conservatives with both Monarchy and Empire.

DISRAELI AND THE CHURCH

Disraeli, a man of Jewish origins and baptised into the Christian faith at the age of 13 on the orders of his sceptical father never possessed the devout faith of someone like Gladstone. However, finding himself at the head of the Conservative party, he was prepared stoutly to defend the privileges of the Church of England. He had opposed Gladstone's disestablishment of the Irish Church and took a considerable interest in **Church appointments** as Prime Minister, preferring not to recommend known Liberals. He sensed that the very high churchmen were not generally popular in the country as a whole and their ritualistic practices were far too close to the Roman Catholic tradition for comfort. The Queen agreed, and wished in fact, to go further than Disraeli in stopping them.

Public Worship Act

The result was the Public Worship Regulation Bill of 1874 which provoked lively discussion in parliament. Certain rituals would be banned, and the thought that clergy defying the ban could ultimately end up in jail troubled many. Gladstone spoke against the Bill on the grounds of religious liberty but it passed both Lords and Commons. After all the dispute that had resulted Disraeli tried to avoid controversial Church issues for the rest of his period of office.

DISRAELI AND THE LANDED INTEREST

As with the Church, Disraeli was an outsider when it came to the English aristocracy, but he took to the idea of a landed life enthusiastically after his father acquired a modest house at Bradenham in Buckinghamshire in 1828. Disraeli himself became the squire of Hughenden, near High Wycombe, in 1848. He enjoyed the conversations and lifestyle of the aristocratic country houses where he was frequently regarded as good company. Where Gladstone, a man of great energy, chopped down trees, Disraeli preferred to watch others. But the two men, for once, agreed on the desirability of having landed aristocrats in government.

However, the landed interest went through a difficult time in the late 1870s, a time that coincided with Disraeli's Premiership.

- A series of cool, wet summers brought very poor harvests.
- Cheap foreign corn imports were now made possible by steam-powered ships.
- Distressed farmers visited Disraeli after the appalling summer of 1879 but he made it clear that the return of Protection (for that is what they desired) was a political non-starter. Free trade was far too popular and far too important for the commercial and industrial interest in the country to consider a change of policy. It was a revealing moment.

DISRAELI AND IRELAND

The agricultural depression also had a major impact in Ireland. Because of it many tenants were evicted and Gladstone's first Land Act of 1870 was now seen as inadequate. By 1879 the activities of the Irish Land League included violent attacks on landlords and their property.

Disraeli's analysis

Back in 1844 Disraeli had accurately summarised the Irish Question as '*a starving population, an absentee aristocracy, and an alien Church and in addition the weakest executive in the world*'. By this he was describing the system whereby the Irish were governed on a day-to-day basis by an English dominated executive (government) with a Viceroy (monarch's deputy) residing in Dublin Castle and a Chief Secretary for Ireland, an English MP who was also a member of the English government travelling backwards and forwards between the two countries. This hardly made for efficient let alone quick government. Moreover, the Dublin Castle Executive was firmly subordinated to the English government.

However, Disraeli showed little sign of turning his analysis into action in office and developing a programme similar to the one Gladstone had proposed to deal with the question. Clear-sighted but short-sighted, as Lord Salisbury once remarked of him in a general context, he appears not to have appreciated fully the growing discontent and nationalist feeling in Ireland until near the end of his premiership.

Disraeli's lack of action

The Irish Home Rule Party led by Isaac Butt had made substantial gains at the 1874 election, but all Disraeli had to offer were Coercion Acts to try to control law and order. Perhaps he was aware of the political reputations Ireland had broken in the past, like Peel's, and how the politicians who had avoided the question as much as possible, such as Palmerston, seemed to have prospered. After the terrible harvest in 1877 economic grievances were increasingly translated into militant political action as Parnell took over the Home Rule Party leadership from Isaac Butt. As a result, Gladstone was to inherit a difficult situation in 1880.

DISRAELI AND THE LIBERAL OPPOSITION

Success

After Disraeli's victory in the 1874 election Gladstone temporarily retired from party politics and the Liberal leader in the Commons was Lord Hartington. Disraeli found him a much easier man to deal with than Gladstone. 'Harty Tarty', as he was referred to by Disraeli and others, was a conscientious statesman but did not possess the debating prowess of Gladstone. Disraeli was therefore in a strong position, and the first two years of government showed a strong ministry capable of passing major reforms.

But when Gladstone returned to the fray to attack Disraeli's foreign policy in 1876 (see below for the Bulgarian Horrors) the Prime Minister had a much tougher time. It was at this point that the Queen offered him an Earldom which would allow him (as the Earl of Beaconsfield) to sit in the quieter pastures of the House of Lords for the remainder of his political career. His years in office from 1876–80 were much harder for Disraeli than the first two:

By-elections Elections that take place when a sitting MP dies or, in the earlier part of the nineteenth century, is promoted to government office. By the 1870s, results of by-elections were seen less to reflect local conditions and more as an indicator of national mood, as is frequently the case today.

- His health was not good.
- Foreign difficulties (see Chapter 9) predominated.
- Gladstone was back with a vengeance, attacking *Beaconsfieldism*. His Midlothian Campaign (see pages 152 and 183), won the Liberals considerable popularity.
- The Government lost a number of **by-elections.**
- Liberal Party organisation rapidly improved, and the government's foreign policy was unpopular in a number of quarters.
- The earlier achievements in social reform were in the past and there was little in the way of domestic achievement.

Dissolution of Parliament Under the Septennial Act of 1716 a General Election had to be held at least every seven years. Technically the monarch dissolved parliament, but in the nineteenth century this decision was normally made by the prime minister. However, he had to make a formal request to do so to the Queen.

The Defeat

When a Liberal Parliamentary seat was won by the Conservatives in a by-election at Southwark (London) early in 1880, Disraeli mistakenly assumed the tide had turned, and asked the Queen for a **Dissolution of Parliament**. However the election in April proved a triumph for the Liberals who returned with a majority of 115 over the Conservatives. Irish Home Rulers again did well with 63 seats. (See Chapter 4 for more on the 1880 election and the reasons for Liberal victory). Although the Queen tried to avoid having Gladstone as her

Prime Minister by sending for Lord Hartington it was known that he would refuse the offer and she would eventually have to ask Gladstone. The latter had made a comeback from his defeat in 1874. Disraeli knew the same would not happen to him. At the age of 77 and suffering from kidney disease, he sensed he had not long left. Of his defeat, Disraeli remarked to the nineteen-year old son of his Foreign Secretary Lord Salisbury *'for you this is an event, for me it is the end'*. A year later, Disraeli died of bronchitis and asthma on 19 April 1881.

CONCLUSION

What had Disraeli's government achieved? It:

- formed the first strong Conservative administration since 1841;
- attracted increasing numbers of middle class voters into the Conservative camp;
- had shown administrative competence or better – Cross was one of the outstanding home secretaries of the century;
- had achieved a great deal of reform and clarity in social reform and its regulations;
- had been active abroad and developed the imperial idea;
- eased the monarchy back into public life;
- continued the Conservative Party's identification with the Church of England and the landed interest.

Why did Disraeli lose the 1880 election despite these successes?

- Disraeli failed to deal with the question of Ireland and Conservative support in that country (outside Ulster) declined as 8 of their 31 seats were lost, with the Home Rule Party making large gains. Moreover, in Scotland and Wales there was a similar collapse with the Conservatives only winning nine out of 90 seats. Even in the English counties where Conservatives were traditionally strong, 27 seats were lost to the Liberals.
- After the surge of social reform in 1875/6 Disraeli's government had run out of steam on domestic reform. There was little now proposed in this area to attract the working class. Not many of those enfranchised by Disraeli in 1867 were actually voting Conservative despite his hopes that they would.

- Disraeli's health was increasingly frail. He was constantly short of breath. This meant he was totally unable to tour the country as Gladstone did. Now that party leaders were of great importance in elections, the contrast with a rampant Gladstone and an exhausted Disraeli in 1874 is striking.
- Though popular after the acquisition of Cyprus in 1878, Disraeli was running into difficulties with his foreign policy in Afghanistan and South Africa (see pages 150–2). The forward foreign policy of the Conservatives now seemed risky and less popular, allowing Gladstone to exploit this brilliantly in his Midlothian campaign (see page 153).
- Gladstone bitterly criticised 'Beaconsfieldism'. This linked economic problems with expense in foreign policy. Gladstone attacked treating overseas peoples as what one historian has called 'pawns of his showy Imperialism' (Roy Jenkins *Gladstone*). Moreover, Gladstone asserted, Disraeli had not been careful with the public purse and had helped to exacerbate the economic difficulties.
- The Church of England and the landowning classes remained the bulwark of the Conservatives: but the Church was undergoing a period of uncertainty and division, especially over 'Ritualism and Romanism' (see page 126).
- The landowning classes were severely weakened by the depression in the late 1870s. Disraeli's rejection of the re-imposition of Protection in 1879 lost him active political support from this area that had been so vital in previous elections.

QUESTIONS TO CONSIDER

1. What were the main achievements of Disraeli's ministry in the field of social reform?
2. What contribution did Disraeli make to the recovery of the monarchy's reputation?

PERIOD STUDY EXAM-STYLE QUESTIONS

1. Access the reasons why Disraeli and the Conservatives were successful in the 1874 general election but were defeated in the one in 1880.
2. Assess the impact of the social reforms introduced by Disraeli's government of 1874–1880.

CHAPTER 9

What were the main principles of British foreign policy 1846–95?

INTRODUCTION

During this time Britain's overseas interests became increasingly wide-ranging and the commitments of the British Empire played a major part in foreign policy. However, this would hardly have been apparent at the start of the period.

Before the 1840s, British colonial control was to be found principally in parts of India, Canada (recently united under British Rule), the southern tip of Africa, the West Indies and, for the deportation of convicts, parts of Australia. By 1895, however, a substantial amount of territory was being added in the Indian sub-continent and Burma, Africa (north, south, east and west), Australia and New Zealand, as well as plans for trading posts on the Chinese coast, such as Hong Kong.

In the 1840s there were two border problems: one with Russia over India and the other with the United States over Canada. In 1895, with the Russian Empire growing, the Indian tensions were just as great, but relations with the US had improved. In 1846 the overseas territories were referred to as 'colonies' but by 1895 they were increasingly seen as part of the **British Empire.**

Sea Power and Trade: the Congress of Vienna

In both 1846 and 1895 British sea power was of the first importance, the British Army often playing what was regarded as a secondary role to the British Navy. Throughout the period a number of vital British naval bases were established around the world to maintain British interests, and frequently also to trade. In fact Britain's maritime reputation in Europe had been a strong one since the sixteenth century. More recently, the naval defeats of Napoleon in the first decade of the nineteenth century in battles such as Trafalgar had emphasised British strength on the world's oceans.

Great Britain had established a reputation as a commercial, trading and maritime nation and the extent of its interests and possessions were evident in 1815 at the **Congress of Vienna** when British ownership of islands and naval bases around the world was confirmed. These included the Cape of Good Hope, Heligoland, Malta, Ceylon, The Ionian Islands, Mauritius and the West Indian Islands such as Trinidad and Tobago and St. Lucia as well as the Demerara area of South America (British Guyana).

KEY EVENTS

Congress of Vienna, 1815
A large meeting of European powers to re-draw the map of Europe (and sometimes beyond) because of the downfall of the Napoleonic Empire.

WHAT WERE THE MAIN AIMS OF BRITISH FOREIGN POLICY?

The aims of British foreign policy were closely linked to the protection of Britain's overseas territories. Aims included:

- Maintaining the British naval supremacy which was so apparent at Vienna. The numerous if scattered territories were useful naval staging posts that provided harbour facilities and vital supplies.

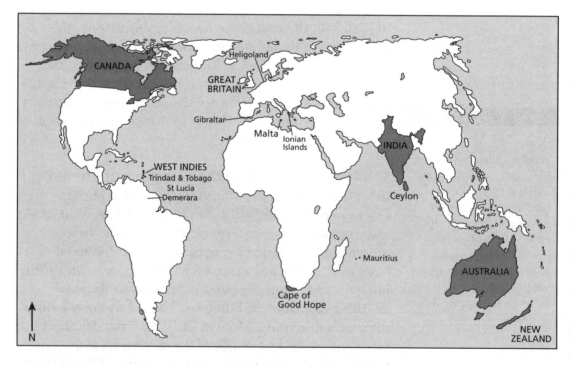

British-held territories in the mid-nineteenth century: reflecting the country's trading interests.

Important sources of raw material for Britain	
West Indies	Sugar, bananas
North Atlantic	Fish
India and the Far East	Cotton, silks, spices and tea
Europe	Wines, naval stores and timber
Australia/ New Zealand	Wool

KEY TERMS

Eastern Question The question of what should be done about the declining Turkish Empire since friendly relations with it were so vital to British trading interests. Should it be propped up? Reformed? Abandoned? How should Russian aggression against it be treated?

Opium Trade Opium was widely used as narcotic drug in the nineteenth century and there were rooms in Britain and elsewhere known as opium dens. British traders were widely involved in its trade in the Far East.

KEY CONCEPTS

Expanding Russian Empire In the 1860s and early 1870s Russia's main external interest was expansion into Asia after their reverses in the Crimean War. They steadily moved their borders south and east reaching the boundaries of Afghanistan, Persia (Iran) and China. The British saw this as a major threat to their interests in India.

- To use the strength of this naval tradition to keep an eye on and protect British trading interests in different parts of the world.
- Attending to British possessions in India and the Colonies where large numbers of British people were settling, especially Canada, Australia, New Zealand and South Africa.

This meant that there were areas around the world of significance to foreign policy and with regard to Empire.

- The Ottoman (Turkish) Empire at the eastern end of the Mediterranean, where it was regarded as vital to preserve the overland trade route to India. This led to the greatest difficulties in this period, such as the Crimean War of the 1850s and the **Eastern Question** of the 1870s.
- The Far East, where relations with China hinged around trade – **the opium trade.**
- The borders with India: Afghanistan was seen as a particularly sensitive area since the **expanding Russian Empire** was seen as potentially dangerous.

EUROPEAN DIPLOMACY

Its international interests were so far-flung that in this period Britain tended to avoid too much involvement with continental Europe. Relations were most difficult with France and Russia:

- With France because of its past history of European expansion and domination which had disrupted British trade through Europe.
- With Russia because of its intermittent interest in expanding south and east towards British trading interests in India and the Turkish Empire.

British involvement in war and European entanglements, however, was generally regarded as best avoided. To maintain both the wider British interest and the general peace in this period was on the whole agreed to be a priority, but there were different schools of thought as to how to approach the various problems, which emphasised different principles. There were three broad and overlapping traditions.

1 **The Concert of Europe** was steadily pursued by Castlereagh (Foreign Secretary 1812–22) and Peel in former times and Aberdeen as Foreign Secretary in the early 1840s and also 1852–5 when, because of the Crimean War, he was singularly unsuccessful. Gladstone's foreign policy at least up until the 1880s was heavily influenced by this view. Britain would take a detached interest in European affairs and hope that the major powers of Europe, of which she was seen as one, would co-operate on important matters of stability and security. There would be an attempt to secure the **balance of power**, and ensure that no one country became too powerful in Europe, as Napoleonic France had done before 1815.

Any danger of this kind of domination would necessitate British intervention, but otherwise the country could stay out of direct action in European affairs. It was the fear that the Russians were upsetting the balance of power that caused the conflict in the Crimea (see page 137–8).

2 The second belief was **to keep out of European affairs as much as possible** and pursue policies relating to British trade and possessions, avoiding wars at all costs. This was the smallest group, led by Cobden and Bright who might be described as international Radicals (the Manchester school) who shared other Radicals' distaste for absolutist governments, but went along with non-intervention as a general rule. They believed that international harmony and peace would grow as countries became more and more dependent on each other in trading terms. They strongly opposed the Crimean War for instance and were generally critical of Palmerston's foreign policy and the more aggressive approach of some of their fellow Radicals such as Roebuck. This view faded considerably in the 1870s and 1880s.

3 **Support for Constitutional states or constitutional movements in states.** This became apparent in the Revolutions of 1848 which tended to have

nationalistic and/or politically liberal demands. In Italy, in 1859, there was British support for liberal nationalism against absolute monarchies trying to suppress unification, though others felt that support for continued Austrian control of parts of northern Italy would be the best means by which to maintain the balance of power.

Palmerston was seen as sympathetic to such movements, much to the delight of the British Radicals who had previously wished to see Britain play a more prominent role on the Continent in support of such developments. However, these sympathies were not shared by many others in the Foreign Office and even Palmerston's sympathies can be exaggerated. They were most in evidence in his period as Foreign Secretary between 1846 and 1851.

Foreign Secretaries 1846–95

Although the office actually changed hands nineteen times there were only nine people who occupied the post in almost fifty years. Except for Palmerston whose Irish peerage did not entitle him to sit in the Lords, all were members of the Upper House.

Palmerston	1846–51		
Granville	1851–2	1870–4	1880–5
Malmesbury	1852 Feb/Dec	1858–9	
Russell	1852–3	1859–65	
Clarendon	1853–8	1865–6	1868–70
Derby (15th Earl)	1866–8	1874–8	
Salisbury	1878–80	1885–6	1887–92
Rosebery	1886 Feb/Aug	1892–4	
Kimberley	1894–5		

FOREIGN POLICY 1846–65

This period was dominated by Lord Palmerston. He was Foreign Secretary from 1846-51: Prime Minister from 1855–8 and 1859–65 when although **Clarendon** and

Russell respectively were his Foreign Secretaries in those periods, Palmerston was clearly very influential indeed in helping to formulate and follow through on foreign policy.

The Palmerston approach saw Britain playing a part, if possible, in upholding constitutional states, but regarded the prime factor in foreign policy as upholding British trading interests abroad. This policy, inherited from Canning (Foreign Secretary 1822–7), was a forceful one. Palmerston had the advantage that some of the Radicals in parliament supported his policy and particularly liked his sideswipes at absolutist states such as his approach to **General Haynau and Louis Kossuth** in the aftermath of the 1848 revolutions in Europe.

Palmerston's forceful attitude towards maintaining the interests of British citizens abroad is seen in its most extreme form in the case of **Don Pacifico**. Palmerston's support for him was much criticised since both Don Pacifico's very slight British connection and very dubious complaint against the Greeks were not considered weighty enough to warrant action. Unusually, both Gladstone and Disraeli were in agreement in opposing what they considered to be the high-handed actions of Palmerston on this occasion. Many other leading political figures were also critical but Palmerston with a four and a half hour speech defending his conduct was triumphant in the vote in the House of Commons

As far as Europe was concerned one of the most significant links was with France. This was a delicate relationship, marked as it was by what one historian has called '*past conflicts, present mistrusts and future fears*'. This was apparent in 1846, the early 1860s, and over Africa in the 1890s. It could be argued that Britain in general and Palmerston in particular considerably exaggerated the French 'threat'.

Palmerston wished to prevent any kind of expansion of French influence.

* In Spain, there had been a marriage linking the French and Spanish royal families in 1846. However, the fear

Haynau and Kossuth The Austrian General Haynau, nicknamed Hyena, had been notoriously violent in suppressing rebels in Italy and Hungary in 1848–9. When he visited England in September 1850, protestors, outraged at reports of his ordering the flogging of women, attacked him at a brewery in Southwark. Palmerston annoyed Queen Victoria by sending only a very mild apology for his treatment in England. In contrast, Palmerston made it clear, when the Hungarian nationalist Kossuth came to England, that he reserved the right (which he never actually exercised) to invite him to his own home despite clear royal disapproval of the visit.

Don Pacifico In 1850 Palmerston ordered a blockade of the Greek navy when a Portuguese moneylender Don Pacifico having been born in the British territory of Gibraltar, claimed the help of Britain over a financial dispute with the Greek government.

Belgian independence and neutrality When Belgium staged a revolt against the Netherlands and gained its independence in 1830, powers such as Russia and Austria considered invading to crush what was seen as a dangerous liberal and nationalist revolt. However, Palmerston, newly appointed as Foreign Secretary, made clear his support of the Belgians. A friendly Belgium would be a great boost for the easy and safe movement of British goods. After a belated attempt by the Netherlands to regain the territory in 1839, Britain formally guaranteed Belgium's independence and neutrality. It was the German invasion of France through Belgium in 1914, rather than French aggression, which brought about a British response to defend Belgium and the widening of the conflict that became the First World War.

of extended French influence was greatly reduced by the downfall of the French monarchy in the revolutions of 1848.

- Belgium and the Netherlands were sensitive areas because of the vast quantity of British exports that went through these two countries. There had been earlier French attempts to increase French influence in this area and Palmerston was anxious to maintain the independence of these two countries. However, this was achieved throughout the period from 1839 to 1914 without great difficulty. The guarantee of **Belgian independence and neutrality** prevented trouble here. When war did break out in 1914 Britain and France found themselves on the same side. They shared a hostility to Russian influence in the Near East for instance, fearing interference with their trading interests. The British also saw Russia as a major threat to their interests in India.

The Crimean War 1854–6

The best example of Anglo-French co-operation as a result of their mutual suspicion of Russia was the Crimean War. Significantly, it occurred at the one time that Palmerston was in government but not at the Foreign Office. This was the only time in the nineteenth century when the Eastern Question spilled over into a major conflict involving Britain. Britain and France fought against Russia's move into Turkish territory.

- The immediate cause of the Crimean War was the dispute over the guardianship of the Christian holy places in Turkish-held Jerusalem: should it consist of French Catholic monks or Russian Orthodox monks?
- But the more long-term cause was a misunderstanding that had occurred when Foreign Secretary Lord Aberdeen had met Tsar Nicholas I of Russia in 1844. Nicholas received the mistaken impression that Britain would accept a partition of the Turkish Empire at some point in the future.
- When Aberdeen became Prime Minister in December 1852 (and Palmerston was no longer Foreign Secretary but Home Secretary), the Tsar thought he saw his chance.
- When Russia made aggressive noises against Turkey in 1853, the Aberdeen government was seen as uncertain in

its opposition, but Nicholas miscalculated by thinking it would never declare war.

- Though it was not the main focus of Britain's strategic interests, most of the war was fought on the Crimean peninsula: this was at the southernmost tip of Russia where only the Black Sea separated it from Turkey. The winter conditions were appalling and the medical facilities for the injured crude in the extreme.
- After the army generals' strategy was viewed as outdated and wasteful of lives, the Aberdeen government was removed by a vote in Parliament in the middle of the war in 1855 and there was a call for reform of the army and the British civil service (see Chapter 6).
- With Palmerston now Prime Minister a peace treaty was signed at the Congress held in Paris. The Treaty of Paris forbade Russia to put its warships or any kind of fortifications in the Black Sea area. Russia abided by this, the most important clause in the peace treaty, until 1870 (see page 143).
- Palmerston was satisfied with the treaty and that Russian expansion had been halted.

Palmerston at the helm again 1855–8 and 1859–65

The hesitant policy of Aberdeen had apparently led to war. It also led to Palmerston becoming Prime Minister and therefore exercising a great influence on foreign policy. His more aggressive style was once again popular. The championing of the cause of liberal and constitutional states continued with support of the moves towards Italian unity in 1859–60. These, however, proved not to be very great, amounting in the end to a friendly neutrality towards the crucial actions of nationalists such as Garibaldi (see page 63) in defeating the opponents of unity. Its main significance for British politics was that it united the Liberal Party (see Chapter 5): for once, Gladstone and Palmerston were on the same side.

China

Palmerston also upheld British trading interests abroad, as in China in 1856 and 1859–60. Following his defeat in the House of Commons over the Arrow incident in 1856 (see page 49) Palmerston had called a general election in 1857 and had been triumphantly returned to power. Armed with a majority he was prepared to order the use of arms, and in 1858 strategic Chinese forts were attacked. The Chinese agreed to a diplomatic mission and to the continuance of foreign trading interests. The opium trade was allowed to continue. The attack was undertaken purely to guarantee British trading interests in the area. Once Palmerston was friendly again with the Chinese Emperor after 1860 he was more than happy to back the Emperor's brutal suppression of a rebellion even though surrendering rebels had been promised their lives.

Conservative policy was similar on this issue. When in office in 1858–9 the Conservatives dropped their previous criticisms of Palmerston's policy, and Derby's government was the one that drew up the terms of the treaty legalising the opium trade. Significantly, Gladstone expressed his reservations about the policy in 1860 but agreed to go along with it.

The Indian Mutiny 1857

Further afield, Palmerston faced his greatest challenge in India where he had to deal with the crisis of the Indian Mutiny.

The general causes of tension in India were:

- Indian resentment at attempts to modify or abolish customs such as suttee – the burning of widows after the death of their husbands;
- the expansionist policies of the British government and the use of Indian troops for this purpose;
- Indian Governor-General Lord Dalhousie's policy of annexing more Indian states when their rulers died, such as Oudh in 1856;
- the discontent of the Indian troops in the British army with their pay and conditions.

The immediate cause of the mutiny was the issue of cartridges for the new rifles used by the troops. The cartridges were smeared with animal fat and had to be bitten open before insertion into the firearm. Both Hindus, to whom cows are sacred, and Muslims, who will not eat pork, objected to having to do this.

The fighting was mainly in north India and there was great brutality on both sides. After English women and children were massacred at Cawnpore the British troops made vicious reprisals. The new Governor-General, Charles Canning, calmed the situation, and though criticised for being too lenient with the rebels (English soldiers called him 'Clemency Canning') he was backed by Palmerston.

In 1858 the Conservatives under Derby reformed the government of India.

- The dual control with the East India Company was abolished: the government would take full authority for the government of India.
- There would be a new ministerial post – the Secretary of State for India.
- Control of India remained effective for another generation or more but a nationalist movement was soon to begin.

Palmerston in difficulties

In the early 1860s Palmerston's aggressive style of policy, which had been so effective in earlier years, began to run into trouble. Poor relations with France in the 1860s were mainly due to Palmerston's great suspicion of the Emperor Napoleon III whom he saw as dangerously aggressive in the Italian crisis in 1859, and when interfering in Syrian affairs in 1860 (in the area of the Turkish Empire). Palmerston obsessively and oddly came to believe that Napoleon III was intent on '*avenging Waterloo*'. Having approved of the coup which brought Napoleon III to power in 1851, Palmerston appears to have felt that a French invasion of Britain was a real possibility in the early 1860s. Thus he organised a volunteer defence movement which recruited 150,000 men, and had new **Martello towers** erected on the south coast of England to watch for signs of French attack. Yet there was no evidence that the French seriously contemplated invasion. The Free Trade Treaty signed in 1860 between the two countries made conflict still more unlikely.

There was an uneasy relationship with the northern states of America in the Civil War. A clash with a northern warship (the Trent) on the high seas at the start of the war was

KEY TERMS

Martello towers These were large round towers originally built for defensive purposes at the time of the first Napoleon.

only smoothed over by the intervention of a dying Prince Albert, and the fact that another ship, the Alabama (see page 144), was allowed to leave an English port in 1862 and attack northern states' ships, proved embarrassing. So did Gladstone's indiscreet remarks about the Civil War in October 1862. In a speech in Newcastle he argued that, although there might be a debate about the rights and wrongs of slavery, the South had 'made a nation'. This not only got the military situation wrong: it gave a misleading impression of the British government's attitude to the issue. Might it intervene to help the South? Palmerston was forced to disown the remarks of his Chancellor.

Palmerston was increasingly unable to influence major world events. In 1863 protests from Palmerston and Russell to Russia about the harsh treatment of rebels in Poland, where there was a nationalist revolt, fell on deaf ears. Moreover, the growing power of Bismarck's Prussia in central Europe meant that Palmerston found his bluff was being called. In the Prussian dispute with Denmark over the ownership of **Schleswig and Holstein** in 1864, Palmerston's promise that if Denmark fought it would not fight alone was seen as a sham, as the Prussians easily overran the Danish forces.

GLADSTONE AND DISRAELI: CHANGES IN FOREIGN POLICY

Significant changes were occurring which would influence the new directions of British foreign policy. Palmerston's death in October 1865, the excitement of the passing of the second Reform Act in 1886/7 and the domestic activities of Gladstone's first ministry, all led to a change in the attitude of both Liberals and Conservatives to foreign policy. Just as the party system had emerged more clearly by 1868 so the different foreign policy approaches of the two parties would become much more apparent. Whereas Gladstone would inherit the tradition of Peel and Aberdeen, Disraeli would pursue more Palmerstonian policies.

Gladstone managed to unite the Liberals over foreign affairs. He combined a belief in the Concert of Europe and the balance of power with a concern for morality in

KEY PLACES

Schleswig and Holstein
Two provinces sandwiched between Denmark and German states. Schleswig was largely Danish in composition and Holstein partly so. The two states had been connected to Denmark in political arrangements of staggering complexity. Palmerston claimed in 1864 that only three people had ever fully understood it: Prince Albert who was dead, a German professor who had become insane, and he himself, who had forgotten the details.

policy and the desirability of an advance in international understanding. This would include a righteous campaign against injustice, most clearly shown in his protest against what he referred to as the *'Bulgarian horrors'* in 1876 (see page 146).

By contrast, Disraeli, the Conservative, adopted the approach of the Whig, Palmerston. The previous Tory approach to foreign policy was of the more cautious Peel/Aberdeen style, but after the death of Palmerston in 1865 (and Derby in 1869) Disraeli saw an opportunity to adopt what he saw as potentially popular foreign-policy principles.

KEY TERMS

A 'forward' foreign policy One which pursued British interests abroad in a vigorous manner, was prepared to intervene in disputes abroad, and sought to extend or at least maintain the colonial possessions of the country.

These principles would be combined in what was seen as a '**forward**' **foreign policy,** which, like Palmerston's, would be popular with many backbench MPs. In addition, however, it could well be popular with the wider electorate Disraeli had himself created with the second Reform Act in 1867. The emphasis, however, had changed from Palmerston's supposed sympathy with '*small nations struggling to be free*' to a concern with the British colonies, or Empire as it was now becoming. This was first apparent in the Manchester and Crystal Palace speeches of 1872 (see Chapter 1). However, Disraeli knew as well as Palmerston or any other diplomat the limitations on an ambitious foreign policy: while Britain's navy was one of the strongest in the world, the permanent army was not large and was ill-equipped for a prolonged continental campaign.

The reasons for changes in foreign policy were not confined to national developments. The political maps of Europe, Africa and the Near East were changing rapidly.

GLADSTONE'S FOREIGN POLICY 1868–74

In what ways did Gladstone face a different Europe?

KEY ISSUES

Gladstone's foreign policy is important for **Key Issue 2** (see page iv).

- The expansion of Prussia in 1864 and 1866 into Denmark and Austria led to a clash with France in 1870 and the final birth of the German state in 1871. The unification of Germany in 1871 after the

Franco-Prussian War brought a powerful European country onto the diplomatic scene and also revealed French military weaknesses.

- The final stage in the unification of Italy in 1870 (when the Pope lost his remaining political power in Rome) meant there was another new major independent country in Europe and a potential ally for Britain.
- There was the more aggressive outlook of a stronger and reformed Russia. The Tsar took the opportunity afforded by the absorption of the major powers in the Franco-Prussian War of 1870–1 to denounce the Black Sea neutralisation clauses of the Treaty of Paris (see page 138) and Russia announced it intended to construct a Black Sea fleet.

Neutrality in the Franco-Prussian War

Neutrality was the only realistic policy in the Franco-Prussian War of 1870, given the geographical circumstances, the divided state of British public opinion, Gladstone's distrust of both Prussian Prime Minister Bismarck and the French Emperor Napoleon III, and the agreement by the Prussians to respect the neutrality of Belgium in the conflict. Yet Gladstone was not as completely non-interventionist as some of his colleagues. His belief in the Concert of Europe became apparent when he tried (unsuccessfully) to persuade his cabinet to oppose Prussia's taking of the French provinces of Alsace and Lorraine at the end of the short war. Gladstone had proposed a stand of neutral countries in Europe against annexation.

Russia and the Black Sea neutralisation

He did manage to convene a conference in London on a related issue in 1871. The Russian denunciation of the Black Sea neutralisation clauses was the kind of unilateral announcement (an announcement without reference to others) that Gladstone disliked. The conference did not reverse the Russian move, but the principle that in future such actions should be subject to international ratification was accepted. Gladstone felt he had made clear the principle but in reality the Russians had got what they wanted.

The *Alabama* incident

Nowhere is Gladstone's internationalist approach better shown than in his acceptance of the Alabama arbitration award which made possible a better future relationship with the United States. After the end of the war the Americans claimed compensation from the British government for the damage done by the *Alabama*. This was at first refused but Gladstone, when prime minister, agreed to an independent international tribunal to assess the claim. He then agreed to pay the figure decided upon: £3.25 million, a third of the figure claimed by the Americans. This arbitration, although it increased Gladstone's unpopularity, was a landmark in the development of international relations.

Disraeli's reaction to Gladstone's foreign policy

Disraeli's opportunism was again given a chance to come to the fore. He sensed the change of atmosphere early in 1872. Victories for the Conservatives in by-elections in middle-class urban seats amidst criticisms of Gladstone's 'concessions' to the Americans over the Alabama arbitration, combined with a renewal in the popularity of the monarchy after the Prince of Wales' recovery from illness, encouraged Disraeli to make his dramatic set piece **speeches at Manchester** and the Crystal Palace (see page 112) which foretold the new direction in foreign policy – an imperial one. Disraeli sensed that it was not merely British economic strength but also public opinion that meant the time was right for a more active foreign policy.

FOREIGN POLICY 1874–86

Disraeli and the Conservatives

Conservative foreign policy, dominated at first by Disraeli, was seen as the more forward-looking and active with a strong emphasis on the traditional principles of maintaining British naval strength and trading interests. But time and circumstances had amended and added to these principles, and after 1880 Gladstone also found himself sucked into a more expansionist policy. In particular, the Eastern Question between 1875 and 1878 produced as much excitement and controversy in Britain over foreign affairs as the Crimean War and more than any other event between 1815 and 1899.

KEY TERMS

The *Alabama* The ship *Alabama* had been built in Liverpool in 1862 and, despite British neutrality in the American Civil War, had been allowed to leave port and sail to the United States where it inflicted major damage on northern shipping. It may be that Gladstone felt personally guilty about the affair because he was in the government that had carelessly allowed the ship to sail out of a British port in the first place.

KEY EVENTS

Disraeli at Manchester 1872 Disraeli related economic strength at home to new opportunities abroad: *'I express here my confident conviction that there never was a moment in our history when the power of England was so great and her resources so inexhaustible. And yet, gentlemen, it is not merely our fleets and armies, our powerful artillery, our accumulated capital and our unlimited credit on which I so much depend as upon that unbroken spirit of her people, which I believe was never prouder of the imperial country to which they belong.'*

KEY ISSUES

Disraeli's foreign and imperial policies of 1879–80 are important for **Key Issue 5** (see page iv).

The Suez Canal shares

The construction of the Suez Canal (opened in 1869) was likely to make the control of the eastern end of the Mediterranean even more significant for Britain. The canal linked the Mediterranean to the Red Sea and thus the Indian Ocean.

Disraeli's dramatic purchase of the Canal Company shares in 1875 (and its popular public reception) seemed to bear out what he had been saying in his earlier speeches. This was a personal triumph for Disraeli since Palmerston had previously been wary of involvement in the canal's construction, seeing it as a French plot to disturb British trade and threaten India. Both Foreign Secretary Lord Derby, son of the former prime minister, and Chancellor Northcote also had their doubts about the policy. Disraeli acted quickly and decisively, arranging at speed the £4 million needed to buy the shares from the bankrupt Khedive (ruler) of Egypt who was desperate to sell his shares. The Prime Minister used his connections to get the money advanced by his old banking friend Lionel de Rothschild: clearly, the idea of the British government effectively being the security for the loan satisfied Rothschild!

The incident brings out particularly clearly the difference between Gladstone and Disraeli at this stage. Gladstone criticised the deal as getting Britain potentially too involved in overseas affairs which might give rise to complications later. In contrast, Disraeli boasted to the Queen of a great triumph. Both had a point.

THE EASTERN CRISIS 1875–8

Background

The most worrying feature of foreign policy for Disraeli was an expanding Russia which Britain wished to hold in check while trying to prop up the increasingly sick Turkish Empire. In the 1860s and early 1870s Russia's main external interest was expansion into Asia after their reverses in the Crimean War. To the new British imperial mind, this threatened India. By the 1870s Russia had emerged as a reformed state (not least having abolished serfdom) and once again looked hungrily towards Turkey. The growth of nationalism in late nineteenth-century Europe had affected the **Slav** areas of eastern Europe which were prepared to back increased Russian influence in the area.

KEY TERMS

Slavs People spread over much of Eastern Europe, including Russians, Bulgarians and Poles.

The Bulgarian atrocities 1876

The feared complications over Russian ambitions and Balkan nationalism presented themselves in 1875 with a nationalist revolt by the Bosnian Serbs against Turkish rule. The Russians, anxious to support Slav nationalism, tried to persuade the Turks to agree to reforms and more self-government for the Serbs. However, the revolt spread to Christian Bulgaria in 1876 with more devastating consequences. Short of troops and money with which to put down the revolt, the Turks allowed the irregular troops of the Bashi-Bazouks to suppress the uprising. This they did with great brutality.

The effect at home: Gladstone and Disraeli clash

This brought foreign policy to the centre stage in a more profound way than Palmerston's antics in the late 1850s, and brought Gladstone out of what now proved to be a temporary retirement to condemn Turkish atrocities. With Disraeli intent on defending the Turks and playing down the news of the massacres of the Christians as *'coffee house babble'*, and Gladstone demanding the Turks leave with *'bag and baggage'* the area they had *'desecrated and profaned'*, the scene was set for a confrontation over foreign policy where the parties were opposed to each other on principle.

Disraeli wanted to maintain the traditional support of Turkey as being in the British interest in general and trading profits in particular. He was suspicious of Russian ambitions and power. Gladstone maintained a concern for moral behaviour in international affairs. Intervention should not be undertaken lightly but the extreme brutality the Turks had been guilty of in Bosnia and Bulgaria should be heavily criticised.

The effect at home: Gladstone's pamphlet

In protest against the Turkish actions, Gladstone produced his pamphlet *The Bulgarian Horrors and the Question of the East* early in September 1876. To Gladstone this was not a question of becoming involved with affairs that

The Eastern Question in the 1870s.

Proposed boundaries of Treaty of San Stefano, 1878

THESSALY (to Greece 1881)

What were the main principles of British foreign policy 1846–95?　　147

were none of Britain's business. Ever since the Crimean War, Gladstone felt Britain was responsible for the fate of Christians in this area. Moreover, the powers of Europe had failed to guarantee their protection in the way that the 1856 Treaty of Paris that had concluded the war had intended. The pamphlet had a dramatic effect. It sold 40,000 copies in the first few days and 400,000 by the end of the month. It struck a chord in the British public, shocked at the revelations of massacres on a scale which the nineteenth century was not used to. Gladstone's move was not without opportunism. He hardly commented on the affair for two months: it was only when protest meetings began in August 1876 that he felt something of a crusade could be launched. He then divided public opinion on the question down the middle.

The public debate

- Much, though not all, of the press backed Disraeli, who also had support from the powerful forces of the monarchy and the majority of high society and city finance.
- But both nonconformist clergymen and Anglican (especially High Anglican) sympathisers with the **Orthodox Bulgarians**, were prominent in their support for Gladstone. He also had much of the academic world on his side, especially the new breed of university historians.

The dislike that Gladstone and Disraeli felt for one another now turned to loathing. Disraeli accused Gladstone of using the agitation to further his own political ends and suggested privately he was '*an unprincipled maniac*', and publicly '*of all Bulgarian horrors the greatest*'. This tasteless remark must have upset Gladstone, although his reaction to insults from Disraeli was publicly muted. His respect for Disraeli at this time was so low that he correspondingly despised any criticisms his opponent might make of him. '*There was nothing,*' said Gladstone, '*serious or sincere in any of his utterances, however vehement*'. Extreme supporters of the Turks even accused Gladstone of being a Russian agent.

Disraeli, who regretted the '*coffee house babble*' remark when the full extent of the unspeakable atrocities became known, had been momentarily wrong-footed. However, the Russian reaction to the atrocities (a military attack on Turkey) gave him a chance to recover. Russia invaded Turkey in 1877 and the excitement in England reached fever pitch. The Treaty of San Stefano early in 1878 created a large Bulgarian state which would be seen as under heavy Russian influence if not control. Now the whole existence of the Turkish Empire seemed threatened. Even Gladstone had only suggested that the Turks leave Bosnia. Gladstone, against all advice, moved Resolutions in the House of Commons arguing that Turkey had forfeited all right to support from the British government. But they were comfortably defeated: the tide of excitement had turned.

Jingoism

Public opinion now began to swing back to the idea that Britain should attempt to stop the Russians. Many supported Disraeli's decision to move a British fleet into the eastern Mediterranean in January 1878, although Derby, his Foreign Secretary, was not among them and subsequently resigned to be replaced by Salisbury. A popular music hall song went:

> *We don't want to fight but by Jingo if we do,*
> *We've got the men, we've got the ships, we've got the money too.*

This first example of jingoism (or aggressive nationalism) seemed to confirm Disraeli's feelings about the way public opinion among both middle and working-class Englishmen (and it was mainly English and mainly men) was going. In February and March 1878 jingoism reached its peak. The windows of Gladstone's house in London were broken by stones thrown by a mob, and on another occasion he and his wife had to be protected from assault by four mounted policemen. His second pamphlet, *Lessons in Massacre*, published in March 1878, sold only 7,000 copies, 393,000 less than his previous one.

The Congress of Berlin

With British hostility towards Russia growing, the German Chancellor Bismarck called an international Congress in Berlin in 1878 where the San Stefano Treaty was revised. Here Britain was backed by Austria who felt the Russians had overreached themselves.

- 'Big Bulgaria' was carved up and Russian influence reduced.
- Britain, represented by Disraeli and Foreign Secretary Salisbury, obtained the island of Cyprus near the eastern end of the Mediterranean.

Disraeli described this as *'peace with honour'* and it emphasised the more imperial mood of the later 1870s. Despite the Congress seeming to be an example of the Concert of Europe in action, Gladstone remained critical: he described gaining Cyprus as *'an act of duplicity not surpassed and rarely equalled in the history of nations'*.

Further complications for British foreign policy

Although the Eastern Question was now at least temporarily settled, other important new factors were coming into play at a time when Britain avoided formal alliances with any other countries:

- The expansion of the great powers into the interior of the African continent widened and complicated the activities of the British government's foreign policy and its diplomatic activity. It added to the possibility of clashes with other European powers.
- The discovery of valuable mineral deposits in areas such as South Africa committed the British presence to this area just at the time when it was becoming less significant strategically.
- The 'white empire', for example Canada, Australia, New Zealand and South Africa, was seen to be moving towards self-government and independence: Canada became self-governing in 1867 and Australia and South Africa at the turn of the century.
- The men on the spot could sometimes push for a more forward policy themselves, not necessarily with the approval of the government back home.

These latter developments in particular were to lead to difficulties for Disraeli in the last 18 months of his ministry, particularly in Afghanistan and South Africa.

Afghanistan

Afghanistan was regarded as a buffer-state against Russian designs upon India.

- In 1878 Lord Lytton, the Viceroy of India, complained to the Amir (ruler) of Afghanistan that a Russian mission (diplomatic group) had been accepted in his country and a British one refused.
- Ignoring orders of caution from London he ordered British troops from India to march on Kabul, the Afghan capital.
- The move was successful at first: the Amir fled, Britain effectively controlled his son and the Russians remained inactive.
- However, in September 1879, civil war broke out, British officials were murdered and there was serious instability in the country.

While Lytton had certainly exceeded instructions, Disraeli's own 'forward' policy must take its share of responsibility for

The crucial position of Afghanistan around 1880.

what occurred. Disraeli had appointed Lytton in 1875 and told him to persuade the Amir to accept a British mission in return for money and assistance against foreign aggression. It is hardly surprising that he refused this obvious attempt to control him, becoming wary when Lytton pressed the terms on him a second and third time.

Gladstone was able to exploit the confusion to the full when he tramped the Scottish roads on the Midlothian campaign (see page 183). He pointed out that '*the sanctity of life in the hill villages of Afghanistan … is as inviolable [untouchable] in the eyes of Almighty God as can be your own,* a simple but powerful statement that transcended the underlying racial assumptions of the time.

The Zulus and the Boers

There was a similar problem with another 'man on the spot'. Sir Bartle Frere, another Disraeli appointment, was made Governor-General of Cape Colony in South Africa in 1877. He behaved in a manner similar to Lytton's when he sent an ultimatum to a ruler he had no right to treat in such a way. This was the Zulu chief Cetawayo, who was commanded to disband his army in December 1878. Although Frere was backed by the new Colonial Secretary, Hicks Beach, Disraeli and his new Foreign Secretary Salisbury (who disapproved of Frere) failed to act decisively: by the beginning of 1879 the British had a Zulu war on their hands.

The first news was of a disaster. Before the end of January, a British force of over 1,000 men had been wiped out at Isandhlwana. Although there was a British victory in July at Ulundi there had by that time been much criticism of the government and what Gladstone termed '**Beaconsfieldism**'. Gladstone again expressed his anger at the treatment of the Zulus; thousands had been slaughtered for no reason other than '*their attempt to defend against your artillery with their naked bodies, their hearths and homes, their wives and families … to call this policy Conservative is in my opinion pure mockery, and abuse of terms. Whatever it may be in its motive … it is in its essence, thoroughly subversive*'.

Gladstone and the Midlothian campaigns

Foreign affairs were proving the undoing of the Conservatives. The Liberal election success in 1880 was partly owing to Gladstone's successful attack on Disraeli's policies. In late November/early December 1879 he undertook the Midlothian campaigns. This was a dramatic tour of the Scottish constituency of Midlothian, a Conservative seat. Gladstone had decided he would contest it at the next election and made a series of brilliant speeches in Edinburgh and other Midlothian towns such as Dalkeith and West Calder. He ruthlessly attacked the economic policies as well as the foreign policies of Disraeli's government. But it was the assault on foreign policy which gained most attention.

When the election loomed the following spring Gladstone undertook a second brilliant campaign in March 1880 and was elected for his adopted constituency. His speeches had produced huge cheering crowds of many thousands (did those at the back hear?). Personality had become both an important part of the political process and a factor in aiding the decision of the electorate.

KEY ISSUES

Gladstone's foreign policy in this period is important for **Key Issue 6** (see page iv).

HOW FAR DID GLADSTONE'S FOREIGN POLICY CHANGE ITS NATURE 1880–6?

Given Gladstone's strong views on Disraeli's behaviour one might have expected a different emphasis in foreign policy in the Liberal Government after 1880. In fact, the forward march of British foreign policy and the degree of their commitment to a complex international policy became apparent in Gladstone's second ministry in the early 1880s.

Afghanistan

Gladstone inherited a tense situation in this area. After the troubles at the end of Disraeli's ministry, Afghanistan reverted to being a buffer state, but tensions were never far from the surface. In 1885 a Russian force attacked and defeated an Afghan one in the disputed border town of Penjdeh. Gladstone and Foreign Secretary Granville threatened retaliation, but negotiated a settlement whereby the Russians acquired Penjdeh but not the important Zufilkar pass which would take them into the heart of the country.

South Africa

If Afghanistan hinted at the difficulties Gladstone might have in extracting himself from Disraeli's imperial commitments, South African affairs brought this home on a grand scale. Gladstone's first government had not been inactive in South Africa: it had annexed the diamond region of the Orange Free State back in 1871. In opposition, as we have seen, he had severely criticised Disraeli's policies in the area. But:

- Frere was not recalled immediately as many expected when the Liberals came to power in 1880. Gladstone's regard for national self-determination apparently did not extend to the Boers (Dutch farming settlers) in the Transvaal.
- A year after Ulundi, with the Zulu threat removed, the Boers declared a republic in the Transvaal, breaking away from British control.
- Gladstone sent a force to resist this move but the force was defeated by the Boers at Majuba Hill in February 1881.
- Now, Gladstone accepted the independence of the Transvaal in reality although still retaining the right to British 'suzerainty', a vague word that suggested ultimate control was still in British hands.
- A Convention in London in 1884 modified the terms but failed to repeat the word 'suzerainty', leading to complications later on that ultimately culminated in the Boer War of 1899–1902.

Gladstone had not handled the situation well. He had, in a historian's words *'conceded to force what he had refused to reason'.*

Egypt

The difficulties Gladstone inherited from Disraeli were not confined to the problems in South Africa and Afghanistan. In fact, Gladstone's greatest problems could be said to have come from one of Disraeli's apparent successes: the acquisition of the Suez Canal shares. For from this, a gradual British-French control over the area of Egypt became apparent. Britain was drawn more and more into Egyptian affairs, exercising an informal control over the country in order to maintain an interest in the now vital

Suez Canal area. This produced a crisis over principle in 1882. Gladstone authorised the bombing of Alexandria and John Bright resigned from the Cabinet. The alliance of the Radical 'Manchester School' of Cobden (no longer alive) and Bright and the now more aggressive Gladstone was over. In practice, Gladstone had adopted a policy at least as interventionist as Disraeli, if not more so.

Gladstone's concern for the Concert of Europe, however, had not disappeared. Britain attended a Conference in Berlin (see below) at the end of 1884 to establish the ground rules for what effectively became the partition of Africa among the major powers, even though Gladstone himself felt that involvement with Egypt and the Boers was quite enough.

As far as Egypt was concerned, however, Britain was not to annex it in a straightforward manner into the British Empire. After long negotiations, a Board of Control was established in March 1885. Although all the major European powers were represented, the presence of the British army and the shrewd command exercised by the British Consul-General Sir Evelyn Baring meant that Britain was effectively in control. This also brought responsibility in times of crisis as with the nationalist revolt in the Sudan, south of Egypt, in 1885. Gladstonian non-intervention had disappeared. Decisive action abroad was increasingly seen as essential to maintain British interests: hesitation shown by the government and resulting in the **death of General Gordon** was much criticised. Gladstone's policy in Egypt had only been cheered while it was successful. Now the GOM – Grand Old Man, had become the MOG – murderer of Gordon.

FOREIGN POLICY AFTER 1886

Salisbury's approach to foreign policy

After 1886 foreign policy was increasingly dominated by Salisbury's Conservatives. The Prime Minister avoided formal alliances in a period when they were common, but this did not mean that Britain was friendless. Salisbury's pact with Italy and Austria in 1887 to defend the status quo in the Mediterranean was a secret one and not formally known about (though suspected in some quarters for a number of years). Salisbury always refused attempts in the late 1880s by Germany's Chancellor Bismarck to draw him into the Triple Alliance of Germany, Austria and Italy. He believed that Britain's lack of definite alliances and commitments was to the country's advantage.

Before 1886 Britain already had formal possessions:

- In the far south of Africa from the first half of the century – Cape Colony and Natal.
- The Ashanti tribes in West Africa which had been attacked in Gladstone's first ministry in 1873: influence in the Nigerian/Ghanaian area had been consolidated.
- Informal influence in Egypt in the far north by the early 1880s.

Growing British influence in Africa

The Berlin Conference of 1884/5, attended by fifteen countries, decided on spheres of influence in Africa for the different European powers. The 'Scramble for Africa' now came to play a central role in political affairs in the ten years between the Berlin conference of 1884/5 and the formal acquisition of Uganda in 1895. The great powers carved up the continent with only Liberia, Libya and Abyssinia remaining independent of colonial rule or domination. A series of further agreements between the major European powers ensured that the carve up of much of African territory was done relatively peacefully, in the sense there was no European war over it. However, the experience was not without violence for the native Africans.

1 Nigeria was formally acquired by Britain in 1886.

2 Britain also held a colonial conference over territory in West Africa with France in 1887.

3 There was a colonial agreement over East Africa with Germany in 1890: Britain was granted the area of Uganda, Kenya and Zanzibar. Uganda was formally annexed to Britain in 1894.

4 Britain, France and Portugal signed more agreements in 1891 to sort out boundary disputes.

Queen Victoria's Golden Jubilee 1887 Held to celebrate the Queen's occupancy of the throne for fifty years, the lavish public celebrations had a military and imperialistic flavour, with all corners of the British Empire represented. A Colonial Conference was held to coincide with the Jubilee.

5 Nyasaland and Northern Rhodesia were formally obtained in1891/2.

Apart from the case of Uganda (see pages 194 and 200), all of these changes were supervised by Salisbury who was his own Foreign Secretary from the start of 1887. The old principle of preferring influence to outright control seems to have been abandoned and the new Imperial atmosphere was well captured by the **Golden Jubilee of Queen Victoria** in 1887.

By 1895 Britain's foreign policy had been transformed and the Empire was assuming an importance unknown before. Significantly, the former Liberal turned Conservative Unionist, Joseph Chamberlain, chose the post of Colonial Secretary in Salisbury's government in 1895. By this time, he saw it as one of major importance.

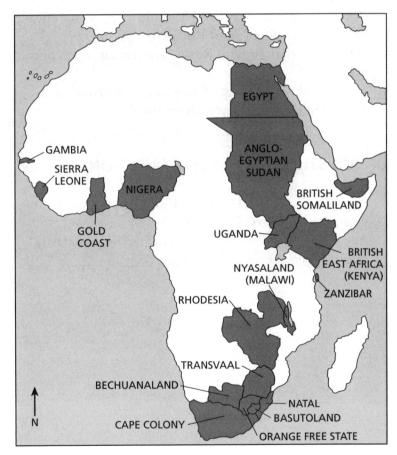

Britain's African Empire at the end of the nineteenth century.

CONCLUSION

- Up to 1895 there was a period of optimism about Empire.
- Relations with Germany were better than relations with France in this period.
- Britain's economic power, spread throughout much of the world, was now being challenged by rapidly industrialising countries like the US and Germany.
- Britain generally avoided formal European alliances.
- Nationalist objections to British control of their territory would loom increasingly large.

QUESTIONS TO CONSIDER

1. What were the main principles of British foreign in the period dominated by Lord Palmerston?
2. Why was the time between 1865 and 1873 so significant for the future direction of British foreign policy?
3. Why were relations with Russia so tense for much of this period?
4. How was there a change of emphasis from colonies to Empire in the late nineteenth century?

PERIOD STUDY EXAM-STYLE QUESTIONS

1. Assess how successful Gladstone's foreign policy was in his second ministry, 1880–85.
2. Assess the relative success of Gladstone's and Disraeli's foreign policy between 1874 and 1885.

CHAPTER 10

What was the importance of the Irish question in the development of Liberalism and Conservatism?

KEY ISSUES

Gladstone and Ireland are important for both **Key Issue 2** and **Key Issue 6** (see page iv).

KEY TERMS

Upas Tree A tree that grows in Java. Its branches were rumoured to spread poison for miles around. Gladstone believed the poisonous branches of Irish life needed to be lopped off.

GLADSTONE'S APPROACH TO THE IRISH QUESTION

At the start of December 1868 Gladstone was chopping down a tree on the Hawarden estate (a favourite pastime) when news came of the Queen's invitation to form a government. After commenting on the significance of this event he continued chopping until the tree was down. Then he stated: '*My mission is to pacify Ireland.*' The tree-felling was not totally incidental. Dealing with the Irish Question, Gladstone believed, was like chopping down a **upas tree**. Three branches needed to be cut: the Church establishment, the land tenure system and educational weaknesses.

- Although Gladstone was aware that governing Ireland was very difficult as early as the 1840s, he did not pay full attention to the issues raised there until he was about to become prime minister in 1868.
- He then saw it as his '*mission*' to deal with 'the Irish Question' in his first ministry of 1868–74.
- After some real achievements early in that ministry, Gladstone found it an increasingly difficult and demanding problem to deal with. It ultimately weakened his government.
- In his second ministry Gladstone was forced into a harsher policy towards Ireland, while still attempting a considerable degree of reform.
- Gladstone's conversion to Home Rule in the mid 1880s brought radical changes to the British political scene, splitting the Liberal Party.
- Gladstone, however, persisted with his attempts to obtain Home Rule for Ireland into advanced old age, but was unsuccessful.

What were Gladstone's views on Ireland before 1868?

As with other issues in his political life, it was difficult to foresee Gladstone's later views and actions from his early voting record on Ireland. In April 1835 as an earnest young Tory in a junior government post, Gladstone unsuccessfully attempted to resist the opposition's successful proposal which brought down Peel's brief Tory government. It was to use Irish Church revenues for non-religious purposes such as education. However, Gladstone's views changed as he became older.

One of his rare references to Ireland in his years in Peel's government in the early 1840s was in a letter to his wife in 1845, just before the Great Famine: '*Ireland, Ireland, that cloud in the west, that coming storm ... Ireland forces upon us ... great social and ... religious questions. God grant that we may have the courage to look them in the face*' (quoted in Magnus, *Gladstone*, 1954, page 75).

Although a fascinating forecast of future problems, these thoughts were not acted upon for over 20 years. Yet the seeds of change were clearly in Gladstone's mind: he was in the process of abandoning his former rigidly held views about the relationship of Church and state. This was shown in his complicated speech accepting the justice of the Maynooth Grant in the same year (1845) (see Chapter 3). From here, Gladstone's views on the Irish Church gradually became more liberal.

But for the moment, economic matters dominated Gladstone's mind. When he was Chancellor in the Aberdeen coalition ministry in 1852–5 he extended the income tax to Ireland in his first budget of 1853. This could be seen as an insensitive measure in a country only just recovering from its catastrophic famine. It is a good example of Gladstone's theoretical analysis of a situation running ahead of a commonsense approach to the question in hand – this happened to him quite often!

Why did Ireland become a more dominant issue for Gladstone in the later 1860s?

By the 1860s the Irish Question had emerged as a more significant factor in British politics than at any time since the famine of 1845–6. This coincided with Gladstone's own developing views. By this time his liberalism in economic matters, which he developed early on, had extended more clearly to other fields. Despite the fact that he was Chancellor of the Exchequer in Palmerston's government he was becoming bolder about making comments that related to his own opinions rather than those of the government he was in.

An example of this was the 'pale of the Constitution' speech in 1864 (see page 62), and another was his support for a private member's bill advocating the disestablishment of the Irish Church in 1865. When defeated for the Oxford University seat in the 1865 general election, he transferred his allegiance to South Lancashire. This, coupled with Palmerston's death soon after the election, seemed to set the stage for a disestablishment measure. Gladstone announced, significantly, to his new constituents: *At last, my friends, I have come amongst you. And **I am come … unmuzzled***.

Once the dust had settled on the 1867 Reform Act, there were good political reasons as well as ones of principle for Gladstone to concentrate on Irish Church disestablishment.

- It would reunite the Liberal Party, wrenched apart by the reform issue, and, in a notoriously fractious (argumentative) party, only six Liberals were to vote against it (see Chapter 5).
- It would also address the increasing challenge from the Irish Nationalist Fenians (see Chapter 5). The extension of their activities to the English mainland was succeeding in drawing their grievances to the attention of a wider English public.

In particular there was the bold plan of Fenian John McCafferty to attack Chester Castle in February 1867, release Irish Nationalist prisoners and seize 2,000 rifles which would immediately have been sent to Ireland. Although it failed, an action of this kind so close to **Gladstone's home at Hawarden**, just over the Welsh border, could hardly have failed to make an impression on him. It reinforced Gladstone's determination to make the Irish question his number one priority when he came to power.

KEY CONCEPTS

Gladstone comes to his new constituents 'unmuzzled' When MP for Oxford University, Gladstone was elected by Oxford University graduates. He was expected to express views in line with those who had voted for him. The majority of these graduates strongly supported the Conservatives in general and in particular wanted to maintain the privileges of the Anglican Church in the whole of Great Britain, including Ireland. Once he was able to represent a more ordinary constituency with a much wider social range of voters Gladstone felt freer to express his increasingly liberal opinions: he no longer felt constricted or 'muzzled' by those he was supposed to represent.

KEY PLACES

Gladstone's home at Hawarden The Gladstone family home in Flintshire, North Wales was not far from the English border and Chester. The property was originally in the possession of the Glynne family. Gladstone had married Catherine Glynne in 1839.

What was the importance of the Irish question?

HOW EFFECTIVE WAS GLADSTONE'S IRISH LEGISLATION IN HIS FIRST MINISTRY?

Gladstone tackled three main areas of Irish policy after 1868. He began successfully with the Church, had mixed fortunes with the land and failed completely with education.

Why was Irish Church disestablishment such a successful measure in 1869?

Gladstone took a good deal of personal interest in Irish legislation in his first ministry. He insisted on completely stripping the Irish Church of all its assets, a point which delayed the appointment of the best Liberal lawyer for the position of Lord Chancellor, Roundell Palmer. Palmer obtained this government post later in October 1872 as Lord Selborne, but back in 1869 he could not accept the disendowment principle (see page 89). Gladstone drew up the Bill himself over Christmas and New Year 1868–9 and then introduced it with a three and a quarter hour speech. A wide variety of people, from Disraeli through to Gladstone's biographer and friend John Morley, thought this speech one of his finest and (despite the length) least long-winded. Gladstone also did a good deal of personal negotiating with awkward Whig peers. It was clearly a personal triumph.

The Act was undoubtedly a success, yet none of Gladstone's subsequent pieces of Irish legislation was as well received in Ireland or as effective in its application. Gladstone faced three major difficulties when trying to introduce subsequent Irish legislation.

- There was the danger of splitting the Liberals. Many of them, such as Robert Lowe, put great emphasis on freedom of property rights and might well resist too radical a change to Irish land arrangements.
- The likely resistance of the House of Lords where property was equally highly regarded and where (unlike the House of Commons) the Conservatives remained in the majority.
- The fact that English public opinion was not very well disposed to further Irish reforms. This was to become increasingly apparent the more Gladstone tried to tackle Irish problems.

How successful was the Irish Land Act?

The Irish Land Act of 1870 demonstrated these difficulties, though it also demonstrated Gladstone's continuing commitment to the Irish question and his mastery of intricate detail. He set himself the task of studying the complications of Irish landownership. The qualities he had previously brought to the mastery of financial complexities were now equally well applied to this extremely tricky issue. His knowledge was entirely theoretical. He had never visited Ireland and was to do so only once, in 1877. However, his success in getting any sort of bill through at all was notable. Between 1835 and 1851 **Tenant Right Bills** had been regularly introduced by the Irish MP Sharman Crawford but were always defeated. The small Tenant Right Party had continued the task in the 1850s, but again with no success. The sticking point had always been that any bill in this area would be seen to be interfering with property rights. As Lord Salisbury put it, the poverty of the Irish tenants did not justify stealing from the landlord. Lord Palmerston took the same line: he once remarked, '*tenant right is landlord wrong*'.

KEY TERMS

Tenant Right Bills Bills put before Parliament to remove absolute rights of property and grant tenants (those who famed the land and paid a rent for the privilege) right of occupation provided they paid that rent.

Gladstone, however, made it clear that he was determined to press on with reform. He clearly appreciated the depth of feeling that the Irish had on the land question, arguing that feelings sustained for so long must have some validity. But difficulties developed. The Liberal Party was less united on this issue than it had been over Church disestablishment. The *Daily News* predicted that Gladstone's Chancellor Robert Lowe was as capable of splitting the party over land as he had been over the Reform Bill in 1866. His eventual agreement stresses the nature of Gladstone's achievement. John Bright inserted clauses in the Act which would enable tenants to purchase land. In the long run this was to be very significant though at this stage not many were able to take advantage of the possibility. The House of Lords found the sections of the Bill that concerned modifications of property rights less than acceptable and insisted on amendments (see pages 90–92).

Why did the Irish Universities Bill fail?

When it came to the third major Irish issue Gladstone wished to tackle, education, it was the House of Commons which Gladstone failed to convince when he introduced the Irish Universities Bill in 1873. Quite a number of Liberal MPs opposed his policy. It indicated both the difficulty of dealing with this very sensitive area and also that the Liberal Party's unity was breaking up.

- Radical members of the party such as Henry Fawcett disliked the restrictive clauses in the Bill.
- Other Liberals were disappointed that Gladstone had not moved on from Ireland to deal with English disestablishment.
- Nonconformists were not inclined to support another controversial educational measure, having been disappointed with the compromises of the England and Wales Education Act of 1870 (see Chapter 6, pages 92–94). Educational concessions to the Catholic Irish did not appeal.
- But neither were the Catholic bishops satisfied with the restrictive clauses in the Bill (see page 92).

HOW DID HOME RULE IDEAS DEVELOP IN THE 1870s?

Developments in Gladstone's ministry 1868–74

Gladstone's Irish reforms in his first ministry, though considerable, did not go far enough for many Irish Liberal MPs to support him to the full. Increasing numbers wanted an opportunity for the Irish to be in charge of their own internal affairs.

- The Home Government Association, set up in 1870, was a group led by Protestant lawyer Isaac Butt (a man of Tory background who had defended accused Fenians) and this organisation was moving towards the idea of self-government with *'full control over our domestic affairs'* – otherwise known as Home Rule for Ireland.
- In passing the Secret Ballot Act of 1872 and reducing Irish landlord electoral influence, Gladstone had made the creation of an Irish Nationalist Party more likely. Voters were much freer to express their true opinions and now found a suitable party grouping to represent them in the English parliament.

**Sir Michael Hicks Beach
1837–1916** Prominent
Conservative politician of
landed background. Became
an MP in 1864. Was Irish
Secretary 1874–8 and 1886–7
when bad eyesight forced
him to resign from the post.
Highly regarded by Salisbury
as an excellent speaker and
debater and retained in the
cabinet without holding office.
Chancellor of the Exchequer
1885–6 and 1895–1902.
Regarded as a moderate on
Irish questions but a lively
character who, it was said,
even *thought* angrily.

Agrarian outrages Attacks
on landlords' property in
the Irish countryside by
Land League supporters or
other nationalist groups or
individuals. Coercion Acts
were partly designed to enable
those suspected of such
outrages to be arrested and
imprisoned without trial.

**Charles Steward Parnell
1845–91** Irish landowner of
Protestant background from
County Wicklow. Became an
MP in 1875 and leader of the
Home Rule Party in 1877.
Controlled 61 nationalist MPs
and obstructed legislation
on Ireland. Continued to
campaign after the failure of
Home Rule Bill. Politically
ruined after being cited as
co-respondent in a divorce
case in 1889–90.

- In November 1873 Butt replaced his Home Government Association with the Home Rule League. As a result, in the 1874 election the Liberal vote in Ireland collapsed, so that the party's strength declined from 65 seats (out of a total of 105 Irish seats) to twelve, with the new Home Rule group winning 59. Although many of these 59 were still prepared to support Gladstone and the Liberals for the moment, it was to be a significant development for the future.
- The most significant factor, however, in the growth of the Home Rule idea was the change in the economic position in Ireland at the close of the 1870s.

Developments in Disraeli's ministry 1874–80

Under **Hicks Beach,** Disraeli's Irish Secretary until 1878, the land question had remained relatively quiet and **agrarian outrages** had remained at a fairly low level. However, Disraeli's government did not develop the kind of detailed policy to tackle Irish questions that Gladstone had persuaded the Liberals was necessary. Moreover, the agricultural depression that, coincidentally, hit Ireland just after Hicks Beach's departure in February 1878 was a serious one. It showed up the inadequacies of the Land Act. For at this point there was a return to wholesale poverty among the Irish tenantry: many of them failed to pay their rents and the number of evictions rose rapidly. Between 1879 and 1883 more tenants were evicted than in the previous 30 years.

These developments were met with a nationalist response. The Land League of Michael Davitt and the militant political leadership of the Home Rule Party under Butt's replacement, **Charles Stewart Parnell**, created a serious situation by the time Gladstone was prime minister again. In the 1880 election Parnell's Irish nationalists had 65 seats and soon made an impact in the House of Commons.

WHY DID GLADSTONE RUN INTO GREATER DIFFICULTIES OVER IRELAND IN HIS SECOND MINISTRY?

When Gladstone was elected for a second time in 1880 he was more concerned with the Eastern Question and the supposed weaknesses of '*Beaconsfieldism*' (see Chapter 11). He had not anticipated Ireland being at the forefront of events but so it proved: Gladstone had hoped that his measures in his first ministry would have greatly eased Irish difficulties but now they were returning, and returning with a vengeance.

How did Gladstone try to deal with the new Irish challenges 1880–1?

Compensation for Disturbance Bill 1880. In his very first piece of Irish legislation on his return to office, Gladstone immediately ran into problems with the House of Lords. His attempt to introduce a measure of compensation for Irish tenants evicted for non-payment of rent in the troubled times of the previous two years was rejected in the Upper House by 282 votes to 51. The Lords saw the measure as an attack on property rights, regarding it as encouraging future non-payment and also aiding those who had supported the **agrarian outrages** and violence of the Land League in the **New Departure** of Davitt.

Coercion and reform: the second Irish Land Act 1881. In taking legal action against Parnell but also planning constructive, reforming legislation, Gladstone's policy was a carrot and stick one. But on the first occasion the stick broke: his attempt at the end of 1880 to prosecute Parnell and other leaders of the nationalist agitation for encouraging non-payment of rent ended in a jury disagreement. With outrages continuing on a large scale, Gladstone's Irish Chief Secretary W.E. Forster introduced a Coercion Act in January 1881. This met such fierce resistance from Parnell's nationalist MPs that the debate on it lasted over 40 continuous hours. Gladstone had had to be persuaded of the necessity for this coercion and wished, as before, to couple it with a more constructive measure. He now felt that a more radical Land Act was required if

Charles Stewart Parnell, leader of the Irish Nationalist Party.

Ireland was to be pacified. This would provide for what became known as the 'three Fs':

- **Fixity of tenure**: this meant that tenants could apply to a special commission for judicial arbitration (judgment) of their rent, the amount being fixed for the next fifteen years.
- **Fair rents**: The second, making it hard to evict except for non-payment of rent, would now be more effective than in the 1870 Act, because the landlord could no longer simply raise the rent and then evict.
- **Free sale**: ensured a fair price for the improvements made, not just in Ulster as in the 1870 Act but all over Ireland.

As in 1870 there was a small section of the Bill to encourage the purchase of land by Irish tenants. Resistance from the Lords was again possible but the senior Irish Conservative Sir Edward Gibson advised against rejection. As one recent historian, Andrew Roberts, has put it, *'the Irish landlords preferred to receive reduced rents than none at all'*. If the bill passed, they hoped the Land League would call off the mass refusal to pay rent. So Gibson's view prevailed.

How effectively did Gladstone deal with the challenge of Parnell in 1881/2?

Parnell's language was still confrontational and aggressive, perhaps to prevent his more extreme supporters from taking the law into their own hands. He planned to test the new Act in the courts and, if it proved unsatisfactory, he threatened further disturbances. Yet Gladstone's concession had been a substantial one and given a little more time might well have taken the sting out of the land campaign. But in October 1881 Parnell's language was so extreme and full of incitement to violence that the government decided to arrest him under the Coercion Laws and imprison him in Kilmainham (Dublin) Jail where he could neither control, nor be blamed for, subsequent outrages. This was clearly a tactical error on Gladstone's part.

- He was making a martyr of Parnell.
- The agrarian violence became worse as the figure of **'Captain Moonlight'** stalked the Irish countryside wreaking havoc.

KEY PEOPLE

Captain Moonlight A mythical name given to an imaginary leader of those Irish protestors who attacked landlord property at night.

Therefore, it was soon regarded as necessary to release Parnell via the unofficial Kilmainham Treaty negotiated by Joseph Chamberlain. In return for Parnell attempting to control the violence of the agitators, an Arrears Act would be passed later (1883) to wipe out previous tenant rent debts.

More difficulties for Gladstone's Irish policy

Gladstone's policies do seem to have persuaded Parnell and the Irish nationalists that their protests could be peaceful and legal rather than violent. In 1882 the land campaign was suspended and this threatened to divide the nationalist movement, as the more extreme members wished to continue their protests.

Problems continued: the tragic **murder** in **Phoenix Park** on 6 May 1882 of Lord Frederick Cavendish, Gladstone's nephew and the new Chief Secretary for Ireland, brought great personal sorrow for Gladstone, but it also brought political difficulty as more coercion was now felt to be necessary because of the unrest following the assassination and the need to catch the murderers. This brought the nationalists back together again in protest against the new measures.

What Gladstone was doing was still trying to 'pacify Ireland' as he had remarked back in 1868. But Ireland's mood was becoming one where this policy was becoming more difficult. Gladstone had reacted to Irish protests by attempting reform on a number of occasions – Ireland was taking up more and more of his political time. What was becoming clearer was that Parnell and the nationalists saw the new laws, however helpful, as treating the symptoms and not the cause of the Irish troubles. They saw the root of the problem as the English landlord system. Only self-government would solve it, and Parnell would campaign until this was achieved. Moreover, Gladstone was beginning to agree with this analysis and moved to favouring Home Rule.

Phoenix Park Murders
Lord Frederick Cavendish, and his Under-Secretary T.H. Burke, were both murdered in Phoenix Park soon after taking up their posts. It was the work of an extremist nationalist group, the 'Invincibles', but clearly made relations between the British government and mainstream Irish nationalists more difficult. Phoenix Park was a large park in Dublin next to where the Irish Viceroy (government official representing the Queen) had his offices. It is said that if the Viceroy, Lord Spencer, had been looking the other way he would have seen the murderers. Thus their very audacity made a major impact on the whole Irish Question.

WHAT WAS THE IMPACT OF THE IDEA OF HOME RULE ON LIBERALISM AND CONSERVATISM?

When did Gladstone become convinced of the need for Home Rule?

- Gladstone had apparently ruled out the possibility of Home Rule at a speech in Aberdeen in 1871.
- However, there is evidence that his conversion to Home Rule in 1885 was not a sudden one.
- The events of 1881–2 seemed to have convinced him that the Irish spirit possessed a genuine need for self-government.
- Despite the fact that Ireland quietened down in 1883 and 1884, Gladstone felt that he had still not '*pacified them*', and that further measures would be required.

Gladstone never used the word 'nationalism' – or hardly any word with 'ism' as Colin Matthew who has studied and edited all Gladstone's diaries pointed out after a careful verbal study of the kind of language the Liberal leader used. But Gladstone did accept the validity of the concept of nationalism to a far greater extent than did Disraeli. This partly helps to explain his greater sympathy with Balkan nationalism in the 1870s. Moreover, Gladstone lived through a time when Liberalism and nationalism often went hand in hand and when strong nationalism was yet to acquire the more sinister and fascist overtones with which it became linked in the following century.

Gladstone wanted Ireland treated as any other part of the United Kingdom; this accounts for his insistence that the vote extension in the third parliamentary Reform Bill of 1884 must be applied to Ireland in exactly the same way as in England. And this was even though he knew it would enfranchise many potential supporters of Parnell's Irish Home Rule Party. In contrast, to avoid further obstruction by Irish members, he did not attempt to redistribute seats in Ireland. But this also benefited the Irish MPs as they were now over-represented in Parliament. Gladstone had come to the conclusion that the nationalists were now the only legitimate source of authority in Ireland: their demands had to be seriously considered.

What were the attitudes of Liberals and Conservatives as a whole to the idea of Home Rule?

Many Liberal MPs were very doubtful about the wisdom of Home Rule but Gladstone appears to have become finally convinced of the need for it after the fall of his Liberal government in June 1885, defeated on an unconnected matter. At this stage Gladstone felt that passing a Home Rule Bill would be best left to the Conservatives if possible. The Liberals would not oppose it and thus the issue could be kept out of party politics.

The Conservative approach to the question of Home Rule was more complex than one might have imagined. There seemed a real (if brief and perhaps mistaken) possibility that a Conservative administration under Salisbury might consider the idea of Home Rule. The new Irish **Viceroy** Lord Carnarvon had secret conversations with Parnell. Since Gladstone was not committing himself publicly to Home Rule at this stage, Parnell instructed supporters of Home Rule to vote Conservative at the election (if there was no Irish Home Rule candidate) Salisbury called in November 1885. This may have lost Gladstone and the Liberals some 20 or more seats. This tactic turned out to be crucial. The Liberal majority of 86 over the Conservatives was exactly matched by the number of Irish nationalist MPs. Parnell now held the balance of power.

KEY TERMS

Viceroy The most senior British government official in Ireland, representing the monarch.

In coming out publicly to support Home Rule did Gladstone act for political motives? The Liberal Party was not in good shape. The stresses and strains of its various coalitions of interests had led to disagreements and splits as had happened at the end of Gladstone's previous government in 1873–4. This had also happened before such as in:

- 1855 over the Crimean War;
- 1858 over the Conspiracy to Murder Bill;
- 1867 over Parliamentary Reform.

Perhaps one great cause such as Home Rule could reunite the Liberals again. Yet Gladstone would surely have anticipated that a controversial bill for Home Rule could have serious consequences for the unity of the Party, making their divisions worse rather than better. Moreover, there was the problem of the approval of the House of Lords. It might be felt more likely that it would reluctantly accept Home Rule if a Conservative leader such as Salisbury himself were to insist on its necessity. Gladstone did not want Home Rule to become a political football but was keen that it should pass by whatever means.

The Hawarden Kite and Liberal opposition to Home Rule

In the middle of December 1885 it became public knowledge that Gladstone had been converted to the need for Home Rule. His youngest son Herbert, a strong believer in Home Rule himself, made indiscreet remarks to the press and the 'secret' conversion was out. This incident became known as the Hawarden Kite. Had Gladstone from his country home in Flintshire deliberately 'flown a kite' to discover whether he could get the Liberals back into power and regain Irish nationalist support? If so, it worked, but only in the short term.

- Salisbury resigned when defeated by a Liberal-inspired vote at the end of January 1886 and Gladstone formed his third ministry.
- Liberal cracks, however, appeared immediately. Joseph Chamberlain had no sooner been appointed to Gladstone's new cabinet in early February than he resigned in March when the terms of the proposed Home Rule Bill became known.
- Gladstone's Home Rule Bill split the Liberal Party and 93 Liberal 'Unionists' voted against the measure, ensuring its defeat by 343 votes to 313. It had failed even to get through the House of Commons.
- Another election had to be called, in effect a **plebiscite** on Home Rule.

This election brought the clearest evidence yet of one of Gladstone's difficulties: public opinion was not sympathetic to Irish reform. The Conservatives won 316 seats, the Liberals 190, the **Liberal Unionists** 79 and the Irish nationalists 85. Salisbury's Conservatives could now form a Government, relying on the support of the Liberal Unionists.

How did the opposition of Ulster Unionists to Home Rule help the Conservatives?

One advantage for the Conservatives was that they could now consistently rely on the support of the Ulster Unionists in an alliance that continued in an amended form up to the 1960s. **The political significance of Ulster** appeared relatively suddenly in 1885–6, since Home Rule was not really regarded as practical politics until Gladstone took up the cause. The people of eastern Ulster had never succumbed to the charms of their fellow Protestant Parnell: their opposition, once roused, was vigorous, with Colonel Edward Saunderson at the head of it. In 1885 he had invited Lord Randolph Churchill (see page 202) to Belfast. Churchill (ever the political opportunist) saw potential support for the Conservatives from Ulster. This was because of:

- religious suspicions of Roman Catholic rule in an area where Protestants were easily more numerous;
- political concerns regarding safety and security;
- economic reservations regarding the backwardness of much of the rest of Ireland.

These factors had produced a profound opposition to the latest Home Rule proposals. Not for nothing did Churchill comment on the question of Protestant Ulster's opposition to Home Rule: '*Ulster will fight and Ulster will be right.*' The fighting occurred with serious rioting in 1886 in Belfast. The early signs of extreme opposition were apparent in discussions about taking a solemn oath and the possibility of military resistance. Not selling the Ulster Protestants short provided one of the main justifications for Conservative opposition to the whole concept of Home Rule.

(see page 202)

KEY TERMS

The political significance of Ulster In around 1800 many Ulster Protestants had been prepared to ally with Roman Catholics in a nationalist movement. But by the 1880s the Protestant majority in the eastern (industrial) part of Ulster had developed more uniformly anti-Catholic views. As late as Easter 1885, however, Ulster Protestants had not believed that Gladstone really would introduce Home Rule.

CONSERVATIVE APPROACHES TO IRELAND AND HOME RULE AFTER 1886

What was Salisbury's attitude towards Ireland?

Churchill was not alone: the Conservative leader Salisbury argued the same in less militant language. '*We cannot desert the loyal people of Ulster*' he argued, and he was concerned

Presbyterians In England, Presbyterians were members of a Protestant nonconformist denomination but in Scotland the established Church was Presbyterian. Presbyters or elders, lay people not ordained, run the Church rather than the clergy. Against the idea of clerical power, e.g. bishops, many Presbyterians were staunchly anti-Roman Catholic. The predominant Protestant denomination in Ulster was Presbyterian.

Hottentots A race from southern Africa, presumably seen by Salisbury as a backward people. His remark caused considerable offence in Ireland.

Guillotine Originally a device used in the French Revolution for beheading by a sudden downward movement of a sharp blade. In parliamentary terms it was when the Speaker (Chair) of the House of Commons used his authority to bring a debate to a sudden end.

about the effects on the rest of the Empire such as India – for Salisbury regarded Ireland as part of the Empire in the same way. Salisbury was careful to keep Ulster Unionists on his side as the 1890s went on, with a privy councillorship for Colonel Saunderson and, later, a post in government for the rising star and future leader of the Ulster Unionists, Edward Carson. Salisbury could also rely on some Scottish votes from Glasgow Protestants, for instance, who sympathised with their fellow **Presbyterians** in Ulster. A quarter of successful candidates in Scottish seats in the 1892 election were Liberal Unionists.

Salisbury, like many other leading political figures of the century, never showed much sympathy for the Irish or much sign that he understood the full nature of their demands. He certainly felt them to be incapable of self-government and caused a stir in 1886 when he referred to their demand for Home Rule as being about as sensible as giving it to **Hottentots.**

He had the advantage of using the parliamentary devices (such as the **guillotine**) developed in Gladstone's second ministry in the early 1880s to bring debates to a rapid halt. When selecting Arthur Balfour for the position of Irish Secretary in 1887 (see below), Salisbury made clear the change of direction. The day before the appointment, Salisbury made a speech in which he argued that as regards Ireland '*too much softness has crept into our proposals*' and that Ireland '*could not be governed by platitudes and rosewater*'.

Salisbury's opposition to Home Rule never faded. Later on, at the time of Gladstone's second bill in 1893, his country home, Hatfield House, was used as the venue for a large demonstration against the legislation, with over 1,500 Ulster people present. Salisbury then made two anti-Home Rule speeches in Ireland, in Belfast and Londonderry. He argued that it would be untrue to the Empire to allow the Bill through and to the '*duty which has descended to you from a splendid ancestry*'. He asserted that the Liberal majority in the Commons was less than the number of nationalist MPs (38) associated with agrarian outrages. He continued to regard Home Rule as a delusion. In private he was even critical of some of the reforms his own administration introduced!

What was the importance of the Irish question?   173

Arthur Balfour as Irish secretary: how different was his policy from the Liberals?

The Conservatives, far from disunited about Ireland, not only had the reassurance of Liberal Unionist support: they also possessed the advantage of a public which did not in the main favour major concessions to Ireland, as the election in 1886 had indicated. Salisbury, with not uncommon pessimism, seemed to view the Irish Question as virtually insoluble. When further economic depression caused more agrarian disturbances in the winter of 1886–87, the Irish Secretary Hicks Beach was inclined to **conciliation** as well as imposing coercion. But on his retirement in 1887 **Arthur Balfour**, Salisbury's nephew, was appointed in his place. Relatively young, and anxious to win his political spurs, Balfour would be faithful to his uncle's wishes. This meant following a policy with very different timing from Gladstone's. It would mean dealing harshly with the disturbances: the original plan was that only when law and order had been fully established would concessions be made. At the very least the 'solution' to the Irish Question would be some time coming.

This delay was politically quite convenient for Salisbury. Whilst Irish issues remained prominent, they reminded the electorate of the political upheaval in 1886 and this made it more likely that the Liberal Unionists would not return to their original party. Balfour's personal aim was to toughen his political reputation so as to be seen as heir apparent to Salisbury in the coming years. His task was difficult in the extreme but it was made slightly less daunting by the fact that Parnell was now committed to gaining Home Rule by political means and thus had the support of the Liberals. Parnell therefore disapproved of the extreme measures in the **Plan of Campaign** begun in October 1886 and conceived by Irish nationalist Tim Harrington and run by William O'Brien and John Dillon. As Parnell would not support the Campaign, its effects were limited both geographically and politically.

By the time of the election of 1895, Ireland was relatively quiet and the more constructive aspects of Balfour's policy, for instance the encouragement of **land purchase**, were paying dividends.

KEY TERMS

Conciliation Trying to obtain an agreement between two warring sides by rational talk and calm discussion.

KEY PEOPLE

Arthur Balfour 1848–1930 Nephew of Lord Salisbury, and acted as his Secretary at the Congress of Berlin. Became an MP in 1880 when he worked with Lord Randolph Churchill and others to put forward ideas that would make the Conservatives more of a reforming party. First entered Cabinet 1886, Irish Secretary 1887–91 and later Prime Minister 1902–5.

KEY TERMS

Plan of Campaign A plan by Irish nationalists to try to force landlords to reduce rents. The landlord's tenants would agree on a fair rent and offer to pay this. If it were not accepted as sufficient, they would refuse to pay anything and risk eviction. If eviction took place, the rent money would be put into a 'fighting fund'.

Land purchase State financed
schemes to aid Irish tenants
to purchase land from their
landlords, quite a number of
whom were happy to sell if
the price was right. The first
land purchase clauses had been
included in Gladstone's first Irish
Land Act of 1870 but this made
little impact. Lord Ashbourne's
Act in Salisbury's brief ministry
of 1885/6, and Acts sponsored
by Balfour in 1888 and 1891
meant that by 1895 the range
of landownership in Ireland was
starting to increase significantly.

Mitchelstown Three
Irishmen were killed and two
seriously injured in September
1887 after police fired on a
crowd. Gladstone more than
once referred to the incident
in subsequent speeches
commenting *'remember
Mitchelstown'*.

Leaseholders Those who
owned land for a set period of
time rather than for life, as in
the case of freeholders.

**Liberal Unionist
influence** Liberal Unionist
opposition to Irish Home
Rule did not always mean
opposition to fair and
constructive treatment for the
Irish. The political reality was
that this was not a period of
Conservative government but
of a Unionist one: Salisbury
had been forced to concede
more constructive measures
earlier than he had planned.

Another government tactic was ultimately less successful.
This was to seek a Roman Catholic condemnation of the
Plan of Campaign and related activities. The outlawing
of the Campaign by Pope Leo XIII in 1888 was accepted
reluctantly by the hierarchy of the Irish Church, though
ordinary parish priests, closer to the heartbeat of the
ordinary tenants, wished to support the Plan.

Balfour had the advantage of a much weakened and divided
nationalist movement. At first there was a complex division:

- John Redmond carried the flag for the old Parnellites
  (he was eventually to lead the reunited movement after
  1900).
- Irish Nationalists who did not accept Redmond's
  leadership were divided between two other leaders, Justin
  McCarthy and Tim Healey.

Irish Nationalists were further weakened when Leading
supporters such as John Dillon and William O'Brien
suffered spells in jail in the early 1890s.

What was the extent and nature of Balfour's legislation?

The nickname 'Bloody Balfour' referred to the overall
severity of the policy rather than to the number of fatalities.
There were some, however, such as at **Mitchelstown.**

Balfour's Crimes Act was to be a permanent law rather than
an emergency Act which would have to be renewed every
year. It increased the power of both the Viceroy and local
magistrates to deal with the landlord-tenant relationship.
Tenants' boycotts, refusal to accept eviction and
intimidation of landlords were all to be illegal. However,
Balfour also followed a more constructive policy with the
Irish Land Act of 1887 which extended Gladstone's 1881
Act to **leaseholders** – over 100,000 of them. This was a
concession earlier than many Conservatives had expected
and reflected **Liberal Unionist influence.**

Land purchase was also encouraged. First made possible in
the Land Act back in 1870, £10 million more was made
available for it in 1888, extended to £33 million in 1891.
The government made buying land from the landlords

What was the importance of the Irish question?   175

easier by giving tenants a 100 per cent loan: when it began it had been a loan of up to a third and then increased to two-thirds in 1880. After 1890 agrarian outrages dropped sharply: this decline was directly related to the number of land purchases.

Balfour also introduced a light railway scheme in 1890 and a **Congested Districts Board** the following year. Both were designed to aid the poverty-stricken areas of western Ireland.

HOW DID LIBERAL ATTITUDES TO IRELAND VARY?

What was the degree of Liberal Unionist co-operation with Salisbury's Government?

Lord Hartington was the prominent Liberal who had broken with Gladstone on the question of Home Rule. He now gave what might be described as independent support to the Conservative government. '*He* [Hartington] *will support the present Government on all critical occasions*', Salisbury assured the Queen soon after he had formed his second ministry. This meant a broad support for Salisbury's policy of coercion. Some Liberal Unionists were no longer only opposed to Home Rule but also backed harsher measures. Only about half a dozen Liberal Unionists opposed coercion sufficiently strongly in 1887 and 1888 to return to their old party, but this made the rest more united in backing government policy. So overall Salisbury's hand was strengthened, even if, as we have seen, the Liberal Unionists may have modified the severity of the Prime Minister's measures at times.

More formal links came with the Arlington Street (London) compact of 1890 when Salisbury for the Conservatives, Hartington for the Liberal Unionists and other prominent party figures agreed to combine the constituency committees of the two parties and to call themselves Unionists. They would not oppose each other at election time. Indeed, the term 'Conservative', while never disappearing, was to take something of a back seat while Irish issues remained prominent. Salisbury, as a staunch Conservative, was probably a more effective leader of this alliance than a more moderate member of his party would have been. His

Congested Districts Board Set up to invest money in poorer areas of western Ireland where the size of the population could not be sustained by the relative poverty of the agriculture in the area. Technical help with agriculture would be given, as well as help with migration and the encouragement of the amalgamation of very small holdings.

mere presence reassured the more traditional landowning members that there would be no sell-out on issues like Ireland and yet he could make realistic compromises when they were necessary.

What kind of Liberals stayed loyal to Gladstone?

- Unlike the Peelites in 1846 the Unionists did not take all the men of talent with them. Although a number of opponents of Gladstone were from the universities and academic world (formerly supporting him over the Bulgarian atrocities), others backed him.
- Radical figures became even more prominent in the higher ranks of the Liberal Party: men such as **Harcourt** and **Morley.**
- Of the leading Whig aristocrats, only Earl Spencer stayed loyal to the Gladstonian idea of Home Rule. Whig influence in the Liberals was fast disappearing: indeed the Whigs were disappearing.

Thus the social differences between the parties became more marked. The trend towards the Conservatives in middle-class suburbia was thus confirmed. (see page 201).

WHAT WAS GLADSTONE'S APPROACH TO HOME RULE AFTER 1886?

Irish representation at Westminster

Gladstone had argued that, if given their own parliament, the Irish would not require representation at Westminster. However, Chamberlain felt that they should still be allowed some say because their country would be affected by decisions that would be taken in the Westminster parliament.

There was little doubt that Gladstone, with the aid of his Irish Secretary John Morley, intended to attempt another Home Rule bill if possible. The party was bogged down in the details of what this might include. Whigs like Earl Spencer wanted to see a renewed emphasis on land purchase and there was also discussion about whether the objection that Irish MPs were no longer to be represented at Westminster could be modified. This had been a particular

KEY PEOPLE

Sir William Harcourt 1827–1904 Liberal politician who first became an MP in 1868. Home Secretary 1880–5 and Chancellor of the Exchequer 1886 and 1892–5; party leader 1896–8. A very capable but sometimes awkward colleague.

John Morley 1838–1923 Liberal politician, writer and thinker, John Morley first held office as Irish Secretary under Gladstone in 1886 and returned to that post between 1892 and 1895. Remained a great admirer of Gladstone and wrote the first (very long) biography of him. He had a strong Liberal dislike of state intervention which he believed infringed the freedom of the individual. He resigned from a Liberal government in 1914 on the outbreak of the First World War.

KEY ISSUES

Gladstone's Home Rule policies are important for **Key Issue 6** (see page iv).

objection that Joseph Chamberlain had raised to Home Rule in 1886. The following year Gladstone considered that the Irish MPs at Westminster might be retained provisionally (for the moment), and the 1893 proposals did allow for this. But Gladstone's concession did not persuade Joseph Chamberlain to support the Bill.

How did Gladstone and the Liberals deal with the Parnell scandal?

Could Parnell's Irish nationalist and the Liberals work together? Events concerning Parnell between 1887 and 1890 ensured that the political focus would remain on Ireland. As the news developed of the **Pigott letters**, the fortunes of Liberals and Unionists swayed back and forth. It was alleged that Parnell had claimed, in a letter, that Under-Secretary T.H. Burke, murdered along with Lord Frederick Cavendish in Phoenix Park in 1881, had received his 'just deserts'. This 'revelation' was initially to the advantage of the government and was exploited by Salisbury. He pointed out that the association between Gladstone and Parnell could imply that Gladstone was linked with a person who had excused murder. The exposure of the Pigott letters as forgeries was something of a setback for the Conservatives, but any increase in sympathy for the wronged Parnell soon evaporated when the news of his involvement in a divorce suit, the **O'Shea case**, came through in November 1890. The political alliance with Gladstone had become close when Parnell visited Gladstone at Hawarden at the end of 1889: the divorce case was to end it. How did this come about?

- The **Nonconformist conscience** reared its head: Wesleyan Methodist Hugh Price Hughes made it clear that support for the Liberals would not be forthcoming if they remained in alliance with the adulterer Parnell.
- Gladstone, under pressure from many Nonconformist supporters, suggested, in his roundabout fashion, to one of Parnell's leading supporters, Justin McCarthy, that if Parnell remained Irish leader the Liberal Party would not be elected next time round and Home Rule would be fatally delayed.
- Gladstone wrote to John Morley, asking him to tell Parnell that he, Gladstone, could no longer lead the Liberals if Parnell continued as leader of the National League.

KEY TERMS

Pigott letters Pigott was the forger of the letters published by *The Times* in 1887–9 to try to blame Parnell for the Phoenix Park murders in May 1882, i.e. associate him with Fenianism and bring about his fall politically.

KEY EVENTS

The O'Shea divorce case Parnell was named as co-respondent in a divorce case brought by a close colleague, Captain O'Shea, against his wife Kitty. Whilst many had known of the affair for years, the wider publicity now resulting produced a general attack on Parnell by many English figures. Gladstone distanced himself from Parnell under pressure from English Nonconformists, who denounced the Irishman as immoral and unfit for public office. Parnell's own party was split over the issue.

KEY TERMS

Nonconformist Conscience A term commonly used in the 1890s to refer to the moral conscience of Nonconformist Christians hoping to *prepare the moral ground for a better kind of politics*. There was a strong belief in social action to help the poor and that those in power must maintain the highest moral standards.

There was some confusion over whether Parnell had read the letter's contents, but when it was clear Parnell was still to be re-elected Irish leader, Gladstone took the major decision to publish his letter: this destroyed Parnell. Irish nationalists now faced a choice between continuing to back Parnell who had achieved so much or clinging to the Liberal alliance that offered the only realistic hope of Home Rule. The majority (54-32) decided to ditch Parnell. The circumstances surrounding the fall of Parnell doubtless affected the by-election at Bassetlaw (a north Nottinghamshire mining district) in December 1890. Despite two major speeches from Gladstone in the constituency the Conservative majority increased. This was a setback for the Liberals.

WHAT WAS THE POLITICAL IMPACT OF THE SECOND HOME RULE BILL IN 1893?

Gladstone persists with Home Rule

For a while, prospects looked bleak for Home Rule. Conservatives were still opposed and the Liberals had looked weak ever since 1886. The fall of Parnell had produced a split in the Irish Home Rule Party (see above). Without his magnetic presence a divided nationalist party was hardly likely to achieve very much.

However, Gladstone's personal mission to try to achieve Home Rule remained undimmed. Moreover, with the **General Election of 1892** the Liberals were able to displace Salisbury. They also had the support of the Irish nationalists while Gladstone remained committed to bringing in a bill. Eighty nationalists were returned, a total figure little different from their number in the Parnell days, but only nine were Parnellites: the other 71 were initially supporters of Justin McCarthy and this made links with the Liberals somewhat easier. Gladstone's majority depended on continued support from Irish Nationalists.

Gladstone's insistence on bringing forward a bill for Home Rule again in 1893 kept the focus on Ireland for a little longer. But the strong opposition of the House of Lords proved far too much. After success, this time in the Commons, by a majority of 34 votes, the proposal was

KEY EVENTS

1892 General Election
The Conservatives and their Liberal Unionist allies had a very clear majority in England and more seats than the Liberals over the whole of Britain. However, in the 'Celtic fringes' of Wales and Scotland the majority of voters still backed Liberal Home Rulers. The Liberals were able to form a government with a parliamentary majority of 39 based on the support of the Irish nationalists.

defeated by a massive number in the Upper House, 419 votes to just 41: a humiliating defeat for Gladstone. Once this had occurred, Home Rule began to fade in the public mind. John Morley wanted to run a campaign attacking the House of Lords, with the slogan *'mend 'em or end 'em'*. However, his colleagues overruled him. Moreover, Gladstone's request that Parliament be dissolved again to focus on Home Rule was rejected by his cabinet. The question simply lacked popular concern. An appeal to the will of the people and a criticism of the hereditary nature of the House of Lords could perhaps strike a chord with a substantial section of the voting community, but not on this particular question. Public opinion still opposed concessions to the Irish.

Moreover, previous omens were not good. In 1888 Gladstone had urged Liberal electors to vote for Home Rule supporter Wilfred Scawen Blunt even though he was in jail for defying the Crimes Act. But the electors of Deptford in south-east London preferred the Unionist candidate. There seemed to be little support for the cause of Irish nationalism.

- An increasingly literate and newspaper-reading public devoured sensational stories in national English newspapers of intimidation by Irish 'Moonlighters'. Their conclusion was that the Irish were not fit for self-government.
- More than this, there was also the imperial mentality of the day. The Irish were seen as part of a United Kingdom, who could not, on a 'whim', demand self-government. The country of the multi-national Empire did not accept that the nationalistic feelings of the Irish were valid.
- In any case many argued that the proposed degree of independence was economically foolhardy. They argued Ireland depended on the close links with the rest of Britain for its economic prosperity.

How did the failure of the second Home Rule Bill affect the Liberals' Irish policy?

After Gladstone's final resignation in 1894 the new Liberal prime minister, Rosebery, soon indicated a change of emphasis in Liberal policy. This was to delay Home Rule until a majority of English public opinion could be brought round to it. This was an interesting idea, since it does not appear to have applied to previous Liberal legislation, some of which had not been particularly popular. Moreover, when the Liberals later obtained a majority in England in 1906, there was no sign of Home Rule forthcoming, perhaps because at that stage the Liberals possessed a large majority and so the Irish nationalists could be ignored. However, even as early as 1895, Irish Home Rule appeared to have been postponed indefinitely.

CONCLUSION

- Gladstone tackled the Irish Question with vigour and, at first, with some degree of success.
- His efforts to deal with the problems of Irish land, though considerable, did not really succeed in getting to the roots of the problem.
- The Liberals had become a divided party over Ireland and were to spend much of the period after 1886 in opposition because of it.
- The Conservatives never really recognised the Irish claims to nationhood but found Ireland easier to control in the early 1890s than it had been in the later 1880s.
- Liberal weaknesses, Gladstone's near obsession with Irish Home Rule, the fall of Parnell leading to the subsequent divisions in the Irish nationalist groups, and the loyal support of much of Ulster, helped to ensure Conservative dominance after 1886.
- A strong nationalist feeling nonetheless remained and a battered and bruised Irish nationalism would revive to make a major impact on British politics early in the next century.

QUESTIONS TO CONSIDER

1. Assess the reasons why Gladstone's Irish Home Rule policy failed.
2. Assess the impact of the failure of the Irish Home Rule bills on Liberalism and Conservatism.

CHAPTER 11

How successful were Gladstone's later ministries – Liberal decline and Conservative revival 1880–95?

INTRODUCTION

When Gladstone was re-elected in 1880 the Liberals seemed the stronger of the two parties as their victory had been comprehensive. Their reverse back in 1874, when the Conservatives had been successful, seemed to have been put behind them. The Liberals were also successful in the 1885 election but a closer examination shows that by this time their difficulties were mounting. Just ten years later, in 1895, the Conservatives were successfully elected for the second time in less than ten years.

The Liberals might have expected that modern political trends would favour them. This was a time when the electorate had been widened to include male householders in both borough and county and when the Conservative party was still strongly associated with a landed interest that was clearly declining in terms of both power and prosperity. Yet they managed to keep out of office a Liberal Party who, with their Whig and Radical supporters, had won more seats than the Conservatives in eleven out of the thirteen elections between 1832 and 1885, the exceptions being in 1841 and 1874. They had also managed to defeat the most popular politician of the day: Gladstone. What caused this change of fortune?

WHY DID THE LIBERALS WIN THE ELECTION OF 1880?

- They had caught up on party organisation. The work of Joseph Chamberlain's National Liberal Federation since 1877 had been very effective (see Chapter 4).
- Nonconformists who had supported and influenced Gladstone's first ministry had generally remained loyal. Their electoral strength and their partially successful

This entire chapter is important for **Key Issue 6** (see page iv).

assault on the dominant position of the Church of England meant that the Liberal 'chapel' vote was just as significant as the Conservatives' 'Church of England' vote.

- There was no separate Labour Party yet and the majority of skilled urban workers tended to favour the Liberals. Only three MPs of working-class origin were elected and they backed the Liberals.
- The Liberals gained 38 county seats as the farmers' deputation to Disraeli which demanded a return to protection failed to move the Prime Minister.
- Personalities were becoming increasingly central in elections. As one historian has remarked: in 1880 there was 'unprecedented public campaigning by party leaders' (K. Theodore Hoppen). Here Gladstone's oratory outshone the somewhat unwell Disraeli (see pages 129–130).

POPULAR POLITICS

Gladstone was now at the peak of his popularity. After his temporary retirement from political life in 1874–76, his campaigns over the Bulgarian atrocities and the campaign in Midlothian in the late 1870s had restored **his popularity among ordinary people.** This was an age when:

- Many families had their head-of-household voting for the first time and interest in political affairs was keen.
- Ordinary working people valued the franchise as new and precious.
- They had become literate and could follow political debate.
- With legislation increasingly limiting working hours, they had the time to attend political functions.
- There were fewer other distractions in terms of popular entertainment.

This period of active political interest by the masses did not last: the next generation generally preferred to attend the Music Hall or a sporting fixture than listen to a prime minister's speech.

Gladstone's popularity among ordinary people
Just a few examples of the adulation in which Gladstone was held on his Midlothian campaign:

- When travelling to Edinburgh he passed through Dalmeny where Gladstone's biographer Philip Magnus recalls '*the town was decorated with arches and the streets were illuminated with fairy lanterns*' (the very latest technology of the day).
- At Edinburgh in November 1879 Gladstone spoke in front of 4,700 people at the Corn Exchange. He reported on the '*eager faces, waving hands and shouting voices*'.
- When Gladstone got back to Chester from this campaign a large crowd was on hand to cheer his arrival.
- 16th March 1880 Gladstone left for his second Midlothian campaign: 2,000 people at the station in London cheered him off.

No other politician of the time could have claimed this degree of attention.

But for the moment the 'People's William' was idolised in many households, where framed pictures and engravings of the great man would appear. In buildings such as public houses, glasses, jugs, plates and other items were adorned with his image. Conservative supporters had to be content with purchasing a chamber pot with Gladstone's face on the inside. However, now in his seventies, Gladstone was visibly ageing. The People's William was becoming the GOM – Grand Old Man.

Gladstone's political career lasted over 50 years. Compare this image from about 1890 with the one on page 76 of Gladstone near the start of his career.

LIBERAL FORTUNES IN GLADSTONE'S SECOND MINISTRY 1880–5

However, the Liberal Party fared less well than in Gladstone's first ministry. The far-reaching domestic legislation so dominant between 1868 and 1874 was not so apparent second time around. All the main issues of the day were to cause difficulties for Liberals who often disagreed among themselves:

- Ireland (see also Chapter 10): nationalist activity was a far more serious threat than before 1880 and Gladstone's increasingly radical policy was also unpopular with English public opinion.
- Foreign policy (see also Chapter 9): Gladstone's previous stance of non-intervention was now much less apparent.
- The growing Radical element in the Liberal Party led by Joseph Chamberlain frequently challenged Gladstone's authority and policies.
- Parliamentary Reform: Gladstone's ministry passed the Corrupt Practices Act (1883) (see page 69), the third Reform Act (1884) and the Re-distribution Act (1885) (see pages 190–1). But these Acts did not help the Liberals electorally as much as some had predicted.

IRELAND

The Conservative Lord Salisbury led the opposition to Gladstone's first piece of Irish legislation after 1880, the Compensation for Disturbance Bill, in the Lords. He commented to his nephew Arthur Balfour on Gladstone's policy: '*there are marks of hurry which in so old a man are inexplicable*'. Another phrase had been born which described Gladstone, this one used by his opponents rather than his supporters: '*an old man in a hurry*'. It was not just Conservatives who were uneasy with the interference with property rights that the Bill was seen to threaten. Seventy Liberals in the Commons had failed to vote for the legislation and Lord Lansdowne had resigned from the government in protest, all of which made it much easier for the Lords to reject this Bill than the Irish Land Act of 1870. Public opinion had also played a part. It was not a measure which the electorate would be likely to support. The following year W.E. Forster resigned as Liberal Irish secretary in protest at the release of Parnell from Kilmainham Jail (see pages 167–8).

Gladstone was still trying to *pacify Ireland*, as he had remarked back in 1868. But Ireland's mood was becoming one where this policy was becoming more difficult. Gladstone had reacted to Irish protests by attempting reform on a number of occasions: the country was taking up more and more of his political time. If he managed to bring peace to Ireland it would be easier for him to justify his policy. However, Gladstone's policy was not radical enough for the Irish Nationalists (see pages 166–8).

FOREIGN POLICY

Just as successive governments were trying to hang on to Ireland, so too they were maintaining and sometimes increasing their control of territory overseas. But more intervention abroad frequently led to greater headaches at home. The problems in Egypt and the Sudan, culminating in the murder of General Gordon, difficult relations with both Bantu (native tribesmen) and Boers (Dutch settlers) in South Africa, even the tensions in Afghanistan (see Chapter 9) threw into doubt Liberal competence, Liberal philosophy and Liberal unity. Many in the party were suspicious of the growth of Empire and felt particular events had been badly handled. Bright's resignation from the Cabinet in 1882 over the bombing of Egypt, brought internal Liberal divisions into the open. Gladstone's foreign policy had changed in its nature. After 1880 he was sucked into the more interventionist policies initiated by Disraeli in the late 1870s but with a notable lack of success and lack of unity.

THE GROWTH OF RADICAL LIBERALISM

The position of the Whigs

Given its very diverse nature, the Liberal Party of Gladstone's first ministry had been a relatively united one. Gladstone had:

Whig politician. Member of Commons 1836–46 when he succeeded to the Earldom. Foreign Secretary 1851–2 holding office under Palmerston. Colonial Secretary 1868–70, Foreign Secretary 1870–4 and 1880–5. Colonial Secretary 1886. A relaxed, sociable figure with sporting and gambling tastes who, perhaps due to the attraction of opposites, got on well with Gladstone whom he once persuaded (it was said no one else could) to attend the Derby. The two men wrote extensively to one another and were mutual supports. It was Granville who once remarked that the Liberal Party were in favour of reform but unsure how far to go.

- placed many Whigs in his Cabinet (such as **Earl Granville**, the Duke of Argyll, the Earl of Kimberley and the Marquess of Ripon);
- pushed through substantial legislation, especially with regard to the removal of unjustified privilege, that the more Radical element in the party found acceptable;
- exerted strong and almost universally accepted leadership.

By 1880, however, tensions in the party were more apparent. The changes begun with the second Reform Act back in 1867 were beginning to work themselves out. The composition of Parliament was changing as aristocratic elements were no longer dominating.

Liberal members in 1880	
Total members	358
About 80 were aristocratic: 71 more were 'great landowners'.	total 151 (43.6%)
Middle class Industrialists and merchants	total 114 (32.6%)
Lawyers	total 93 (26.9%)

Although 151 Liberal members of the Commons were still those with landed interests, they were now outnumbered for the first time by those with business and commercial dealings. The latter would naturally expect the party to look after their interests. Still, even if landowners were now outnumbered by those from other backgrounds they were sufficiently numerous to be able to resist measures they felt to be too radical. The landed influence of the Whigs was still crucial in getting electoral support and financing candidates. A Whig/Liberal supporter in one county remarked that if the leading Whigs in the area deserted to the Conservatives then '*a Liberal candidate might as well stand for the moon*' because of all the help, financial and otherwise, that would be lost. Since these Whigs contributed so much, they in turn would also assume that the Liberal Party would follow their lines of thought.

Gladstone was anxious to use Whig talent:

- He held the traditional belief that **aristocrats had a natural talent** for government.
- The landowning Whigs contributed more to the Liberal election effort in 1880 than they did in 1874 and the party fared much better.
- The House of Lords was still significant in political debate and decision making. Without Whig aristocratic peers in this Upper House the Liberals would be very weak indeed in the Upper Chamber, which had a large Conservative majority anyway.

Joseph Chamberlain and Radical Liberalism

However, the Radical element in the party was becoming increasingly prominent. In 1880 Gladstone clearly signalled the importance of Joseph Chamberlain by putting him (without **junior ministerial experience**) straight into the Cabinet as President of the Board of Trade. But the two never got on and regarded each other with mutual suspicion. Gladstone never confided in Chamberlain as he did with some of his more Whiggish colleagues such as Lord Granville. For his part Chamberlain felt that Gladstone was insufficiently Radical. Chamberlain no longer saw him as the 'People's William' assaulting the privileges of aristocratic society as he had done in his first ministry, and gradually developed his own ideas for a new direction in Liberal policy. His social reforms in Birmingham had showed him keener on the role of government than Gladstone and he was more positive than the G.O.M. (see page 184) about further political reform.

Chamberlain's position in the Liberal Party in the 1880s bore some resemblance to Gladstone's himself twenty years before in the 1860s. As a senior Cabinet Minister Gladstone at that time seemed to be striking out on his own in advocating parliamentary reform and finding Prime Minister Palmerston old and out of touch. Now in the mid 1880s it was Chamberlain's turn to suggest new Radical policies not yet officially approved by the Liberal Party. This took the form of his Unauthorised Programme. The principal elements were:

Aristocratic talent for government A widely held belief (among aristocrats) that their leisured, well educated and careful upbringing, together with their financial independence, made them ideally suited to exercise the responsibility and cope with the demands of governing the country.

Junior ministerial experience At this time junior ministers were general assistants to more senior ministers in charge of Departments. It was normal to occupy one of these posts as a first step on the political ladder unless the party in question came into government after a long period in opposition. To be put straight into the Cabinet by being immediately given a very senior post suggested a person was regarded as exceptionally able.

- Free elementary education for all.
- The extension of house building and public sanitation by local authorities paid for by rate increases.
- Higher taxation of the wealthy and the landed in particular.
- Church disestablishment in England and Wales.
- More democratic local government.
- Manhood (though not female) suffrage.
- Payment of MPs.

The programme was unauthorised in the sense that Chamberlain was a cabinet minister and yet his ideas had been put forward without reference to, or approval of, his cabinet colleagues. The differences between advanced Chamberlainite Liberals and traditional Gladstonian supporters were widening all the time. It was on Ireland that the break was to come (see below page 200), but the nature of the party's split was hardly predictable, owing as much to personalities as to policies. Ironically, it was Gladstone's more Radical solution of Home Rule which split the party, not the programme of Chamberlain. But Ireland was never the only source of tension in the Liberal Party.

PARLIAMENTARY REFORM: THE 1884 REFORM ACT

Causes

- The rather haphazard passing of the 1867 Reform Act with its extensive increase in the borough rather than the county franchise was always likely to lead to a demand for further legislation. One aspect of the 1867 Act had been to extend the boundaries of many small boroughs out into the countryside. The Conservative thinking behind this had been that rural Tory votes might then outweigh Liberal town votes. However, it led to **anomalies**. Neighbours would find themselves in one case as a borough householder and thus entitled to vote, while down the road just outside the borough boundary, a county dweller was still denied the franchise. It was difficult to defend this system.
- By the early 1880s the improving educational standards of the rural working classes, especially after the Education Act of 1870 (see page 92) also helped to remove objections to their enfranchisement though opponents

KEY TERMS

Anomalies Unevenness or irregularity. In the context of the nineteenth-century electoral system it is a term frequently used to describe the haphazard nature of voting rights and seat distribution.

claimed they had not 'earned' the vote as their more sophisticated town cousins had done. Even on this issue Liberals were not completely united, though many Liberals were now keen to push ahead with further change.

- More radical Liberals saw party advantage in further reform. After the Secret Ballot Act and the Corrupt Practices Act (see Chapter 4) they hoped the independent rural voters would now favour them rather than opting for the Conservatism of their landowning masters. However, the remaining Whigs in the party had reservations about this move towards more democracy in the countryside.

How easy was it to pass reform this time?

Gladstone had no great difficulty in passing the Bill of 1884 through the Commons. Its main terms were that the householder vote in the counties would be granted on the same terms as in the boroughs. However, the Lords provided resistance to the proposals. This was not surprising:

- The Conservative-dominated Lords feared the decline of the landed aristocratic influence if the Bill were to be passed.
- A Liberal-Radical government always had more difficulty in passing major reform through the Lords (for example in 1832) than did a Conservative administration, which could argue that if it considered it necessary the Lords should agree (such as in 1867). Nevertheless the Bill eventually became law as follows:

Redistribution Act 1885

- Boroughs with fewer than 15,000 people lost both MPs.
- Boroughs with fewer than 50,000 people lost one MP.
- Of 670 constituencies all but 23 became single-member seats.
- The Bill passed the Commons without difficulty at the end of February 1884 by a comfortable majority of 130.
- In June, the Lords voted for Salisbury's motion of outright rejection of the Bill by a majority of 59. They refused to budge unless there was also a Redistribution Bill passing at the same time as the Reform Bill.
- Until October there was a tense atmosphere. There was talk of the **creation of peers** to get the Bill through the Lords, and Radical Liberals such as John Morley were hostile. Reform disturbances occurred in Aston, Birmingham, and a

Creation of peers Peers
(Lords) were created by the
monarch. Very occasionally in
a time of political crisis (1832,
1911) the elected government
whose wishes were being
thwarted by the House of
Lords would ask the monarch
to consider appointing
large numbers of its own
supporters as peers in order
to get controversial legislation
through. The threat always
proved enough.

Liberal rally for reform was held near Chatsworth, the stately
home of the Duke of Devonshire, a leading Whig opponent
of further reform. The atmosphere had been briefly
reminiscent of 1866/7 though never as serious or prolonged.
One difference was that on this occasion it was Gladstone
who was following through his own Reform Bill and further
cementing his reputation as the People's William.

What was the importance of the Election of 1885?

In the election of 1885, fought on the new electoral register,
the Liberals, even without the usual Irish Home Rule Party
support (see page 170), did well enough to form another
government and had a majority of 86 over the Conservatives
(see page 171). This election victory traditionally receives less
attention than its predecessors perhaps because the Home
Rule issue soon rendered its result irrelevant. Yet it shows
that, despite Irish and Imperial setbacks (see Chapters 9
and 10) Gladstone and the Liberals were still popular: in
many differing social circles the Prime Minister remained
the 'People's William'. However, in much of middle-class
(and sometimes working-class) England this reputation
was then suddenly lost when Gladstone announced his
conversion to Home Rule (see pages 170–1). There followed
a dramatic slide in popularity: for all the affectionate use
of the alternative phrase to describe him, the 'Grand Old
Man' which persisted until his death, Gladstone never quite
regained his popularity of the previous period.

How did the Re-Distribution Act affect the Whigs and the Liberals?

**Lord Hartington 1833–
1908** Politician seen as the
last of the leading Whigs, with
a very conscientious approach
to public service. Held various
cabinet posts under Gladstone
but became a Liberal Unionist
after the split with Gladstone
over Home Rule. Continued
in government until 1903
when he resigned over the
perceived threat to free trade.
Succeeded his father as Duke
of Devonshire in 1891.

Another problem Gladstone and the Liberals faced in gaining
support was the long-term effects of the Re-Distribution Act
of 1885. It was to work against the Liberals because of the
decision to go for single-member rather than the double-
member constituencies that had remained the common
if not universal method of election. In the boroughs, this
created a single member for the more prosperous area of
town or suburb and gave the Conservatives an opportunity
to gain representation in urban areas previously dominated
by the Liberals. For the Whigs, it was particularly bad news.
They frequently had an arrangement with more Radical
Liberals in the two-member seats whereby they would have
one candidate each. This would no longer be possible, and
Whigs such as **Hartington** feared that they would lose

out badly in the new single-member seats. It seems that Salisbury's calculation that the Conservatives would gain seats was more accurate than that of the Liberal **Sir Charles Dilke**, who estimated that the Liberals would benefit from the single-member constituencies more than they did. But complications over Ireland were to change the whole political scene and render these calculations irrelevant.

1886–95: WHY DID THE LIBERALS ENCOUNTER FURTHER DIFFICULTIES IN THIS PERIOD?

Ireland

Despite having been successfully re-elected in 1885, the Liberals split over the Irish question within six months: it was to put them out of power for the next six years. Even when they returned to power in 1892, Ireland remained a problem. A weak Liberal government lasted barely three years and finally lost Gladstone on its way out.

In 1886 Gladstone's Home Rule Bill split the Party badly:

- The Whig element in the party, led by Lord Hartington and including a number of Irish landowners, could not accept the idea of Home Rule. Hartington saw it not as a chance for the Irish to govern themselves but as a dereliction of duty by the English government.
- In addition, a Radical element led by Chamberlain and (for a time) **Trevelyan** also broke with the Party over the issue. They felt Home Rule to be unnecessary: the Westminster government should itself attempt to bring about further reform and improvement in Ireland.
- These Liberal Unionists remained without a party, rather like the Peelites after 1846. Many were never to return and gradually connected themselves to the Conservatives over the next few years, as did Chamberlain by 1895.
- But unlike the Peelites in 1846 the Unionists did not take all the men of talent with them. Harcourt and Morley remained.

With Home Rule remaining a prominent political issue, the Liberals faced other problems as a result:

- The downfall of the Home Rule leader Parnell after the divorce case in 1890 (see page 178) meant the end of

KEY PEOPLE

Sir Charles Dilke 1843–1911 Prominent advanced Liberal and ally of Joseph Chamberlain in the early 1880s. Supported Home Rule, imperialism and social reform but a divorce scandal made a future ministerial career impossible, although he remained an MP.

KEY PEOPLE

George Otto Trevelyan 1838–1928 Son of Sir Charles Trevelyan of the Northcote/Trevelyan report into the Civil Service in 1853. Appointed Chief Secretary for Ireland 1882–4. Opposed Home Rule, like Joseph Chamberlain, despite his advanced Liberal opinions and resigned from the government in April 1886. However, unlike Chamberlain, he returned to the Liberal fold in 1887. Served briefly as Scottish Secretary in 1886 (before resigning) and again in 1892–5.

friendly relations between Liberals and many nationalists.

- Gladstone remained as leader into his eighties because he believed he must try to obtain the Home Rule he failed to achieve in 1886. This became something of an obsession with him and compromised the development of the party in other more constructive ways.
- Liberals increasingly lacked English support, where Home Rule remained unpopular. Even when he became Prime Minister for the fourth time in 1892, Gladstone had to rely on the votes of Irish nationalists as well as Scottish and Welsh MPs.
- The House of Lords remained strongly opposed to Home Rule and, in truth, were never likely at this stage to agree to its passage.

British public opinion's indifference to Ireland's problems remained. Gladstone's plea at the end of the 1880s 'Remember Mitchelstown' (see page 175) was a call for some sort of moral outrage campaign against Salisbury's Irish policy. It never got anywhere near the Bulgarian-type excitements of the 1870s. Neither the scale of the deaths nor their location could produce that kind of reaction.

How effective was Liberal leadership?

Gladstone was largely remaining in politics to try to deal with Ireland through granting Home Rule: he often failed to provide the necessary direction in other areas. The Liberals had also lost a number of their ablest supporters such as Chamberlain and Hartington as a result of the Home Rule split. But there were other difficulties. Sir Charles Dilke was a match for Chamberlain in ability and remained loyal to Gladstone. But he suddenly faded from the political scene in Parnell-like manner in 1886, when cited in a divorce case. Although remaining as an MP, his influence was lost. Harcourt was a very capable figure but his short temper frequently made him an awkward colleague. By 1895 the next generation of Liberal leaders, Asquith and Lloyd George, were starting to make an impression but their great days were in the future.

How much working-class support was there for the Liberals?

The Liberals hoped to consolidate their support in the working class. But the rise of socialism in the 1880s threatened to provide alternatives for this kind of voter. Some

Liberals, notably Gladstone, were keen to see working men as candidates for the party, but few were selected. A well-connected Liberal with a private income was always a more attractive proposition than a working man, where the lack of a parliamentary salary would handicap him. After the Scottish ex-miner Keir Hardie was rejected for a Liberal seat in 1888 he turned to socialism and formed the Scottish Labour Party in 1892, and the Independent Labour Party in Bradford the following year. Trade Union support for the Liberals from men such as Henry Broadhurst, Secretary of the Trades Union Congress, was challenged, and he was forced to retire in 1890 to make way for more radical, socialist figures. Automatic Trade Union support for the Liberals was fast disappearing. Socialist sympathisers were increasingly feeling they could not live with a Liberal Party where major employers of labour such as Sir Alfred Illingworth, MP for Bradford, and Sir James Kitson, the Leeds president of the National Liberal Federation, were so prominent. John Morley, a fervent believer in laissez-faire, found workers campaigning against him at Newcastle in the 1892 election.

Imperialism

- The public's perception was that Salisbury had inherited from Disraeli the more forward-looking (and popular) foreign and imperial policy that became particularly associated with the Conservatives.
- By contrast, the Liberals were seen, not altogether accurately, as 'Little Englanders', whose vision was small, who played down the greatness of the English race and who had insufficient regard for the great British Empire.
- In fact a number of Liberals such as **Lord Rosebery** were keen imperialists but therein lay the problem: the Liberals were divided on the issue.

In the brief Liberal ministry of 1892–5 their splits over imperial policy were apparent. As Foreign Secretary, Rosebery's policy of supporting the aggressive colonialism of Cecil Rhodes in South Africa was opposed by the 'Little Englanders' Harcourt and Morley. On the question of Uganda there was a major split over whether Great Britain should formally annex the territory from the struggling East Africa Company. The result was that the decision was delayed for two years. Only when Rosebery replaced Gladstone as Prime Minister in 1894 was the territory annexed to the Crown.

Earl of Rosebery 1847–1929 Inherited the title as a child. Assisted Gladstone in his Midlothian Campaign in 1879; Lord Privy Seal 1885; Foreign Secretary 1886, 1892–4, Prime Minister 1894–5, the choice of Queen Victoria. First Chairman of the London County Council. Handsome, rich and personable, he cut quite a dash in the Liberal Party but remained essentially a Whig with imperialist views and little interest in social reform. He gave up the Liberal leadership soon after the party's defeat in 1895.

LIBERAL PRINCIPLES: ACHIEVED OR OUTDATED?

Liberals not only experienced difficulties in approaching specific political issues. Their whole philosophy (one which had brought them so much success in the middle years of the century) was going through a period of difficulty.

Political Liberalism

Apart from Disraeli in 1867, it was the Liberals who had been more associated with the extension of the franchise than had the Conservatives. But with the passing of the Third Reform Act in 1884 and the Corrupt Practices Act the previous year they had run out of steam on the issue.

- There were divisions in the Party on whether to extend the franchise to all men. There was a disagreement as to whether the vote was a privilege or a right.
- The question of votes for women put the Liberals in difficulties. More radical Liberals were sympathetic but were opposed to a limited franchise for just wealthier women which they feared would benefit the Conservatives.

Economic Liberalism

Liberal belief in free trade remained as strong as ever. Unlike issues surrounding Ireland and imperialism it was also popular in the country as a whole. However, throughout the late-nineteenth century the Conservatives remained attached to it, despite some murmuring in the ranks in the 1880s. So the Liberals were unable to gain any significant electoral advantage from this commitment. Moreover, as imperial and military commitments grew by the early 1890s the Liberal association with cheap government became harder and harder to sustain. In 1895 the Liberal Chancellor of the Exchequer, Harcourt, developed the principle of taxing large inheritances and the modern idea of death duties was born. This would hit the landed interest most and there was still sufficient anti-aristocratic feeling among many radical Liberals for them to accept the measure. But others were worried the new tax undermined laissez-faire. Gladstone (who had plenty to compare it with) regarded it as the most radical measure passed in his lifetime.

Religious Liberalism

Liberals had long stood for the removal of the religious discrimination still apparent in public life, and Gladstone's great 1868–74 ministry had clearly demonstrated this commitment. But here, Liberals were really victims of their own success. By the 1870s Nonconformists, for instance, could feel that their chances of social, political or economic advance were no longer hampered by their religious background. After the **Burials Act of 1880** few major Nonconformist grievances remained. Although **prejudice against Roman Catholics** remained in areas like **Liverpool** and **Glasgow**, it was becoming more informal than institutional. Back in 1861, Lord Salisbury had complained when a civil servant was dismissed from his post for no better reason than he was a Roman Catholic. Attitudes had changed by 1886 when Salisbury, as prime minister, appointed Henry Matthews as Home Secretary, the first Roman Catholic to hold a cabinet post.

Feelings of informal discrimination, however, lead to another significant development. In the past, Liberals could rely on the Nonconformist vote because they were the party looking after their interests. It was Nonconformists who pushed for the Licensing Act of 1872, unpopular with many other groups. But now:

- As they rose socially, many Nonconformists turned to Anglicanism, for social as much as religious reasons.
- The Nonconformist Church's strength had peaked mid-century and was starting to decline by 1895.
- Religious issues were less prominent in politics, though they could surface at times over issues such as education: the Liberals could no longer rely on the Nonconformist vote.

Social questions

The demand for state action on social problems was increasingly evident in the last years of the century. Moreover, the Liberals had an opportunity to associate themselves with the need for further change, as Salisbury's range of social reforms was limited. But there was a problem. Social reform in areas such as housing, pensions, poor law reform or concern for children's welfare would involve state intervention on a scale many Liberals such as Gladstone's disciple John Morley found incompatible with their traditional views on the freedom of the individual. Gladstone's resistance in this area

Burials Act of 1880
This legislation, for which Nonconformists had been pressing for some time, allowed non-Anglicans to be buried with their own religious service inside Anglican burial grounds. Demand for this concession was particularly strong in Wales where the proportion of non-Anglicans was high and alternative places of burial especially limited in many more rural areas.

Anti-Catholic prejudice in Liverpool and Glasgow
Prejudice against Roman Catholic immigrants from Ireland was common in these two cities. There was tension between Protestant and Catholic communities which extended to the rival football teams of Everton (Catholic 1878) and Liverpool (Protestant 1892) and Celtic (founded by Catholic Irish immigrants 1888) and Rangers (Protestant 1872). Conservatives, with their anti Home Rule policy gained support from Protestants in these areas.

was obviously influential, and the **Newcastle Programme** of 1891 highlighted the struggle between traditional and more radical Liberals in the mixed agenda it presented.

Writers such as T.H. Green and L.T. Hobhouse were moving towards **'New Liberalism'** which argued that a minimum standard of living for ordinary people was necessary if the true fruits of freedom were to be enjoyed. For many voters, a party divided on such an important issue and debating changes to its fundamental philosophy was hardly one to be entrusted with the government of the country.

POSSIBLE PROBLEMS FOR THE CONSERVATIVES

For most of this period the Conservatives were led by the Marquis of Salisbury (until his retirement in 1902), who came from the heart of the English landowning aristocracy. He always used the word 'English' rather than 'British', and indeed it was in England that the Conservatives were the most successful electorally. Salisbury held traditional Conservative views, opposing parliamentary reform strongly in 1867. He also resigned from Disraeli's Government rather than support the urban household suffrage that ultimately expanded when he was prime minister. Until the mid 1890s he faced Gladstone as leader of the Liberal party but proved more successful than the 'People's William'.

Circumstances did not appear to favour a long period of Conservative rule. It surprised many that this is what they achieved, not least the pessimistic Salisbury who constantly lamented the decline of aristocratic power. The signs of future problems for the Conservatives, however, were all too apparent:

- After the Corrupt Practices Act of 1883 (see page 69) the landed interest and the wealthy industrial class would find it harder to exert their traditional 'influence' at elections and it was thought this would count against the Conservatives.
- Economically, Salisbury presided over a period when **British industrial power** and prosperity was perceived to be less dominant than earlier in the century.

Newcastle Programme 1891 At a conference in Newcastle the National Liberal Federation called for the Liberal Party to adopt a number of measures. Some of these were traditional ideas such as the disestablishment of the Welsh Church, Home Rule for Ireland, and Licensing reform. Others were newer such as parliaments to be elected every three years (it was seven at the time) and employers' liability for accidents at work.

New Liberalism The attempt by Liberal writers and politicians to reconcile their traditional belief in freedom and laissez-faire with the new support for widespread social reform, involving a clear extension of the role of the state. The crux of the argument was that without the state's aid to attain a minimum standard of living the joys of freedom were not likely to be properly appreciated. These views eventually became accepted by many party members, but often not until after 1895.

British industrial power It has been argued that, in Britain, the 1880s in particular were a time of industrial depression. Certainly there was a slowing of growth compared to previous decades. However, while wages were not rising, the general fall in prices, helped by cheap imports of food from abroad, ensured that living standards increased for all but the worst-off classes whose poverty relative to other social groups was greater.

- There were increasingly widespread calls for a greater degree of social reform as **greater awareness of the extent of poverty** among the lower working-classes became apparent.
- There was a major nationalist challenge in Ireland to Britain's refusal to grant them Home Rule.
- Demands for a further extension of the franchise in general and to women in particular, though as yet expressed in moderate language, were quite apparent.
- Trade Unionism spread rapidly to unskilled workers and grew in militancy, with more strikes in the late 1880s and 1890s.
- Socialist ideas, supported by few before the mid 1880s, were gaining ground strongly by the early 1890s as arguments grew that 'labour' should be represented.

Lord Randolph Churchill and Tory democracy

In opposition between 1880 and 1885, the Conservatives experienced some internal difficulties. Sir Stafford Northcote, their leader in the Commons, was criticised for being ineffective in his criticisms of Gladstone's second ministry. The '**Fourth Party**', led by Lord Randolph Churchill, challenged Northcote's leadership. How far did this group in general and Churchill in particular have democratic ideas?

- They idolised Disraeli, viewed him as having democratic instincts and wished to see his social reform extended further, arguing that this is what he would have wished.
- Churchill used the phrase 'Tory Democracy', first mentioned at the time of Disraeli's passing of the second Reform Bill in 1867 (see Chapter 7), to launch an attack on Liberal policies, suggesting they were not always in the interest of the majority of the people.
- To reverse the Liberal victory of 1880, the group argued that the ordinary people needed to be trusted. This argument was extended to Ireland where, by 1884/5 Churchill was arguing that coercion would no longer work.
- Churchill helped to form the Primrose League (see page 202) and saw an increased role for women in the party.
- Churchill adopted the National Union of Conservative Associations (an organisation similar to the National Liberal Federation) as his power base. In 1884 he challenged the policies of the official leaders of the party by resigning from the chair of the National Union, only to be triumphantly re-elected within a fortnight.

KEY CONCEPTS

Greater awareness of the extent of poverty

The surveys of Charles Booth in London in the 1880s and Seebown Rowntree in York at the turn of the century confirmed a growing feeling that the extent of severe poverty at the lower end of the working class was more severe than many had previously realised. It was gradually becoming accepted that those out of work may have been victims of the economic system rather than lazy. Moreover, the surveys revealed that those in work could be extremely poor because of very low wages.

KEY TERMS

The Fourth Party A very small but influential group of Conservative MPs in the early 1880s led by Lord Randolph Churchill and including Sir Henry Drummond Wood, John Gorst and, sometimes, Arthur Balfour. Their chief aim seems to have been to attack what they saw as the weak leadership of the Party in the Commons by Sir Stafford Northcote

- At times, Churchill seemed to be suggesting an alliance of the aristocracy and the working classes against the grasping middle classes.

But it can be questioned how far this really was Tory Democracy in general and how far they were the true beliefs of Lord Randolph in particular.

- True the Fourth Party was frequently seen as more dynamic in their parliamentary activities than Northcote. For instance they took the lead in trying to oppose the entry of the atheist, Charles Bradlaugh, to the House of Commons. Yet this was hardly a democratic move and hypocritical given Churchill's lack of definite religious belief.
- Disraeli might just have talked in terms of an alliance of upper and lower classes against a wealthy industrial group but Churchill and his fellow Conservatives clearly wanted the money and talents of a middle class who were increasingly more prosperous than the landed interest by the 1880s. Disraeli was praised in order to damn Northcote.
- Other views were not always consistent. For example Churchill, having argued for more reasonable treatment for Irish nationalists then proceeded to back the Ulster opposition to Home Rule.
- As a result Churchill has been described essentially as an opportunist. In late 1884 he agreed to stop using the National Union as a body which kept challenging Conservative policy. It seems that Salisbury had bought him off by promising him a Cabinet post when the Conservatives next formed a Government.

Tory Democracy was never very coherently formulated; it was based upon the idea *'trust the people and they will trust you'*. It differed from ordinary Radicalism (with which it shared an interest in reform) in strongly supporting the Crown, Church and the House of Lords.

However, it was not by becoming a democratic party that the Conservatives achieved success (this had to wait for the twentieth century). In both 1886 and 1895 Salisbury and the Conservatives won elections quite comfortably, yet by 1887 Churchill had been defeated politically and the aristocratic and anti-democratic Salisbury was secure in the post of Conservative leader and Prime Minister. In Gladstone's final ministry (1892–5), the Liberals had to rely on Irish nationalist support. The Conservatives remained the majority party in England.

WHY WERE SALISBURY AND THE CONSERVATIVES SO SUCCESSFUL IN THE LAST YEARS OF THE NINETEENTH CENTURY?

Elections 1886–95

Date	Prime Minister	Party	Result	
1886	Salisbury	Conservative	Con/Lib. Unionist	405
			Liberals	190
			Irish	85
1892	Gladstone	Liberal	Con/Lib. Unionists	314
			Liberals	272
			Irish	81
1895	Salisbury	Conservative	Con/Lib. Unionists	411
			Liberals	177
			Irish	82

Policy controversies: Ireland and imperialism
Ireland

The establishment of Conservative rule in 1886 was caused by the Irish Question. English public opinion in particular was not in general pro-Roman Catholic or pro-Irish and the hostile reaction to Gladstone's proposal to Irish Home Rule demonstrated this clearly. The substantial Conservative victory in 1886 was, in effect, the electorate's verdict on the desirability of Home Rule and the decision was clear: it was not wanted. Salisbury's Government's firm policy in putting down the Irish Nationalist disturbances in the late 1880s also won electoral support.

Imperialism

The substantial gains made with the European carve-up of Africa were well received by the public at the end of the 1880s and the Conservatives took much of the credit. It was certainly to their advantage in the election of 1895. The association of Conservatives with imperialism also attracted support in dockyard towns such as Chatham, Plymouth,

Portsmouth, Southampton and the great shipbuilding centre of Newcastle. Conservative support was also found among the manufacturers and labourers in the armaments factories in towns such as Woolwich. The Golden Jubilee celebrations of Queen Victoria in 1887 marked a high point of pride in the Empire, and were extremely popular.

Middle class support

Ever since the General Election of 1868 there had been indications that the **growing urban middle-class** was turning away from the Liberals and giving its support (and money) to the Conservatives:

- Wealthy commercial businessmen, (sometimes known as plutocrats) City bankers, lawyers and a growing professional class of doctors, architects and university teachers whose parents or grandparents may well have come from humble backgrounds had now 'arrived' in society and had lost their Radical edge and Liberal instincts.
- They tended to imitate the landed classes by sending their children to board at the **public schools** that had developed thanks to the growth of the railway system.
- They liked the relatively low-cost government with careful expenditure which Salisbury managed to retain well into the 1890s. Here, Salisbury owed a good deal to the financial skills of his Chancellor from 1887 onwards, George Goschen.

Working-class support

Though this was never as great as middle-class support, a solid minority of the working electorate after 1885 voted Conservative. This was evident in towns such as Coventry and Sheffield which had been hit by Liberal free-trade policies and particularly in industrial Lancashire where anti-Irish feelings and strong Protestantism combined to produce a pro-Conservative culture among many working men. Twelve out of thirteen cotton-spinning towns in Lancashire regularly returned Conservatives. Workers also joined the numerous Conservative clubs where (frequently) alcohol flowed more freely than in Liberal ones. In some areas, the public house was the vital component in attracting potential members to meetings. Since Gladstone's unpopular Licensing Act in 1872, the drink

KEY THEMES

The growing urban middle class As early as 1868 two election results had indicated the potential support for Conservatives in the new middle-class suburban areas: bookseller W.H. Smith defeated the Radical Liberal J.S. Mill and, in Middlesex, another Radical, Henry Labouchere, was defeated by Lord George Hamilton. These results were against the national trend towards the Liberals. 20 years later the situation was reversed: the 56 wealthiest constituencies after 1885 were Conservative.

KEY TERMS

Public schools In reality private schools, though open to all who could pay the fees. Barely a dozen of them operated in the early part of the century but the number of schools rose sharply from the 1840s onwards as the railway made boarding at them a practical proposition.

trade had generally been very happy to let its premises for Conservative rather than Liberal meetings.

The effects of parliamentary reform

- The Redistribution Act of 1885, following on from the 1884 Parliamentary Reform Act, proved to be of considerable benefit to the Conservatives. By creating many single-member constituencies and removing most of the double-member ones, larger towns were divided up. The middle-class area would now be a separate constituency and given the social trends we have just noted would probably return a Conservative.
- In addition, the Conservatives had an army of volunteer supporters, including many women. Organisations like the **Primrose League** as well as the National Union would do a great deal to turn out Conservative voters when the need arose.
- Even one aspect of the Corrupt Practices Act (1883) helped the Conservatives. Limitations on expenses only applied to *local* seats: national fund-raising at election time was beginning to take on the increasingly significant role it has had ever since. The Conservatives were the party with the greatest resources for this.
- Moreover, these resources were used effectively. Under the overall control of 'Captain' Richard Middleton, Conservative party organisation again edged ahead of the Liberals in the late 1880s and early 1890s. This was not an easy task. As late as 1890 a vote on a budget clause was almost lost because so many Conservative MPs were at the Ascot races. But Middleton provided a constant stream of good advice to Salisbury while leaving policy decisions to his leader.

Political Skills of Salisbury

For all his throwaway style and prophetic gloom, Salisbury was in fact a shrewd operator who handled his colleagues effectively on most occasions. In particular, the way he handled the **resignation of Randolph Churchill** and enticed Joseph Chamberlain permanently into Conservative ranks by 1895 illustrates his abilities.

Salisbury's selection of W.H. Smith in 1887 to be First Lord of the Treasury (a post usually reserved for the prime minister) and run business in the House of Commons

KEY TERMS

Primrose League Not officially a Conservative party organisation until 1914, it nevertheless acted as if it was one. Founded in 1883 by Lord Randolph Churchill in memory of Disraeli and, supposedly, his favourite flower. By the mid 1890s it had about a million members, many of them middle-class women who were willing to do voluntary unpaid work for the party of the envelope licking variety. Its social activities linked the party with many ordinary voters and even non-voters.

KEY EVENTS

The Resignation of Randolph Churchill
Churchill was made Chancellor of the Exchequer in Salisbury's second ministry in 1886. He dramatically resigned at the end of that year when he wished to make greater economies in the military budget than other ministers wanted. He had thought he was indispensable to Salisbury but Salisbury, who found Churchill a difficult colleague, accepted his resignation and appointed Goschen in Churchill's place. Churchill never regained office: his behaviour became increasingly erratic and he died of syphilis in 1895.

showed his shrewd judgement of men from a social group different from his own. Smith proved a reliable and loyal colleague until his untimely death in 1891, after which he was sorely missed by Salisbury.

Social changes in the Conservative Party

The downfall of the duke's son and the rise of the newsagent's boy emphasised social changes in the Conservative Party. Salisbury's appointment of peers from a business rather than a landed background also showed a thoughtful assessment of a changing political landscape. Gladstone had traditional views on this matter and only a handful of 'business' peers had been appointed before 1886: Salisbury now led the way. His numerous appointments included a brewer (Henry Allsopp from Burton-on-Trent who was created Baron Hindlip in 1889) and a textile manufacturer (Bradford's

Aristocratic Prime Minister, Lord Salisbury.

Samuel Cunliffe-Lister, creator of the vast Manningham mills, who became Lord Masham in 1891). Nonetheless, the Conservatives retained the bulk of landowning support. Whereas the decline in landowning Liberal MPs was particularly noticeable, this trend was less marked in the Conservative Party.

Clearly the biggest battle was for the middle-class vote, and here the defection of Chamberlain to the Conservatives was significant. Birmingham, for instance, became a Conservative city for a time as the Chamberlain electoral machine changed political sides.

Conservative domestic reform

Despite the fact that Salisbury gave the impression of wishing to stem the tide of reform once he was prime minister, his first ministry (1886–92) introduced a few significant changes which would have commanded the support of some of the electorate and which frequently aided the ordinary citizen:

- The **Local Government Act** of 1888 introduced a more uniform and democratic system of local authorities, consistent with the national change to Householder franchise in 1884. In particular, the long overdue reform of the government of London was undertaken. The government of the City of London had not been reformed as were other Corporations in 1835. The growth of London way outside the city boundary, as well as the vast increase in population, had made for confused and complex administration.
- Elementary state education, which had been rapidly growing since the Act of 1870 was now to be made free in all areas (as it already was in some) with legislation to this effect passed in 1891.
- The **Tithe** Act of 1891, by requiring (generally Anglican) landlords rather than (frequently Nonconformist) tenant farmers to pay the tithe, pleased many different sectors of the community.
- The Housing of the Working Classes Act 1890 extended the Artisans Dwelling Act of 1875 by consolidating powers of compulsory purchase and enforcing the requirement that local authorities replace the demolished buildings.

KEY EVENTS

Local Government Act of 1888 The most important piece of domestic legislation passed by Salisbury. It:

- Created County Councils for all areas of England elected by ratepayers (male and female) and modelled on the existing municipal boroughs.
- Greatly reduced the administrative role of Justices of the Peace – magistrates.
- The London County Council was created.
- There would be a group of nominated senior Council members called Aldermen.

The changes were extended in 1894 by the Liberals who created a further tier of local government with the creation of urban and rural district Councils as well as the very local Parish Councils

The reforms lasted until 1965 in the case of London, with the creation of the Greater London Council, and until 1972 for other areas when there were changes in the size and functions of the County Councils, though most still continued to exist.

KEY TERMS

Tithe Literally a tenth. Traditionally, the tenth of the produce of the land given to the Church as a form of tax. It had long been changed to a payment on land and, like Church Rates, was especially resented by Nonconformists.

CONCLUSION

- Gladstone formed a strong Liberal Government in 1880 though there were many tensions within the Liberal ranks.
- The difficulties in dealing with the Irish question were much greater than in his first ministry.
- Liberal foreign policy became more like the Conservatives: more involved with a wide range of imperial affairs, not always successfully.
- The Conservatives benefited from Ireland and imperialism being major political issues throughout this period.
- Lord Salisbury proved an able leader of the Party and Conservative party organisation again moved ahead of the Liberals.
- A wider and wider social range of people became involved in the political process.

QUESTIONS TO CONSIDER

1. Why did the Liberals run into difficulty in this period?
2. How far was Gladstone's weakness in domestic, foreign and Irish policy responsible for the decline of the Liberals?

PERIOD STUDY EXAM-STYLE QUESTIONS

1. Assess to what extent Gladstone's ministries after 1880 were dominated by Irish questions.

SUMMARY

The late-nineteenth century was the period when the Liberals and the Conservatives were the two dominant political parties in Britain. Except in times of political revolution (which Great Britain has avoided since the seventeenth century) parties tend to evolve rather than suddenly appear or disappear. The Liberal Party gradually emerged from the traditional Whig Party and Radical groups that had developed steadily in the period up to 1846. The Conservative Party emerged from the old Tories in the 1830s and 1840s.

This process was complex and the various twists and turns need careful study. However, this does not mean there are no periods of excitement and dramatic development. For a party to be successful in an age when the (still all male) electorate was increasing, it had to appeal to a range of voters who held a variety of views and empathised with different aspects of the party's policies. A party with a range of views can attract a wide range of support, but this can also lead to strains and tensions and splits within its ranks.

At the start of the period this happened to the Tories/ Conservatives with the division over Corn Law repeal in 1846 and towards the end of the period it happened again with the Liberal split over Irish Home Rule in 1886. On both occasions the divided party was weakened and its rival held political power for some years afterwards. Yet in the end both parties recovered to hold office with a strong government again – the Conservatives in the 1870s and the Liberals likewise at the end of 1905.

Some of the political apparatus with which we are familiar today developed at this time, as parties produced a clearer philosophy, became more cohesive, more disciplined, better organised and developed national and local organisations with a popular following. The growth of railway travel, increasing literacy and the emergence of a popular press brought politicians to the people and encouraged the appearance of political personalities such as Gladstone and Disraeli: men with enthusiastic supporters, though also detractors. The right to vote was an increasingly valued prize and many families found themselves with a first time male voter during this period. By the end of the period many women were inspired to campaign for similar rights for themselves.

1846–95 was a period of general educational advance and more leisure time (as working hours decreased and conditions improved) but it was before professional sport and other pastimes provided major distractions on a large scale. As a result, there was a keen and widespread public interest in the political process that has rarely been repeated since and is certainly not apparent in the present day!

After 1895 a Labour Party emerged that was to take the place of the Liberal party as the main opposition to the Conservatives, a situation that still prevails well over 100 years later. More Parliamentary Reform Acts have enfranchised almost all adults and a good deal of Britain's current political system can be seen to have developed in this period.

The time from the downfall of Peel's Conservative Government in 1846 to the emergence of a strong Liberal Government under Gladstone in 1868 was one of political and social transition. Liberals, Whigs, Peelites and Radicals jostled for power and influence while Protectionist Tories struggled to come to terms with the triumph of free trade and the growing political importance of the already economically powerful middle-class and its challenge to landed-wealth power and influence.

With politics in a state of flux and party discipline fluid, these 22 years saw many changes of government, eight in total, but only two of these (December 1852 and 1858) were linked closely with general election results. Though increasingly aware of parties, MPs still showed a good deal of independence in the way they thought and voted. The political skills of Lord Palmerston dominated the period. He was a Whig who attracted Liberal, Radical and even Tory support, belonging to an age before more disciplined party allegiances. He cultivated a broad popular appeal for a political leader. Because he was Prime Minister for most of the period 1855–65 the more confused position with regard to political parties lasted well into the 1860s. This also delayed further changes in the franchise that would have hastened other more democratic developments.

Palmerston died in 1865. Two years later, after the second Reform Act of 1867, a clear two-party political system emerged. Liberals and Conservatives locked horns in Parliament, in election battles and in individual clashes. Examples of this include some of Gladstone's controversial domestic legislation between 1869 and 1873 and the disputes over Disraeli's foreign policy in the late 1870s.

Gladstone's ability to hold together a wide range of Liberal opinion, despite major differences over political priorities, led to Liberal success in the 1868 election, and his first ministry succeeded in passing major reforms based on the relatively clear philosophy of Gladstonian Liberalism. The emphasis on equality of opportunity and the removal of unjustified privilege fitted the spirit of the age and reflected the social changes taking place. All this excited a good deal of popular support: hence the term People's William. His moralistic approach to foreign policy also struck a chord with many, though opposition arose as he seemed to succumb to the imperialistic feelings of the 1880s and developed the radical policy towards Ireland that was eventually to split his party.

Disraeli also managed to develop a sense of direction for the Conservative Party after its disasters in 1846 as protection was gradually dropped in the 1850s. The party, based previously on protecting the landed interest, adapted to the increasingly wide franchise by attracting middle-class voters who backed support for traditional institutions such as the monarchy and the Church. Its pursuit of British interests abroad was also coupled with a paternalistic social concern for the poor at home. This brought support for Conservatism from all social classes (albeit somewhat unevenly) and enabled the party to survive, win the election of 1874 and prosper into the democratic age of the twentieth century. Conservatives continued to look to the time of Disraeli, to the origins of Tory Democracy and One Nation Conservatism in orchestrating their successes in the next century.

BIBLIOGRAPHY

Straightforward

Christopher Harvie and Colin Matthew, *Nineteenth-century Britain: A Very Short Introduction*, Oxford University Press, 2000

Michael Lynch, *An introduction to 19th Century Britain*, Hodder and Stoughton, 1999

Derrick Murphy, *Britain, 1815–1918: A-level*, Flagship History Series, Collins, 1998

More complex

Eric Evans and Chris Culpin, *The Birth Of Modern Britain 1780–1914*, Longman, 1997

W.D. Rubenstein, *Britain's Century A Political and Social History 1815–1905*, Arnold, 1998

Robert Pearce and Roger Stearn, *Government and Reform: Britain, 1815–1918*, Access to History series, Hodder Murray, 1999

Michael Willis, *Britain 1851–1918: A Leap in the Dark?*, SHP Advanced History, 2006

A.N. Wilson, *The Victorians*, Arrow, 2003

Gladstone and Disraeli compared

Paul Adelman, *Gladstone, Disraeli and Later Victorian Politics*, 3rd ed., Longman, 1997

Richard Aldous, *The Lion and the Unicorn: Gladstone Vs Disraeli*, Pimlico, 2007

Stephen J. Lee, *Gladstone and Disraeli*, Routledge Questions & Analysis in History, 2005

Michael Willis, *Gladstone and Disraeli Principles and Policies*, Cambridge University Press, 1989

Parties

Paul Adelman, *Victorian Radicalism: The Middle-class Experience, 1830–1914*, Longman, 1984

Robert Blake, *The Conservative Party from Peel to Major*, Fontana, 1996

T.A. Jenkins, *Disraeli and Victorian Conservatism*, British History in Perspective, 1996

Duncan Watts, *Whigs, Radicals and Liberals 1815–1914*, Access to History series, Hodder, 2002

Duncan Watts, *Tories, Unionists and Conservatives, 1815–1914*, Access to History series, Hodder, 2002

Michael Winstanley, *Gladstone and the Liberal Party*,
   Routledge, 1990

Biographies

Robert Blake, *Disraeli*, Eyre and Spottiswoode, 1966,
   Reprinted Prion Books, 1998
Roy Jenkins, *Gladstone*, Macmillan, 1995
Chris Culpin and Pat Tweedie, *Gladstone*, Longman
   History in Depth, 1998
Graham Goodlad, *Gladstone*, Flagship Historymakers
   Collins, 2004
Mary Dicken, *Disraeli*, Flagship Historymakers Collins,
   2004
H.C.G. Matthew, *Gladstone 1809–1898*, Clarendon, 1997
Jonathan Parry, *Benjamin Disraeli*, Very Interesting People
   series, Oxford, 2007
I. Machin, *Disraeli*, Profiles In Power, Longman, 1994
Michael Partridge, *Gladstone*, Routledge Historical
   Biographies, 2007
E.J. Feuchtwanger, *Disraeli*, Reputations series, Hodder
   Arnold, 2000
James Chambers, *Palmerston: The People's Darling*, John
   Murray, 2004

Ireland

Chris Culpin and Tim Hodge, *Parnell and the Irish
   Question*, Longman History in Depth, 1998
Paul Adelman, Mike Byrne, *Great Britain and the Irish
   Question, 1798–1921*, Access to History series, Hodder
   Murray, 2008
F.S.L. Lyons, *Charles Stewart Parnell*, Gill and Macmillan,
   2005

Parliamentary Reform

Sean Lang, *Parliamentary Reform 1785–1928*, Questions &
   Analysis in History, 1999
Annette Mayer, *The Growth of Democracy in Britain*, Access
   to History – Themes, 1999
Eric Evans, *Parliamentary Reform in Britain, C.1770–1918*,
   Seminar Studies In History, 1999

Foreign Policy

Graham Goodlad, British *Foreign and Imperial Policy, 1865–1919*, Questions & Analysis in History, Routledge, 1999

J.C. Lowe, *Britain and Foreign Affairs, 1815–85: Europe and Overseas*, Lancaster Pamphlets, 1998

Exam Café

Relax, refresh, result

Relax and prepare

Student tips – Stage 1 Note-taking

Serena

When I started the course I wondered why other students were taking lots of notes. I retain information well and I thought I would remember the main ideas. I just put down a few detailed things; but now I am coming to revise I don't always understand the context in which the notes were written. You need to make sure you have adequate notes on every topic as you go along. Don't leave it 'till later

Mark

My problem was different: I had written a lot down but my notes weren't very structured. It was all there but somewhat jumbled. I needed to make bold headings and subheadings so that I could see the outline of each topic more clearly.

Arvind

I have found highlighter pens really useful: it breaks up the text and makes it more manageable to revise from. It has helped me to remember the main causes of an important event much more easily. In thinking about what to highlight it forces you to consider what material is really vital.

Becky

I think I had good notes but they were quite extensive. So I have found it really useful to take a section of notes I am revising and summarise them: make notes from notes. This really tests your ability to write down the essentials. It also assesses how well you understand the topic. The more thoroughly you understand it the easier it is to summarise. It's also useful to read though these summaries as it's a quick way of revising the essentials.

Student tips - Stage 2 Revision

Serena

I think it's important to develop a variety of techniques when you are revising. Don't just passively read your notes through; be more active by looking at some period study questions and writing out a short plan on how you would tackle them. This makes you focus on how to answer the question rather than just stick down all the information you know.

Becky

Yes, I also found that useful. I realised that, while I could manage to plan an outline answer, when it came to making notes of details to illustrate the points that I'd made, I found it hard to recall the necessary factual information. It really identified areas of weakness and what I still had to learn.

Arvind

One method I found helpful was, for each revision session, to focus on one of the key issues and write down four important ideas about each of them. It really made me think and helped me to focus on assessing the material and the relative importance of causes of events for instance.

Mark

My friend told me about a really good website with interactive quizzes on Gladstone and Disraeli: I fancy that type of revision – more fun.

Serena

We need to remember what our teacher said: we have to be careful about using certain websites. I found contradictory statistics on two different websites and I'm uncertain which are correct. We need to cross reference with other sources.

Becky

I felt very rushed trying to write the essay in the time allowed. It wasn't that I hadn't prepared the material but there seemed so much to include that I panicked a bit and found myself out of time before I got to the final paragraph.

Arvind

The crucial thing is to relate your material to the question set. Having worked hard revising the material it is very tempting to put down all you know about a topic, thinking it must be relevant. You can easily answer the question you practiced before: it was similar but not the same.

Serena

That's what happened to me writing the previous essay. But this time I approached it differently. Once I saw what the question was I made a swift plan based on a theme for each paragraph and made sure I spent about the same amount of time on each section. I had written a brief sentence summarising the theme of the paragraph and one or two factual illustrations which I then developed when writing the whole thing out. Although you spend a little of your time preparing this, it enables you to write more quickly as you constantly have prompts for the next section.

Becky

I suppose it's like taking time to write the plan. It pays dividends to spend a few moments just thinking about the precise phrasing of the question before you launch into your answer.

Mark

I'm not very good at remembering details, especially statistics, so what I do at the start is to write some I have managed to remember down in the margin and then use them in the essay if and when appropriate.

Revision checklist

Key Issue 1 How were the Whigs transformed into the Liberals (1846–68)?

You should:
- Be confident about political terminology such as Whigs, Liberals and Radicals, understand their relationship and appreciate the differences between the three words.
- Come to some conclusion about why Radicals did not succeed in permanently forming their own party.
- Realise why Palmerston was such a successful and popular politician in this period.
- Understand why the Whig Party was disappearing by the 1860s.
- Think about how the Liberal Party emerged and why Gladstone became its leader by 1868.
- Consider what Liberal beliefs were by 1868 and compare and contrast this to the policies of the Whigs earlier in the period.

Key Issue 2 What was Gladstonian Liberalism and how successful was Gladstone's first ministry (1868–74)?

You should:
- Examine how Gladstone's political views developed and changed up to 1868.
- Understand clearly what constituted the different aspects of Gladstonian Liberalism.
- Apply this understanding to the different reforms of Gladstone's first ministry.
- Gauge the widespread impact of the ministry's reforms.
- Appreciate the popular appeal of both Liberal policies and the People's William himself.
- Analyse why the Liberals still lost the election of 1874.

Key Issue 3 Why did Disraeli become the Conservative leader?

You should:
- Understand the nature and significance of the Conservative Party split in 1846 and why it was so damaging to them.
- Follow the complexities of the disputes and divisions in the Tory Party after 1846.
- Consider the role of Palmerston in keeping the Conservatives out of office in this period (see also Key Issue 1).
- Be aware of the significant position of Lord Derby in the Conservative Party from 1846 to 1868.
- Appreciate why Disraeli was mistrusted by many Conservatives.
- But see why nevertheless he came to hold a prominent position in the party.

Key Issue 4 What was Disraelian Conservatism?

You should:
- Come to a full understanding of the main principles underlying Conservative beliefs.
- Apply these principles to specific policies such as foreign affairs and parliamentary reform.
- Study carefully the meaning and significance of the phrases One Nation conservatism and Tory Democracy.
- Study Disraeli's view of parliamentary reform.

- Judge the significance of the passing of the 1867 Reform Act in relation to both the Conservative Party in general and the position of Disraeli within it in particular.
- Examine the reasons why Disraeli and the Conservatives were elected in 1874.

Key Issue 5 How successful was Disraeli's second ministry?

You should:
- Follow the reasons for the social reforms of Disraeli's second ministry and judge their significance.
- Assess how Disraeli's foreign policy fits into his overall Conservative philosophy.
- Come to a verdict about the overall degree of success of both Disraeli's domestic and foreign policies.
- Analyse how far Disraeli himself took a personal interest in the social reforms of his ministry.
- Understand the factors that lost Disraeli and the Conservatives the election of 1880.

Key Issue 6 How successful were Gladstone's later ministries?

You should:
- Be able to compare Gladstone's reforms of 1880–85 with his earlier ministry.
- Analyse carefully Gladstone's policies with particular regard to parliamentary reform and foreign policy.
- Form a view about how the Liberal Party's ideas were developing in this period and to what extent they were running into difficulties.
- Assess the specific problems of the final Liberal ministry of Gladstone between 1892 and 1895.
- Judge how far Ireland dominated Gladstone's policies during his later ministries.

Get the result!

Examiner's tips

There are two common types of questions on this paper. The first type asks for reasons for an event, events or developments. These questions often start:

- Assess the reasons for...
- Assess the importance of...

Let's look at an example:

Assess the reasons why Palmerston was able to stay in power as Prime Minister for most of the period 1855–65.

How might you answer this question?

Think about the question – what type is it? You are asked to assess a range of reasons that will account for Palmerston's survival at the top. You need to weigh up the relative significance of the different reasons and also make links between them.

In answering any question you can start by actually asking yourself two questions to get your thought processes going. Firstly,

'Do I understand what the question is getting at?'

If the answer is 'yes' then you need to think about developing an analytical framework for your answer.

The second question is:

'Have I enough knowledge to illustrate and justify my argument?'

Asking these two questions is a useful exercise when you are faced with a choice of questions. If you are well prepared you might think you could attempt any of the questions. This thought process might help you to choose which question you could answer best.

ANALYTICAL FRAMEWORK

Below are some possible themes for the different paragraphs in the answer to the question above. Think about these carefully and decide whether they would be suitable for your answer. If so, you need to judge their relative importance and also decide in what order they should appear?

Serena's paragraph headings

- Popular foreign policy – find examples.
- Moderate domestic policy – persuaded Tories to support him.
- Successful postponement of parliamentary reform.
- Attuned to the modern world despite his regency background.
- Attracted more Liberal and Radical support in his final term.
- Relative weakness of alternative political leaders.

About half a dozen points – well made, illustrated and linked, should be enough.

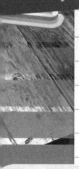

KNOWLEDGE TO ILLUSTRATE THE POINTS

It is vital that you have sufficient relevant evidence to justify your assessment of the points you have made and their relative importance. So there are some crucial points which will need to appear somewhere in the answer:

Serena's knowledge for the answer

1855: the offer to Palmerston to form a ministry — others discredited.

1857: the election result which showed his popularity among voters.

1859: Liberals under Palmerston now more united with both Gladstone and the Radicals supporting him.

1865: Palmerston was re-elected — could he have gone on even further?

Note: Palmerston held on to power despite not always possessing a large majority.

Can you match these dates and specific events to some of the paragraph headings on page 217?

WRITING IT OUT

You need a decisive first sentence in the paragraph.

Here is Serena's first sentence for a paragraph on foreign policy:

Serena's answer

Palmerston's successful appeal to the country in 1857 showed the popularity of his foreign policy among the middle class voters.

Examiner's comment

This kind of opening sentence attacks the heart of the question making a strong assertion. From here it is clear what the subject matter will be. Serena will need to illustrate her theme by explaining why the strong emphasis on British trading interests was so popular with the enfranchised middle-classes and give appropriate examples of Palmerston's policy in 1855–7 such as ending the Crimean War and his aggressive policy towards China.

Here is a sentence from Mark's essay: For which point could **this** be the opening sentence?

Mark's answer

The meeting at Willis's rooms in 1859 gave Palmerston a sound basis for parliamentary support.

Now can you write an opening sentence for the remaining themes from the analytical framework?

Think carefully about the order of your points bearing in mind their relative importance and the ease with which they can be linked. For example, a paragraph on Palmerston's political success in persuading many Tories to give him an 'independent' support could be followed by one on Liberal and Radical support increasing after 1859.

See below how Arvind does this:

Arvind's answer

Not only did Palmerston stay in office with Tory support: a reinvigorated Liberal party was also prepared to back him.

Examiner's comment

Note how this sentence not only links with the previous point: it relates directly to the question and invites detailed back-up of the point in the next few sentences.

What illustration would *you* provide?

When considering a ten year time period, different factors may be important at different times: you may need to point this out. For instance, Palmerston's foreign policy was less successful in his last years: so at this stage other factors in his survival may be more significant. To put it bluntly, were some opponents waiting for Palmerston to die in the 1860s?

Judgement questions

The second type of question involves a greater sense of judgement rather than a list of reasons. Common stems for this type of question include:

- Assess the view that...?
- To what extent...?
- Assess the significance/importance of...
- A quotation that gives a view and you are asked to comment on this and say how far you agree with it.

For this type of question you can adopt the same initial thought process and approach as with the previous question. However, you will also need to think about your degree of agreement with the view which will affect the balance of your answer.

Let's have a closer look at one of these questions:

> To what extent was Gladstone's Liberalism the dominant force behind the domestic legislation of his first ministry (1868–74)?

Becky's opening paragraph

Examiner's comment
The start of the answer is brief and to the point. It immediately makes clear what Gladstone's Liberalism consists of and introduces a clear theme: that this Liberalism played a 'major part in the legislation of Gladstone's first ministry'. Given that this is her view, Becky could go even further and use the word from the title, 'dominant', rather than the word 'major'.

> The ideas known as Gladstonian Liberalism played a major part in the legislation of Gladstone's first ministry, influencing many areas of policy, religious, economic and political. Also, significant measures were passed concerning the removal of unjustified privilege, administrative efficiency and a desire for economy in government.

Becky's answer (of about a thousand words) went on to look at religious liberalism, political liberalism, removal of unjustified privilege, administrative efficiency and economy in government. For this to be an effective answer it needs both to have a clear analytical point for each paragraph and appropriate material to illustrate and justify the point. This justification of the point approach should result in a well argued, convincing, balanced and well-illustrated answer.

POINT: The opening sentences in each paragraph are vital. They outline the relevant theme, directly answering the question in general terms. If these opening sentences are put together and they have been well planned they should form a skeleton answer as seen below in Mark's effort where we have selected the first sentences in each of his main paragraphs.

Mark's POINTS

1. Religious liberalism for instance was central to Liberal Party beliefs and was a significantly unifying factor in a party always prone to splits.

2. Politically too, Gladstone had changed his opinions late and (though not a democrat) had convinced himself that a greater proportion of increasingly respectable working men were qualified to exercise the franchise.

3. Another Liberal move was to assist men in their working relations and remove unjustified privilege.

4. Other legislation showed more than one aspect of Gladstonian Liberalism.

5. Underlying all these Liberal moves was the economic belief in laissez-faire — which, significantly, went well beyond the confines of the Liberal Party.

6. Gladstone's less successful legislation often lacked these liberalising impulses.

JUSTIFICATION From this framework that Mark has planned, it should be possible to illustrate each point with one or more pieces of legislation from Gladstone's first ministry. Note how at the start of the second point, by using the simple short word, 'too,' Mark establishes a useful link with the previous paragraph. Other linking words or phrases such as 'moreover,' 'also', 'in addition to' and 'as well as' can be used for the same purpose.

Look at Mark's numbered paragraphs above and the lettered pieces of legislation below. Which lettered pieces of legislation could illustrate the numbered paragraphs above?

Mark's PROOF

A	1872	Ballot Act
B	1870	Civil Service Act
C	1871	University Tests Act
D	1872	Licensing Act
E	1870	The Education Act
F	1873	Irish Universities Bill
G	1869	Disestablishment of the Anglican Church in Ireland
H	1869–71	Army reforms of Edward Cardwell
I	1870	The Irish Land Act
J	1871	The Trade Union Act

In an assessment/judgement type question rather than a list of reasons type question, you need to look at the balance of your material. If a view is made, how far is it true? You might want most of your material to agree with the question, but towards the end include a section to show it is not always true. For instance, in this question on Gladstone you could show that there were also less liberal pieces of legislation:

Examiner's comment

This is a useful modification to the idea that all Gladstone's legislation in his first ministry was Liberal, making this point clearly. It has useful link words such as 'however' and 'in addition.' It has two relevant and accurate examples with just sufficient detail to reinforce the argument. Arvind could also point out that the occasions when Gladstone's proposals were less liberal were also the occasions when he seemed to run into more trouble. He could also mention exactly which subjects were not going to be taught in the proposed new university.

Arvind's answer

However, not all Gladstone's legislation was of a liberal kind. His Licensing Act of 1872 to restrict pub opening hours had been unpopular from the first and the initial attempt at a Bill in 1871 had been defeated. 'Better an England free than an England sober' said the Bishop of Peterborough in the House of Lords, reflecting a common public view at the time. In addition, although the Irish Universities Bill of 1873 was a genuine attempt to improve the quality of Irish education, the restrictive clauses of the legislation (such as trying to stop certain subjects being taught in the new Universities) was what persuaded the House of Commons to reject it.

Let's look at another example:

To what extent had Disraeli assumed a prominent position in the Conservative Party by the end of 1852?

In preparation for this you need to consider the points for and against the prominence of Disraeli's position by the end of 1852.

The question requires you to make a judgement. Clearly this is open to debate but it is up to you to judge how prominent Disraeli had become and justify your argument with relevant material.

Serena's points for and against

FOR:
- Disraeli had become leader of the Conservatives in the House of Commons by this time.
- The Conservative leader Lord Derby gave Disraeli his complete confidence.
- Disraeli's assumption of the position of Chancellor of the Exchequer in 1852 cemented his position near the top of the Party.

AGAINST:
- At this stage there was no chance of Disraeli becoming leader of the Party as a whole: this was clearly Derby's position.
- There was a lot of suspicion against Disraeli in Conservative circles because of his style, his background and suspicions about the nature of his political ambition. This was clearly indicated in the delay in making him the Party's leader in the Commons.

This exercise might lead you to a fairly definite conclusion. For example you might argue that, on balance, Disraeli was a prominent Conservative to a large degree by the end of 1852 and that the points against are merely minor qualifications to this. Your judgement does not need to sit on the fence. However, in coming down on one side or the other you need to ensure you have the evidence to sustain your argument. Moreover, you should not ignore the points on the other side of the argument. A 'to what extent' or a 'how far' question usually requires you to make points on both sides of the argument. The weight of points and your overall conclusion is a matter of judgement for you and depends on your use and interpretation of evidence. Look for statements that relate clearly and directly to the question, such as :

'By the end of 1852 Disraeli was clearly number two in the Party to Derby and number one in the House of Commons.'

Here is a part of an answer to the question by different students: which do you consider to be the best effort – and why?

Mark's paragraph

Disraeli's emergence as leader of the Protectionist Conservatives in the House of Commons by 1851 was a clear sign that he had, against all odds, succeeded in becoming a prominent Conservative. From 1848 to 1851 Granby and Herries had shown none of Disraeli's parliamentary skills yet both had been given equal or higher positions in the party. Despite this treatment Disraeli had shown great loyalty to Lord Derby especially with his forbearance in tolerating these complex and unhelpful party leadership arrangements in the previous few years. For instance Disraeli accepted the 'triumvirate' he had to form with Granby and Herries in 1849 to run the Commons' party jointly. This not only showed the hostility to Disraeli in some parts of the party but also Derby's determination to insist on some authority for Disraeli. Disraeli gradually emerged from the triumvirate to be the clear leader of the party in the Commons by the middle of 1851.

Disraeli was annoyed when he was not given the leadership of the party in the House of Commons in 1848. It was given to the Marquis of Granby instead. When Granby soon proved unequal to the task of leadership and resigned within a month, Disraeli was still not given the position. After a short period when there was no Commons leader at all, Disraeli then had to accept a rule of three with himself, Granby and J.C. Herries in 1849. For two or three more years Disraeli had to wait to become Commons' leader and many Conservatives continued to be suspicious of him. By 1852 when Disraeli was appointed to be Chancellor of the Exchequer his position in the party had improved to some extent.

Other possible questions include:

- To what extent had the Liberals replaced the Whigs as the main opponents of the Conservatives by 1868?
- Assess the view that the successes of Gladstone's first ministry were due to Gladstonian Liberalism.
- Assess the reasons why Disraeli and the Conservatives were successful in the 1874 general election but defeated in the one in 1880.

GLOSSARY

Absolute monarchy An absolute monarchy has complete power to make and enforce laws and control a country's domestic and foreign policy.

Advanced Liberals Liberals whose views bordered on Radical.

Agrarian outrages Attacks on landlord property in the Irish countryside by Land League supporters or other nationalist groups or individuals. Coercion Acts were partly designed to enable those suspected of such outrages to be arrested and imprisoned without trial.

Artisan Originally, anyone practicing an industrial art. It had become a word for the skilled working class.

Back benchers In the British political system government ministers are normally taken from the membership of the majority in the House of Commons. (or Lords).They occupy the benches at the front of the chamber (House). Those MPs who support them occupy the benches behind them and are known as back benchers.

Balance of Power The idea of ensuring that no one power in Europe (or the wider world) should exert too much influence over events.

Beaconsfieldism Disraeli had become the Earl of Beaconsfield in 1876. Gladstone associated the next four years of foreign policy as meddling, expensive and unsuccessful British interference abroad and used the term 'Beaconsfieldism' to describe it.

Borough A town or village granted a Royal Charter giving it the privilege of electing its own two MPs.

British Empire The idea of a grand and coherent Empire which was co-ordinated and controlled by Britain was a later-nineteenth-century development from the earlier idea of individual colonies. Hence, in 1852 Disraeli could remark that 'colonies are millstones round our necks' but later on be enthusiastic for Empire.

Budget Annual financial statement by the Chancellor of the Exchequer. In the mid-nineteenth century the normal aim of these Budgets was to ensure that government expenditure was matched by government income from taxation and trade.

By-elections Elections that take place when a sitting MP dies or, in the earlier part of the nineteenth century, is promoted to government office.

Cabinet The most important ministers in a government who meet regularly together and agree important policy decisions. The prime minister chairs cabinet discussions.

Catholic Emancipation An Act of Parliament passed in 1829. By removing an MP's obligation to take an oath upholding the Protestant faith, it enabled Roman Catholics to take seats in parliament. Preceding the Great Reform Act, Emancipation can be seen as the first real break with the constitution of 1688–9.

Chartists Chartism was a working class movement most prominent between 1838 and 1848. It requested universal male suffrage and related demands such as the secret ballot in the form of three petitions in 1839, 1842, and 1848. Its near collapse in 1848 weakened the working class movement for political reform until the 1860s. However, its decline also meant that governments could now propose parliamentary reform without being accused of caving in to Chartist demands.

Chief Whip The politician who is responsible for trying to get party supporters to vote for his party's measures.

Civil Service Encompassed all direct employees of the government apart from the armed forces. After being reduced in numbers earlier in the century to curb corruption, the service was now expanding steadily in the nineteenth century as government intervention in social life increased. As a result of the Northcote/Trevelyan Report, a Civil Service Commission was set up in 1855 to unify the departments and make it possible to move from one to another.

Commoners Ordinary citizens who did not possess a peerage (title). Entitled to sit in the House of Commons rather than the House of Lords.

Compound householders Householders (around 400,000 of them) who paid their rent to their landlord and then added on (compounded) their rate – local tax. This meant they did not qualify for the vote as technically they did not pay tax, their landlord did.

Concert of Europe The idea that the major powers of Europe should act in concert (together) as much as possible to prevent minor disputes becoming serious wars. It was a popular idea in the nineteenth century from the end of the Napoleonic Wars in 1815.

Congested Districts Board Set up in 1891 to invest money and technical help in poorer areas of western Ireland where the size of the population could not be sustained by the relative poverty of the agriculture in the area.

Conservative The word conservative can be used with a small 'c' to describe a particular attitude to a problem, question or situation. This attitude:

- is cautious, careful and apprehensive of too much change all at once;
- has regard for past traditions and ideas;
- believes that rapid upheaval may produce instability and uncertainty;
- feels that, at national level. This kind of alteration could result in the loss of valuable ideas or institutions.

Constituents All the people who live in the constituency (area) represented by an MP.

Constitutional Monarchy A constitution is a set of rules and laws by which a country is governed. Therefore in a constitutional monarchy, the monarch's powers are carefully defined and restricted.

Creation of peers Peers (Lords) were created by the monarch. Very occasionally in a time of political crisis (such as 1832, 1911) the elected government whose wishes were being thwarted by the House of Lords would ask the monarch to consider appointing large numbers of its own supporters as peers in order to get controversial legislation through. The threat always proved enough.

Dissolution of Parliament Under the Septennial Act of 1716 a General Election had to be held at least every seven years. Technically the monarch dissolved parliament, but in the nineteenth century this decision was normally made by the prime minister. However, he had to make a formal request to do so to the Queen.

Eastern Question The question of what should be done about the declining Turkish Empire since friendly relations with it were so vital to British trading interests.

Electoral influence Landowners and (sometimes) factory owners felt it was quite legitimate to influence how their workforce should vote if they were enfranchised. This could be a mild hint, outright bribery or a threat that a wrongly directly vote could lead to the end of their employment. By the 1860s this 'influence' was becoming more and more morally unacceptable.

Established Church of England A Church established by Act of Parliament by Henry VIII in the 1530s when he broke away from the Roman Catholic Church. In organisation, if not always in belief, it retained many of the features of the Roman Catholic Church.

Evangelicals A group within the Church of England who stressed the importance of individual faith and the authority of the Bible and preaching, rather than the Catholic emphasis on the authority of the Church as a body and the importance of sacraments.

Food adulteration Mixing harmful, unwanted or unmentioned ingredients into food. Salt in beer to make the drinker thirstier or watering down milk to save expense were unwanted ingredients but more harmful substances could also be added.

The Fourth Party A very small but influential group of Conservative MPs in the early 1880s led by Lord Randolph Churchill and including Sir Henry Drummond Wood, John Gorst and, sometimes, Arthur Balfour. Their chief aim seems to have been to attack what they saw as the weak leadership of the Party in the Commons by Sir Stafford Northcote.

Franchise The right to vote.

Free trade Allowing trade between and within nations to flourish without artificial restrictions by government such as import duties or tariff barriers.

Friendly Societies Associations whose members pay fixed contributions to insure they receive help in sickness and old age and ensure provision for their families in the event of death.

Front bench The benches at the front of the House of Commons on either side of which sit senior government ministers and the leading figures of the main opposition party.

General Staff A body of Officers controlling the Army from Headquarters under the control of the Commander-in-Chief.

GOM Grand old Man: a term frequently used to describe Gladstone in his later years from about 1880.

Household suffrage Voting rights for the head of any household rather than those occupying a property of particular rateable value such as £10.

Income Tax Tax paid by individuals to government in proportion to the size of their own income. First used in wartime 1797–1816 it was re-introduced as a temporary measure 1842. In the 1850s it had still not been established as a permanent tax.

Irish Home Rule The idea of giving Ireland their own parliament back (it had been abolished in 1800) and making them responsible for running their own domestic affairs. Defence and foreign policy would be left in the hands of the Westminster government.

Jewish Disabilities The inability of Jews to take their seat if elected to parliament. This was because the parliamentary oath included the phrase 'on the faith of a Christian'. This was removed in 1857 and MPs could then restrict themselves to an oath swearing by Almighty God.

Laissez-faire A French term meaning 'leave it alone'. In this book it refers to the idea that governments should not intervene with the natural workings of the economy or society but leave things to natural (or market) forces.

Land purchase State financed schemes to aid Irish tenants to purchase land from their landlords. The first land purchase clauses had been included in Gladstone's first Irish Land Act of 1870 but this made little impact. Lord Ashbourne's Act in Salisbury's brief ministry of 1885/6, and Acts sponsored by Balfour in 1888 and 1891 meant that by 1895 the range of landownership in Ireland was starting to increase significantly.

Leaseholders Those who owned land for a set period of time rather than for life, as in the case of freeholders.

Liberal The word liberal with a small 'l' suggests:
- an open-minded and flexible approach to a problem;
- plenty of scope for free interpretation of the question in hand;
- that tradition, though respected, should not be adhered to over-rigidly;
- that change may be seen as desirable to prevent frustration and anger from building up.

Liberal Unionists Those Liberals who opposed Home Rule for Ireland, supporting the continued Union of the parliaments of England, Scotland, Wales and Ireland.

Lodger vote Voting in Boroughs was based on *occupancy* not ownership of a house. Lodgers in a house, especially common in the larger cities, were not qualified to vote at all.

Magistrates Members of the local community who preside over criminal hearings performing unpaid work in local courts normally dealing with small scale offences. At this time magistrates tended to come from the landed classes, though wealthy industrialists and businessmen had now begun to sit on the magistrates' bench.

Manchester School Originally a group who came from Manchester and industrial Lancashire who believed in a school of thought which championed free trade and as little government interference with the workings of the British economy as possible. Cobden and Bright were leading representatives.

Minority administration A government that did not have majority support in the House of Commons. Since the Conservatives won no election between 1841 and 1874, the three brief administrations of Lord Derby in 1852, 1858–9 and 1866–8 were all minority ones.

Municipal Corporations A Royal Charter had granted the right of local self-government to particular boroughs run by a mayor and local worthies who came together (were incorporated) to organise services in their local town (or municipality). The range of their responsibilities was increasing rapidly in the mid- to late nineteenth century.

New Liberalism The attempt by Liberal writers and politicians to reconcile the traditional beliefs in freedom and laissez-faire with the new support for widespread social reform, involving a clear extension of the role of the state. The crux of the argument was that without the state's aid to attain a minimum standard of living the joys of freedom were not likely to be properly appreciated. These views eventually became accepted by party members, but often not until after 1895.

Nonconformist conscience A term commonly used in the 1890s to refer to the moral conscience of Nonconformist Christians hoping to '*prepare the moral ground for a better kind of politics*'. There was a strong belief in social action to help the poor and that those in power must maintain the highest moral standards.

Nonconformist denominations Those Protestant groups who did not wish to conform to the beliefs and organisation of the Church of England. Among the most numerous and influential of these groups were Methodists, Presbyterians, Congregationalists, Baptists, Unitarians and Quakers.

Pacifists Those opposed to war in all circumstances.

Parliamentary Mandate A twentieth century political concept whereby if a party is elected into power at a General Election having set out its policies to the electorate, it is seen to have obtained a mandate (permission) to carry those policies through. Occasionally in the nineteenth century, as with the Great Reform Act of 1832, a party elected to government was expected to introduce a certain measure.

The **People's William** Popular name for Gladstone in the 1860s and beyond. Gladstone was seen as the senior politician most representative of the views of ordinary people.

Peelites Followers of Sir Robert Peel who had broken with the rest of the Conservatives by supporting Peel in repealing the Corn Laws. They often stayed independent of other parties, though a number of them such as Gladstone eventually became Liberals after a long period of political uncertainty.

Plebiscite A vote by the people to decide one particular issue. Normally elections were fought on a range of issues rather than a dominant one, though this could happen, as in 1831 over parliamentary reform and in 1857 over Palmerston's style in foreign policy.

Poor Law Board of Guardians Locally elected administrators of the workhouses set up by the 1834 Poor Law Act.

Prime ministerial ecclesiastical appointments By the mid-nineteenth century the prime minister rather than the monarch had the greater say in Church appointments such as bishops.

Primrose League Not officially a Conservative Party organisation until 1914, it usually acted as if it was one. Founded in 1883 by Lord Randolph Churchill in memory of Disraeli and supposedly his favourite flower. By the mid 1890s it had about a million members, many of them middle-class women who were willing to do voluntary unpaid work for the party of the envelope licking variety. Its social activities linked the party with many ordinary voters and even non-voters.

Protectionist Conservatives The name given to those Conservatives who refused to support the repeal of the Corn Laws and remained general supporters of the principle of protection for a few more years. In particular, they wished to 'protect' English farmers from cheap foreign competition in corn.

Purchase of Commissions To attain officer rank in the Army, the Commission (official authorization of appointment as an officer) had to be bought. The higher the rank, the more expensive the fee. Thus the top ranks of the army were confined to the wealthy, landed classes.

Radical Literally means 'by the roots'. After 1832, it was used to describe MPs who supported further reform of parliament and other extensive administrative alterations. They wished to see major change from the root of things rather than minor adjustments to the existing system. Never forming a definite, coherent party, the term 'Radical' remained in use to describe certain MPs for much of the rest of the century though the term is used less frequently after about 1870.

Reactionary In general political terms someone who reacts against change and wants to return to how the system used to be. Since 1789 many Tory politicians had reacted against the French Revolution and all it stood for. So, partly on these grounds, they had opposed parliamentary reform and many other changes in the previous fifty years.

Religious Toleration Allowing religious minorities the right to worship in their own way but not necessarily providing true equality of opportunity for them in society.

Resolutions in the House of Commons An expression of opinion by the Commons on any issue: it does not go before the Upper House (House of Lords) and so does not have the force of law.

Rotten and pocket boroughs Rotten boroughs were very small or deserted towns and villages which still returned two members to parliament who were effectively nominated by the local landowner, since there were hardly any voters. Pocket boroughs might be larger, but the landlord's control was still the predominant factor. He has the borough in his pocket (under his control).

Rule of law The idea that everyone, whatever their status or position in society, must keep to the laws of the land. Everyone of whatever social status is equally bound by these laws and would all be punished to the same degree if they broke them.

Secret ballot The right to cast your vote in secret in a polling booth instead of publicly on a hustings (platform). It was believed that a secret ballot would drastically reduce aristocratic influence and bribery and corruption at election time. The Secret Ballot Act was passed in 1872.

Tariff barriers Limit put on the free movement of goods by a government-imposed duty on their importation. This could be either to increase government revenue or to restrict imports of goods that might compete with British-made ones.

Tenant Right Bills Bills put before Parliament to remove absolute rights of property and grant tenants (those who farmed the land and paid a rent for the privilege) right of occupation provided they paid that rent.

Tithe Literally a tenth. Traditionally, the tenth of the produce of the land given to the Church as a form of tax. It had long been changed to a payment on land and, like Church Rates, was especially resented by Nonconformists.

Trade unions At this time, the 1860s and 70s, efforts to ensure decent pay and conditions were generally confined to associations of skilled workers but their numbers were growing steadily.

Treating The giving of generous amounts of free food and drink by candidates to potential voters shortly before an election.

Two member seats Before 1885 many, though not all, parliamentary seats were represented by two MPs. Quite often a close and potentially expensive contest could be avoided by an agreement for each side to share the representation.

Viceroy The most senior British government official in Ireland, representing the monarch.

INDEX